I0729643

Try to Tell a Fish About Water

THE ART, MUSIC, AND THIRD LIFE OF NORMA TANEGA

Anthology Editions
New York

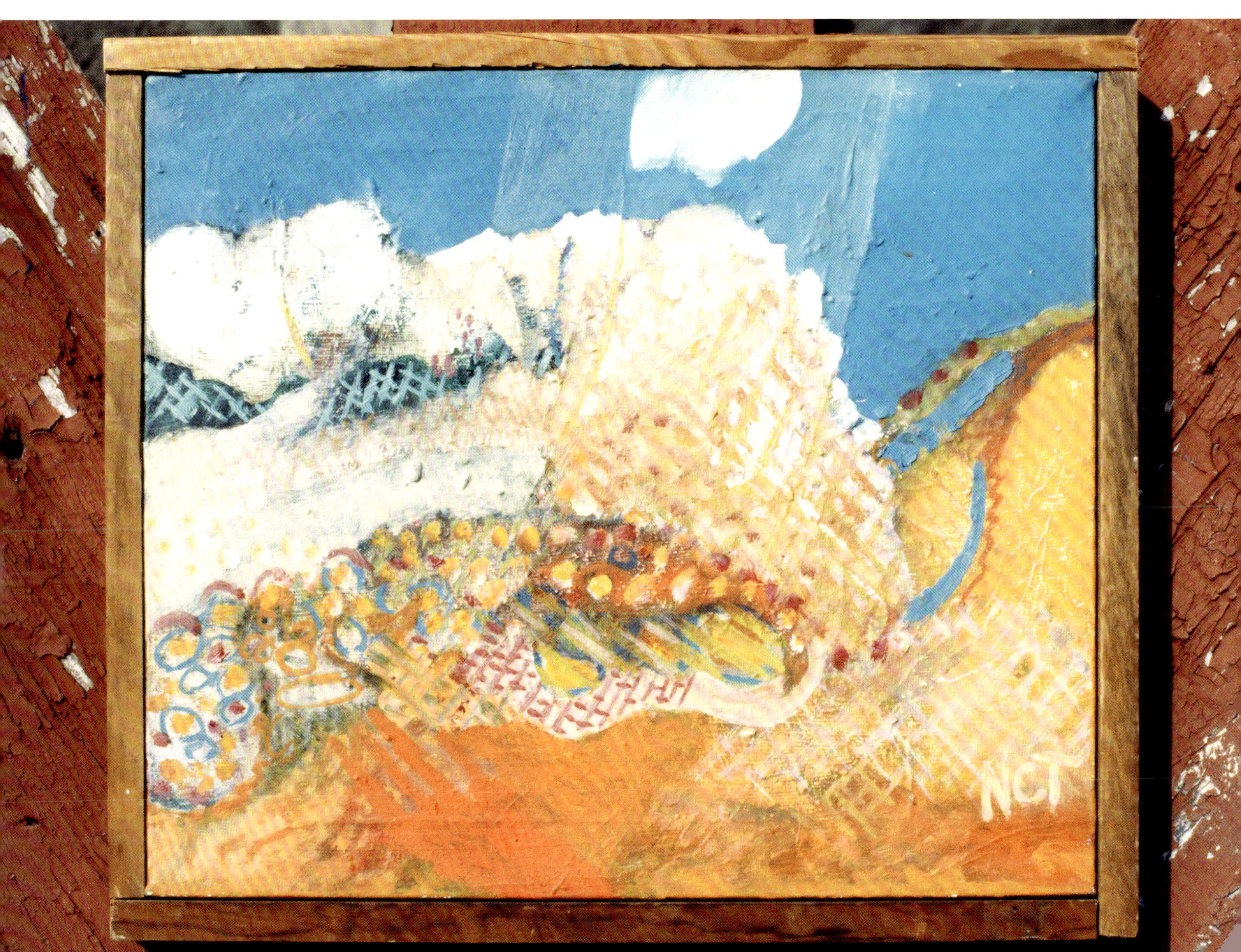

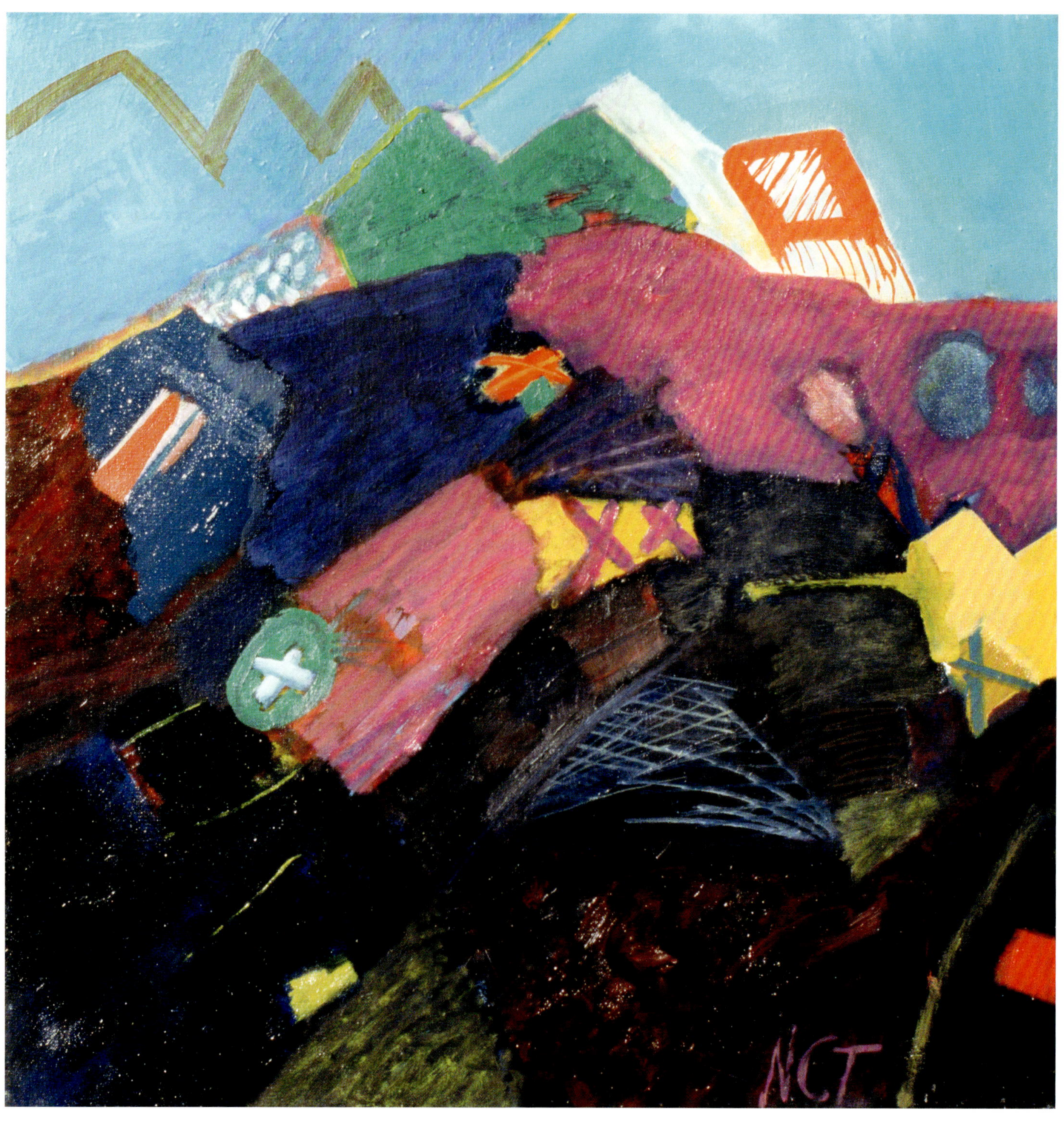

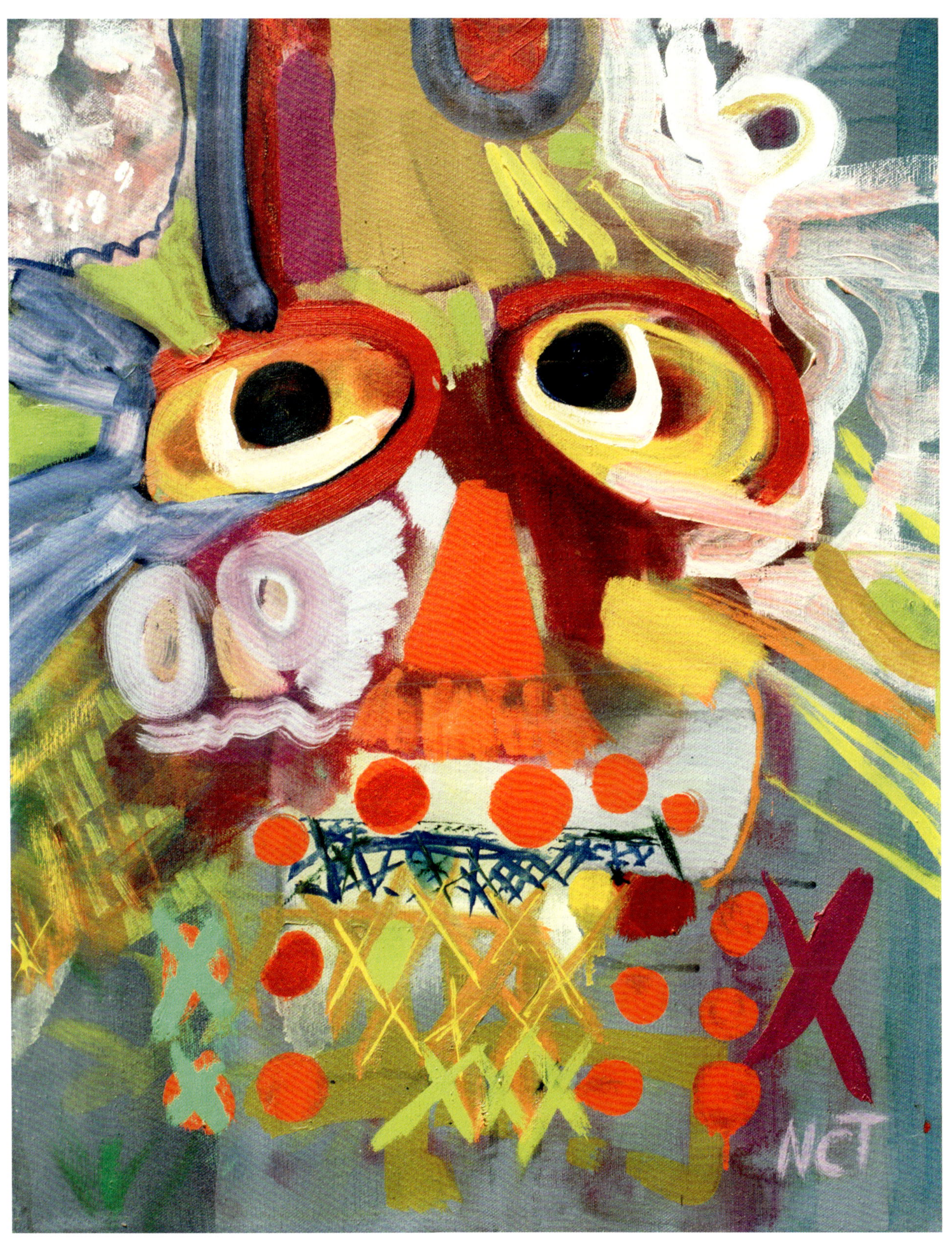

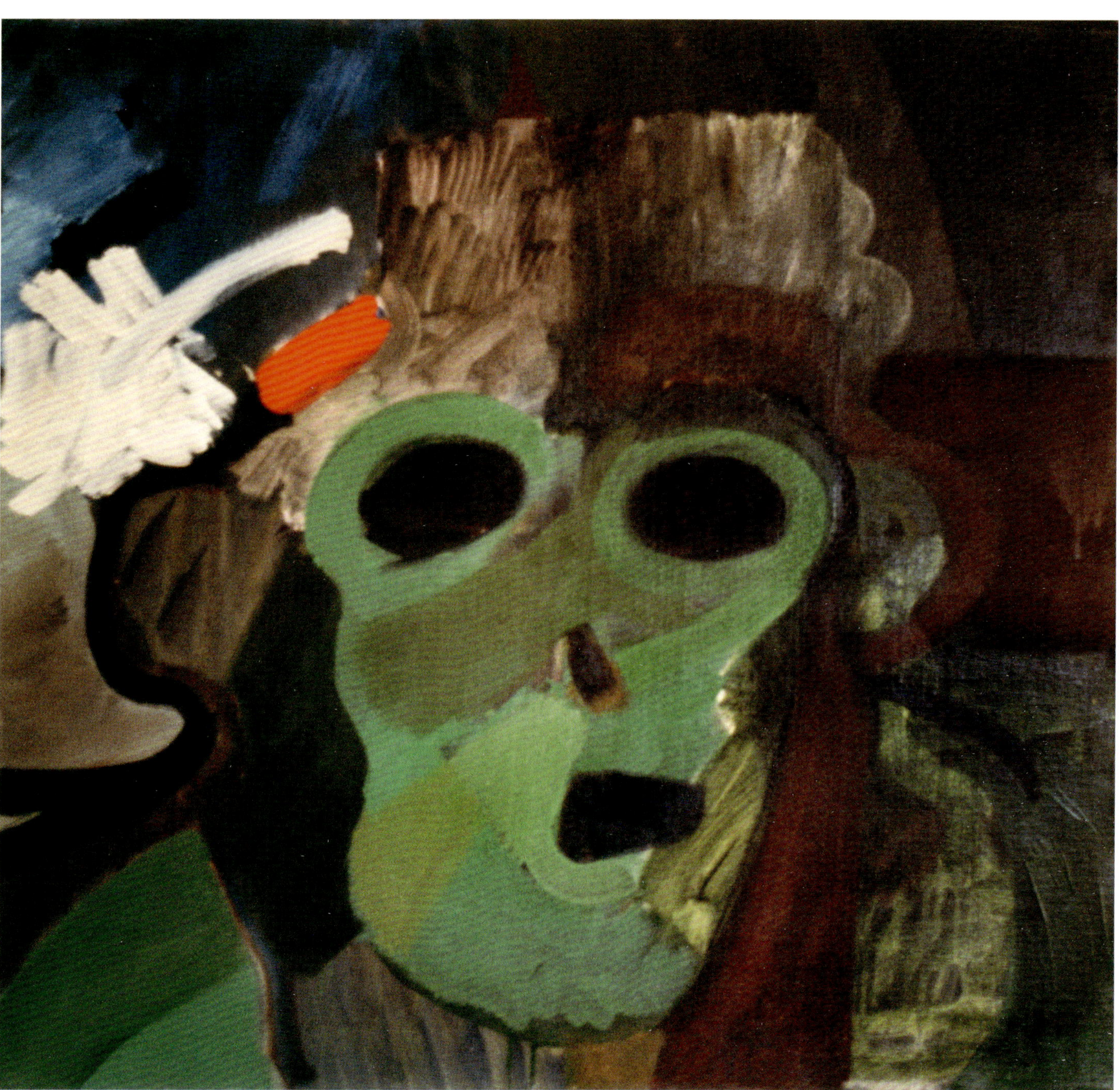

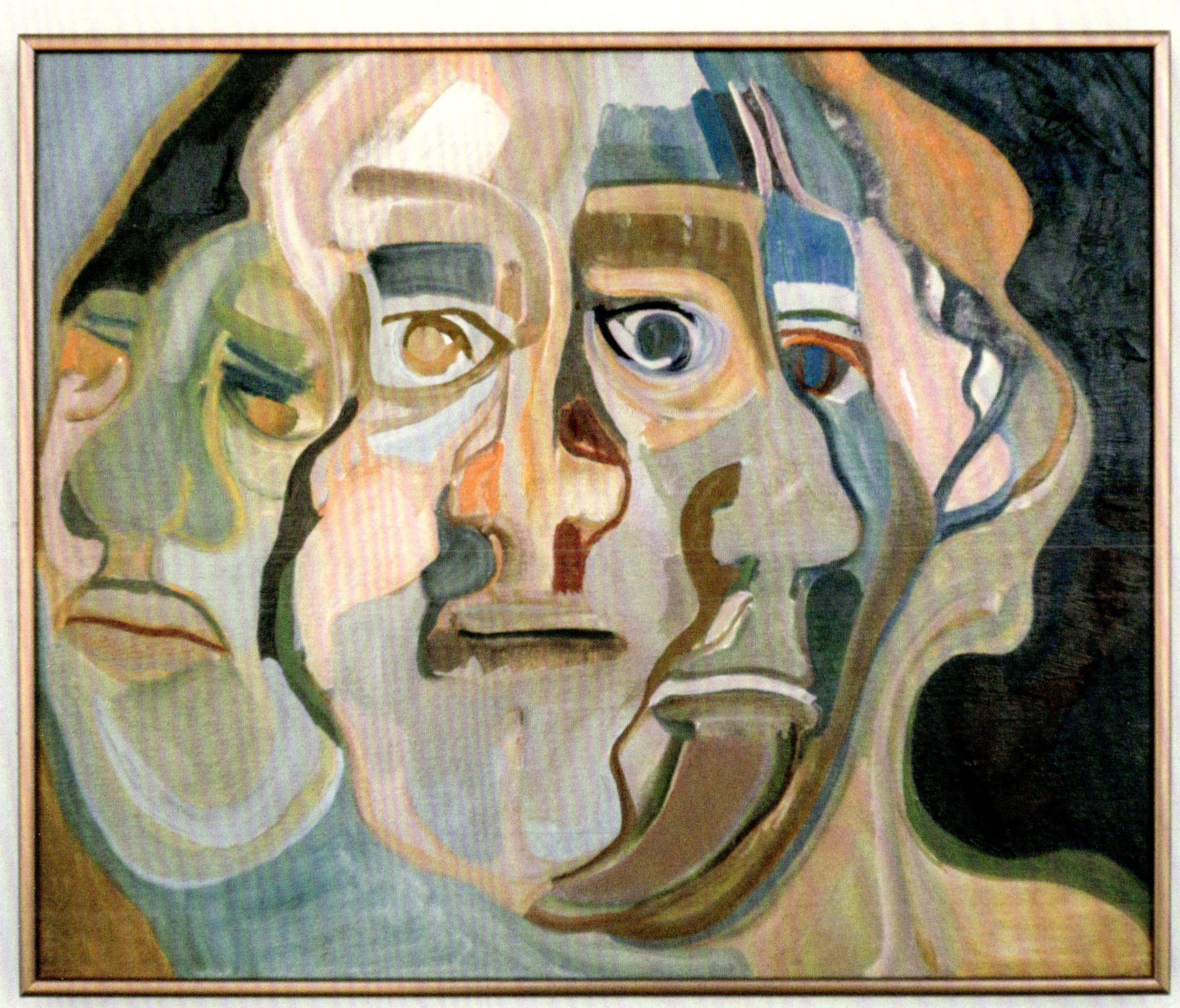

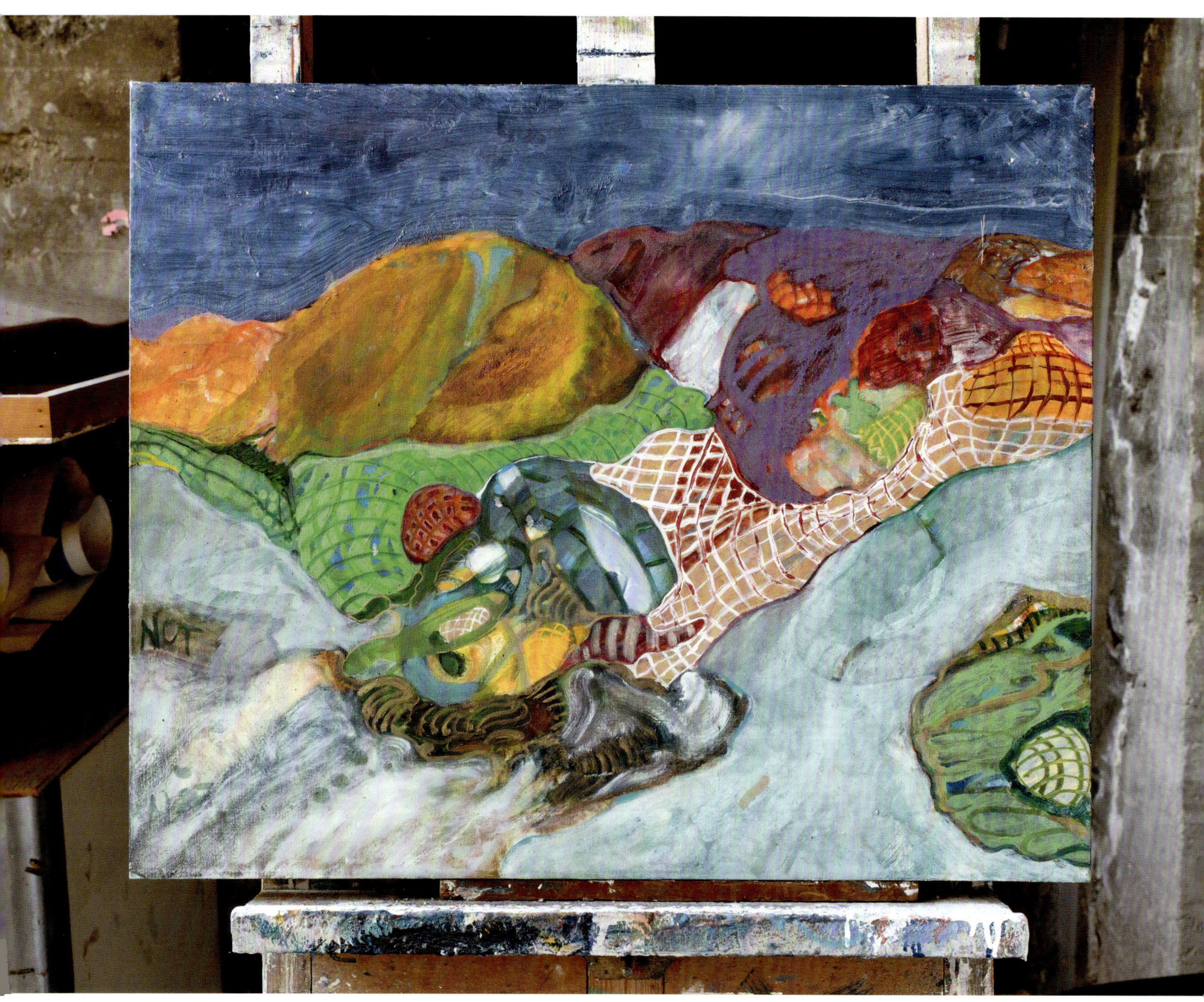
NOT

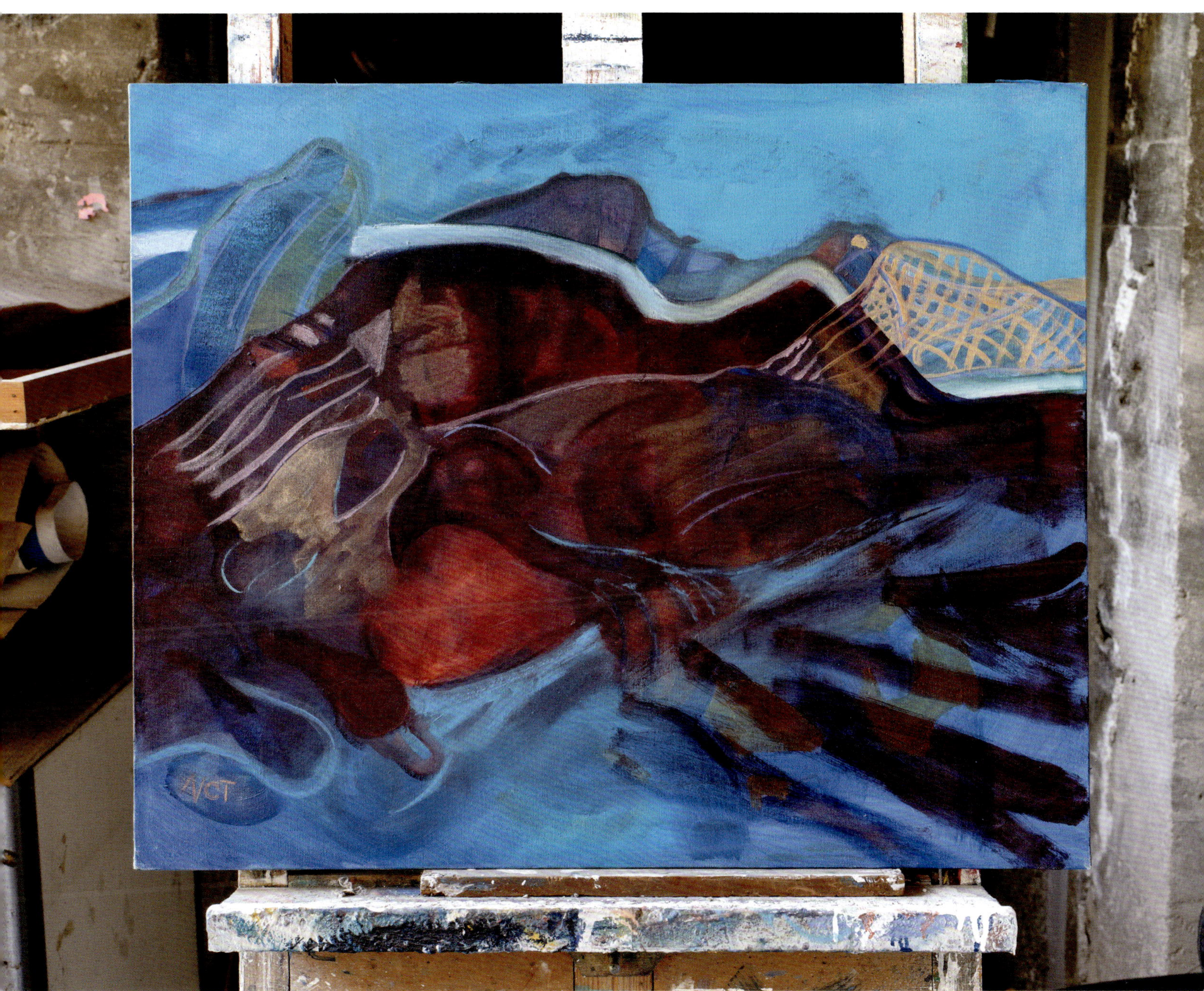

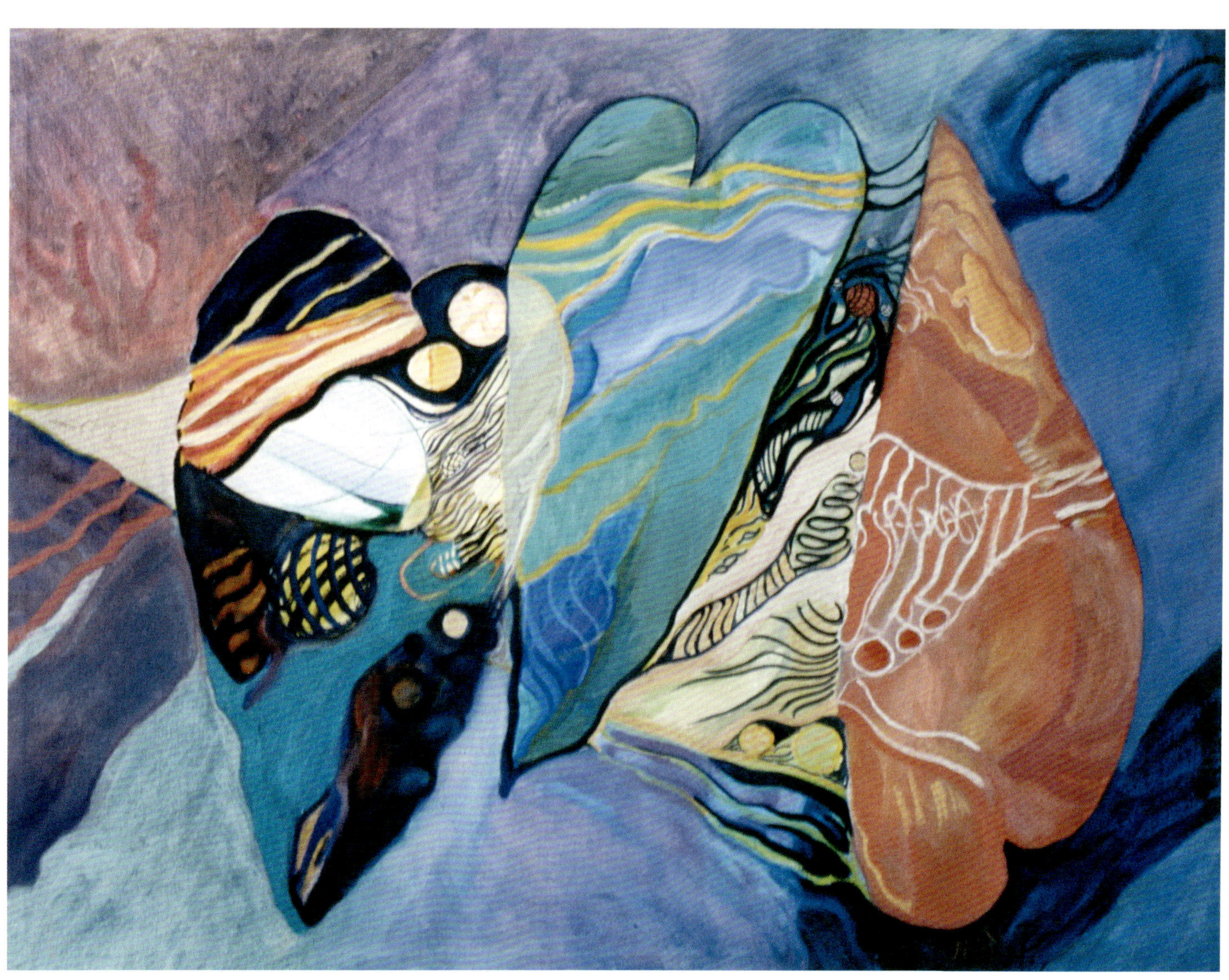

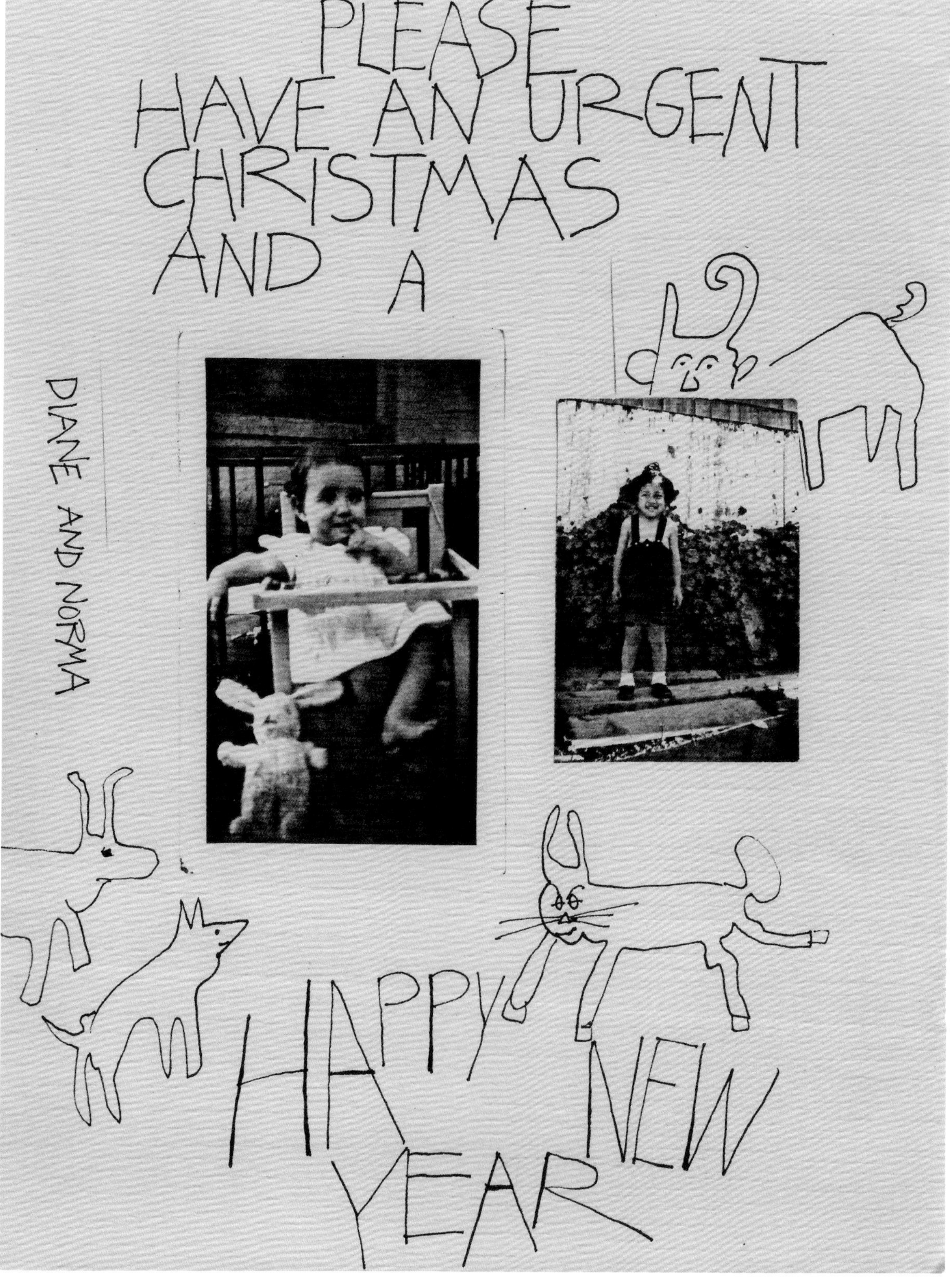

PLEASE
HAVE AN URGENT
CHRISTMAS
AND A
DIANE AND NORMA
HAPPY
NEW
YEAR

Introduction

Diane Divelbess

Norma the visual artist and Norma the musician.

Norma the complicated—or was she simple? Was she tough, or simply resilient? Always generous, she could be selfishly honest. Usually playful and outgoing, she could be moody. Creative, of course. Devious, never.

What was she? Who was she? Where to begin . . .

Norma was true. She was proud. She was loyal. Her friendships were many, with some going back to her high school years. She had close relationships as well, but when she was ready to move on, she moved on; most remained as friends. Norma was fun to be around, and she loved to entertain. She once collected a crowd in a department store while "struggling" to put on a sports bra, and at a shoe clearance sale she entertained everyone with a zany dance routine while wearing her new checkered Vans. When she was a young woman in New York City in the sixties, Norma gave a spontaneous performance at a party and the hostess gave her a check for $1,000 (a fortune in those days) and told her to go hitchhiking in Europe. So off she went!

Norma loved to eat, and she appreciated good food. Like her father, she was a great cook. If there were unexpected guests, she could always whip something up; there was always room for another at her table. It was also from her father, a bandmaster in the US Navy, that she inherited her musical ability. Her sense of pride, fierce independence, and ambition were instilled by her mother. From both parents came her love of celebration.

When Norma was performing, she always had a big smile. A great smile. She always gave her performances everything she had. When she was on, she was on. When she was creating, however—whether painting in the studio or composing in the music room—she was quiet. One could be painting in the same studio with her and there would be only a comfortable silence. Rarely would she fall into a dark mood, but when she did she would announce it. The solution would be to give her a bottle of Johnny Walker Black Label and ignore her for a couple of days.

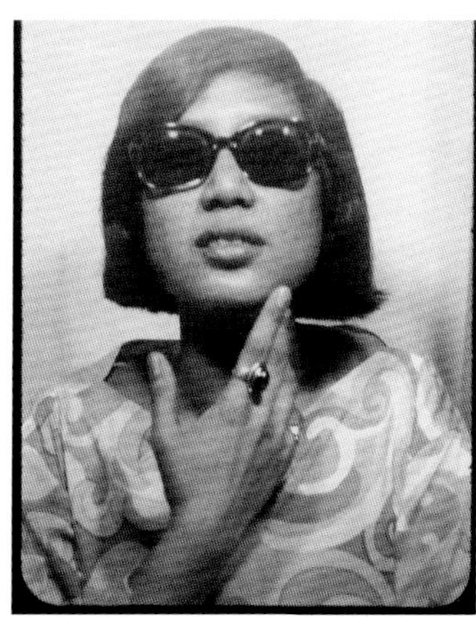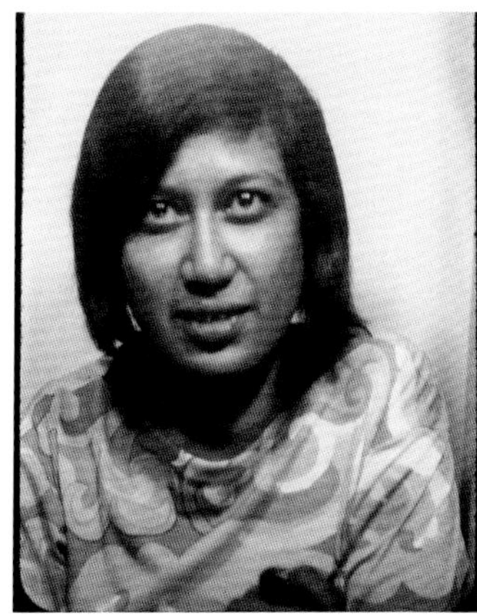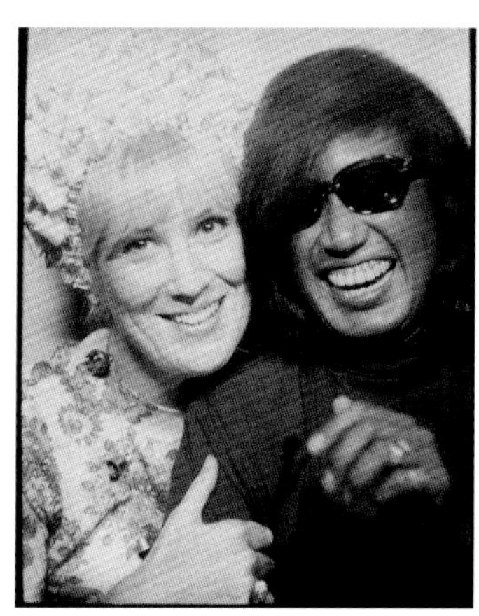

NCT with Dusty Springfield

It was while living on NYC's Lower East Side that she composed her best-known song, "Walkin' My Cat Named Dog," the sixth track on the album of the same name. Of that album's twelve songs, four were composed exclusively by her, and eight were composed with her good friend Norma Kutzer. After touring in this country for two years, Tanega went to England, where she met Dusty Springfield. She continued to compose songs, some of which were recorded by Dusty, and at least one of which was recorded by Blossom Dearie. In London, she released an album, *I Don't Think It Will Hurt If You Smile*. Although it never became a hit, the album did have several very good songs. It was also while living in London that Norma recorded the hauntingly beautiful *Snow Cycle*, a small set of songs never released by Capitol Records.

Upon her return to this country in 1972, Norma settled in Claremont, California, where she had gone to Scripps College and the Claremont Graduate School (now Claremont Graduate University). She loved living there, and she never

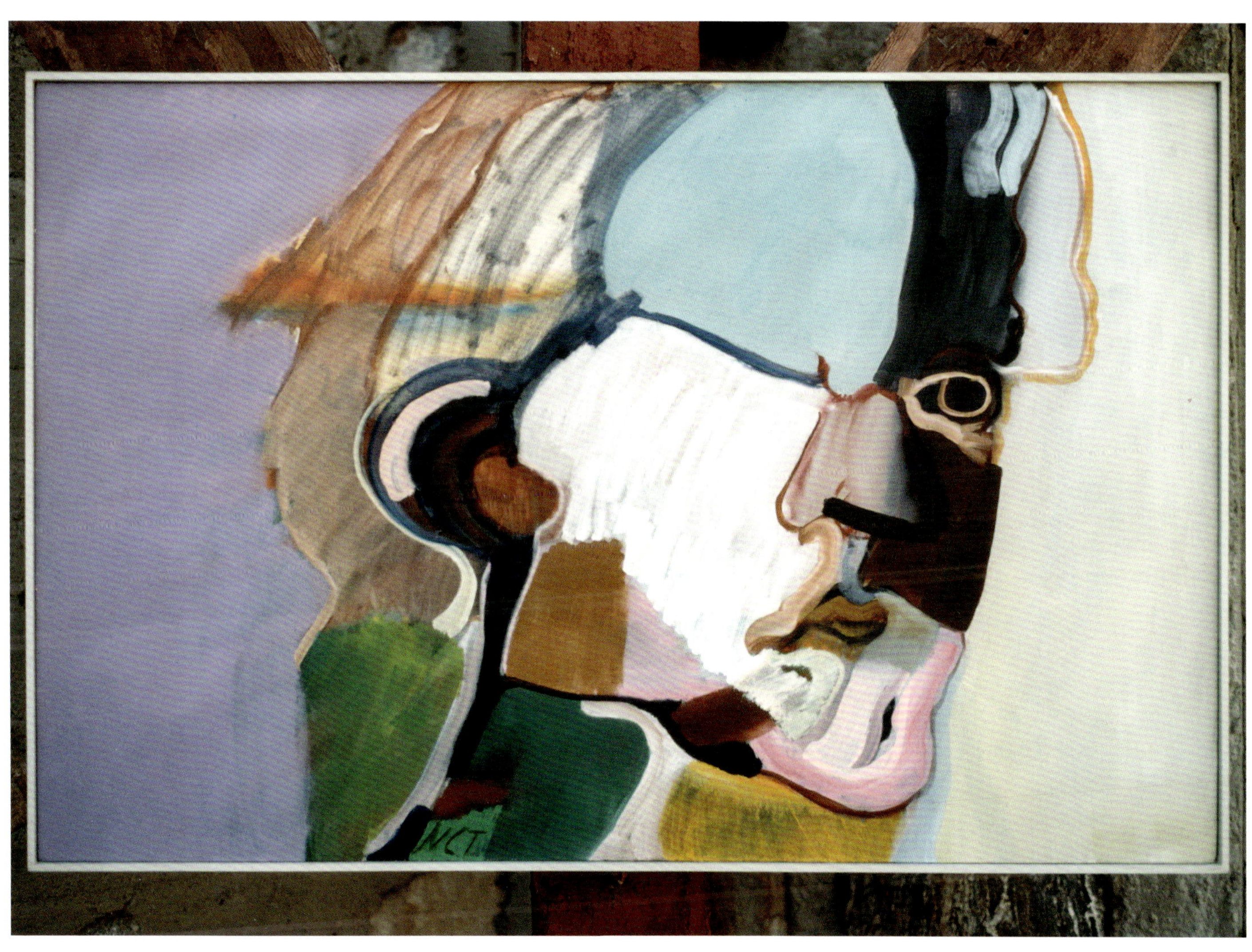

left. However, like anybody living in Southern California, she spent a lot of time as a "freeway flyer." During one of those times—a period of some seven or so years—Norma drove daily to Redondo Beach, where she and Daniel Maher ran a successful gallery and framing business, the Tanega-Maher Gallery. The exhibits changed monthly, which involved a lot of work, but it was also an exciting period of meeting new artists and making many new friendships. As time allowed, Norma worked on her own art and music. When she had compiled a collection of new songs, she played them for a former producer in LA one afternoon. After the session, he told her his interests had turned to country western and he was really hoping to hear something more like "D-I-V-O-R-C-E" by Tammy Wynette. Norma was stunned and hurt. It was a kick in the gut. Nevertheless, she refused the suggestion to write for the marketplace. Instead, she began to collaborate with musicians she knew and admired: people who were skilled, creative, and alive.

What people may not realize when they think of Norma as a musician is that she was not only a composer, vocalist, and guitarist; she was also a fantastic percussionist. She could play anything that made a sound when struck, strummed, or shaken, from keyboards to drum kits, from bongos or hand-held drums to autoharp or the melodic Caribbean oil drum. If the instruments were ethnic or individually created, all the better. She was a person of exquisite musicianship, with a fabulous ear. A friend, Aida Pavletich, once produced a show for a local public television station that featured only Norma on the bongos. It was terrific!

From 1990 to 2014, Norma's records were collaborations, and she was almost always listed on percussion. With Brian Ransom (as the Ceramic Ensemble) and with John Zeretzke, the music was otherworldly and avant-garde. With Mike Henderson (as Hybrid Vigor), Tom Skelly and Mario Verlangieri (as Baboonz), and Robert Grajeda (as the Latin Lizards), compositions were original or experimentally recorded. It was only when playing percussion with the Egyptian oud musician Emad Gabra that Norma was more ethnic-traditional. All these bands played gigs, of course, and Norma loved that. She not only loved performing, she enthusiastically appreciated other performers. She was always happy in their company.

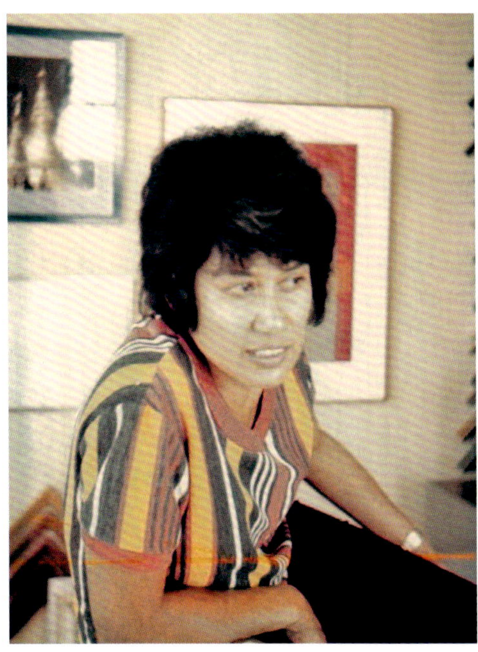

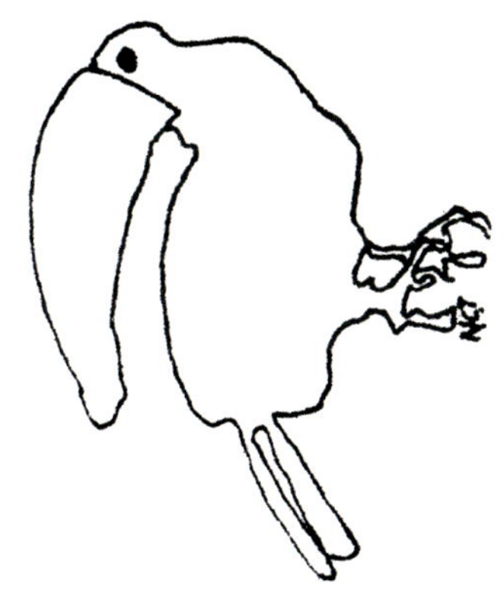

Norma's degree from Scripps College was in Humanities and Fine Arts, not music. Her emphasis in fine arts was painting and printmaking, and her MFA from the Claremont Graduate School was primarily in painting. It is true that when Norma was in graduate school, she always had her guitar with her and entertained undergraduate students with renditions of folk songs. Nevertheless, when she moved to NYC a couple years after graduate school, no one in Claremont expected to hear her singing "Walkin' My Cat Named Dog" over their radio! Suddenly, and then for a long time, everyone had to think of her as a singer-songwriter. It was not until she returned to Claremont and eventually shared a studio that she could return to painting, at which point everyone realized that Norma was both a musician and a visual artist.

Norma was no longer working with Dan Maher, who had moved to Los Angeles, so she had time to teach private music lessons. She was also an adjunct instructor in the Art Department at Cal Poly State University, Pomona, and a teacher of English as a second language for the Claremont Adult School for thirty years. She absolutely loved to teach, and her students loved her.

In those years, our Taliesin West–style house/studio on Mt. Baldy Road was a magnet for creative people, filled with good conversation and gatherings around the patio. There was always music. There were publishing parties and poetry readings, as well as house concerts and art events. Friends dropped in from everywhere, it seemed. The magic of this house in the Padua Hills cast its spell on everyone.

Like many artists, Norma painted series of works over the years; in other words, she would become interested in a subject or theme and develop a body of work around it. For example, she did a wonderful series of paintings of bridges. This happened after she took a trip to Northern California and became enchanted by the steel grid patterns of the railroad bridges spanning canyons. Her work was always more expressionistic than realistic in style, very strong and usually colorful. Her brushwork was generally loose, not slick, the paint more fluid than tight. She is probably best known for her faces—the series of "killers" and the series of "hockey mask" faces. Many were simply titled "portraits." They are striking, as are her expressionistic landscapes. Over time, those landscapes morphed into large, nonobjective, very colorful art works. Heart shapes, X's, and texture marks were frequent. Many times Norma incorporated words into her paintings—perhaps meaningful, or perhaps nonsensical, or perhaps because the letters made interesting shapes. When the words were meaningful they had a haiku quality; when nonsensical, they might be riddles. A favorite childhood book had been *Riddle Me This* by Frances Chrystie. Her college senior thesis was on the book of Ecclesiastes. Go figure.

Norma's work was exhibited in numerous shows and events, such as the annual Padua Hills Art Fiesta and the Claremont Museum of Art's OpenART Studio Tours. She also had work in several galleries over the years and was regularly represented in the faculty art exhibits at Cal Poly. Her last exhibit, titled *SuperNova*, was at the Ginger Elliott Center in Claremont in April 2019.

Over the years from 1977 to 1999, Norma worked on the words to "The True Believer," later titled "Testament." At first it probably seemed heavy, labored, and maybe even pretentious, but as the years rolled by it became apparent that "Testament" was the expression of Norma's thinking at its best. Norma was a free spirit—yes. She was joyous and creative. But she was also very smart, brilliant even; a woman of depth and understanding.

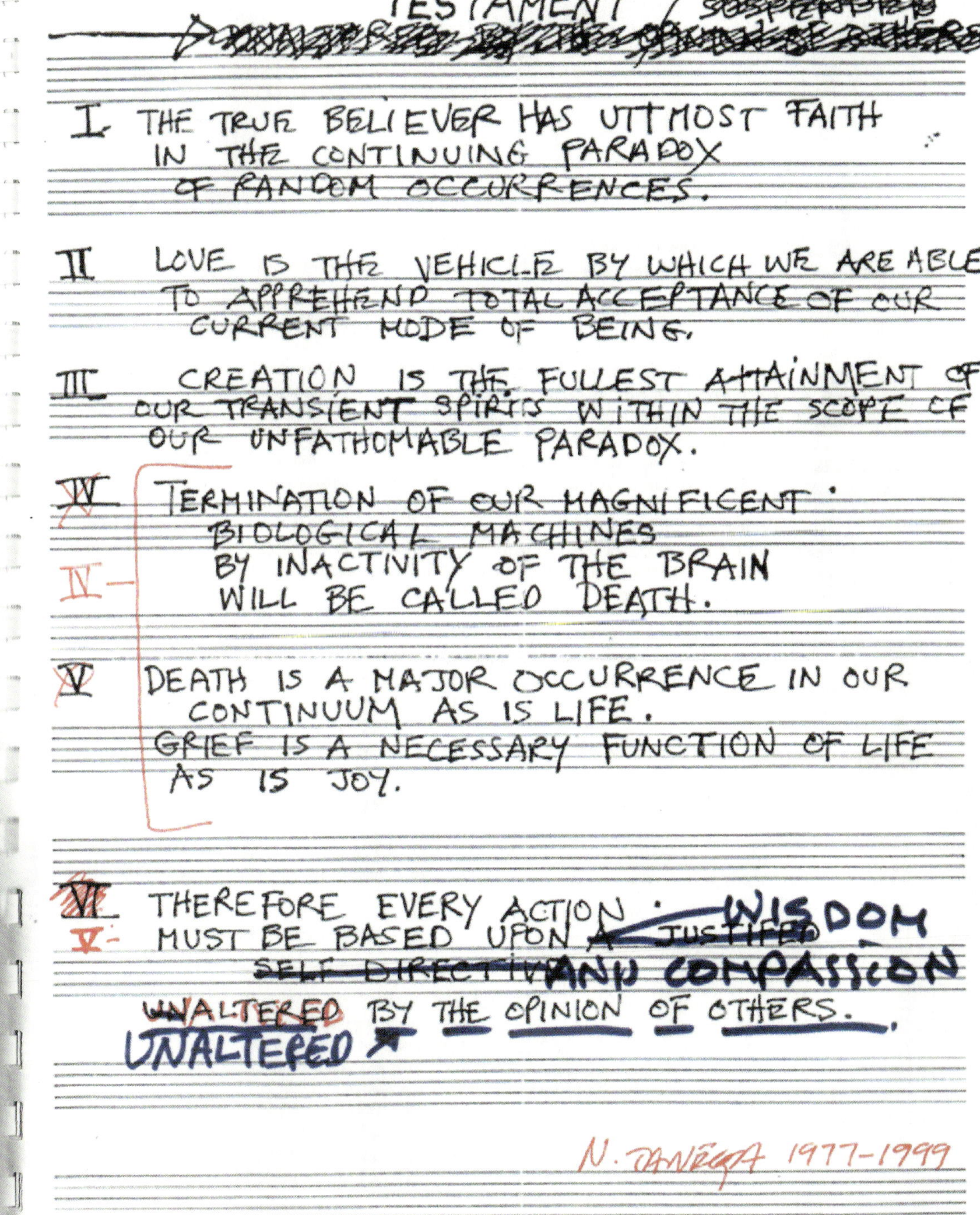

TESTAMENT

I   THE TRUE BELIEVER HAS UTTMOST FAITH
    IN THE CONTINUING PARADOX
    OF RANDOM OCCURRENCES.

II LOVE IS THE VEHICLE BY WHICH WE ARE ABLE
    TO APPREHEND TOTAL ACCEPTANCE OF OUR
    CURRENT MODE OF BEING.

III CREATION IS THE FULLEST ATTAINMENT OF
    OUR TRANSIENT SPIRITS WITHIN THE SCOPE OF
    OUR UNFATHOMABLE PARADOX.

IV TERMINATION OF OUR MAGNIFICENT
      BIOLOGICAL MACHINES
      BY INACTIVITY OF THE BRAIN
      WILL BE CALLED DEATH.

V   DEATH IS A MAJOR OCCURRENCE IN OUR
    CONTINUUM AS IS LIFE.
    GRIEF IS A NECESSARY FUNCTION OF LIFE
    AS IS JOY.

VI THEREFORE EVERY ACTION
    MUST BE BASED UPON A WISDOM
    AND COMPASSION
    UNALTERED BY THE OPINION OF OTHERS.
    UNALTERED

N. DANREGA 1977-1999

1987	Chaffey Community Art Association, Ontario, CA
	Claremont Graduate School, Claremont, CA
	University Union Gallery, Cal Poly Pomona
1986	University Union Gallery, Cal Poly Pomona
	Allauch, France
1985	Chaffey Community Art Association, Ontario, CA
	University Union Art Gallery, Cal Poly Pomona
1984	Chrysalis Gallery, Claremont, CA
	Daniel Maher Gallery, LosAngeles, CA
1983	University Union Gallery, Cal Poly Pomona
	Laguna Beach School of Art, Laguna, CA
1982	Chaffey Community Art Association, Ontario, CA
	Los Angeles City College, Los Angeles, CA
	Daniel Maher Gallery, Los Angeles, CA
	Roberts Art Gallery, Santa Monica, CA
1981	Wild Blue Gallery, Los Angeles, CA
	Chaffey Community Art Association, Ontario, CA
	University Union Gallery, Cal Poly Pomona
	Abraxas Gallery, Newport Beach, CA
1980	Downey Museum of Art, Downey, CA
	University Union Gallery, Cal Poly Pomona, CA
1979	Brand Library Art Galleries, Glendale, CA
1962	Lang Art Gallery, Scripps College, Claremont, CA
1960	Lang Art Gallery, Scripps College, Claremont, CA

SELECTED COLLECTIONS:

Diane Divelbess, Seattle, WA
Downey Museum of Art, Permanent Collection, Downey, CA
Dennis Garcia, Claremont, CA
Dr. Barbara Goldstein, New York, NY
Col. James Jones Collection, Cal Poly Pomona, CA
Barbara Pascal, Los Angeles, CA
Dr. Lynn Sakai, Beaverton, OR
Dr. David W. Scott, Whitehaven, MD
Dusty Springfield, London, England

MUSIC AFFILIATIONS:

1996	Member, Tanega and Henderson;
	Partner, TH Music
1994-present	Member, The Latin Lizards
1988-present	Partner, Addictive Audio
1985-1995	Member, The Ceramic Ensemble
	Partner, RT Music
	Owner, Producer, Engineer: Tanega Recording Studio
1980-present	Instructor of piano, drums, guitar and bass.
1967-1972	Partner, Jubilation Music, Ltd. , London, England
	Songwriter, Essex Music, London, England
1962-1967	Composer/Recording Artist, New York, NY

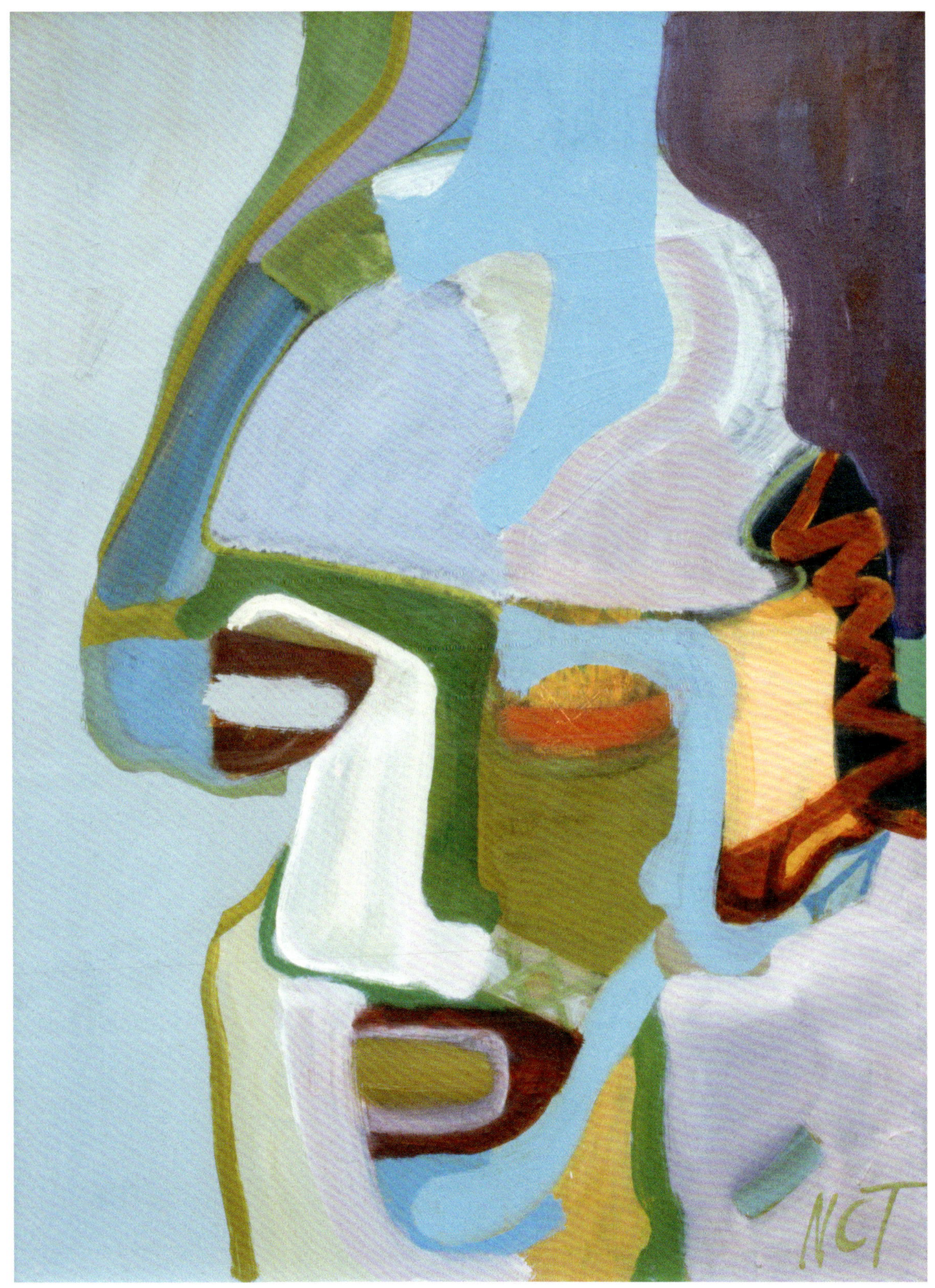

NCT

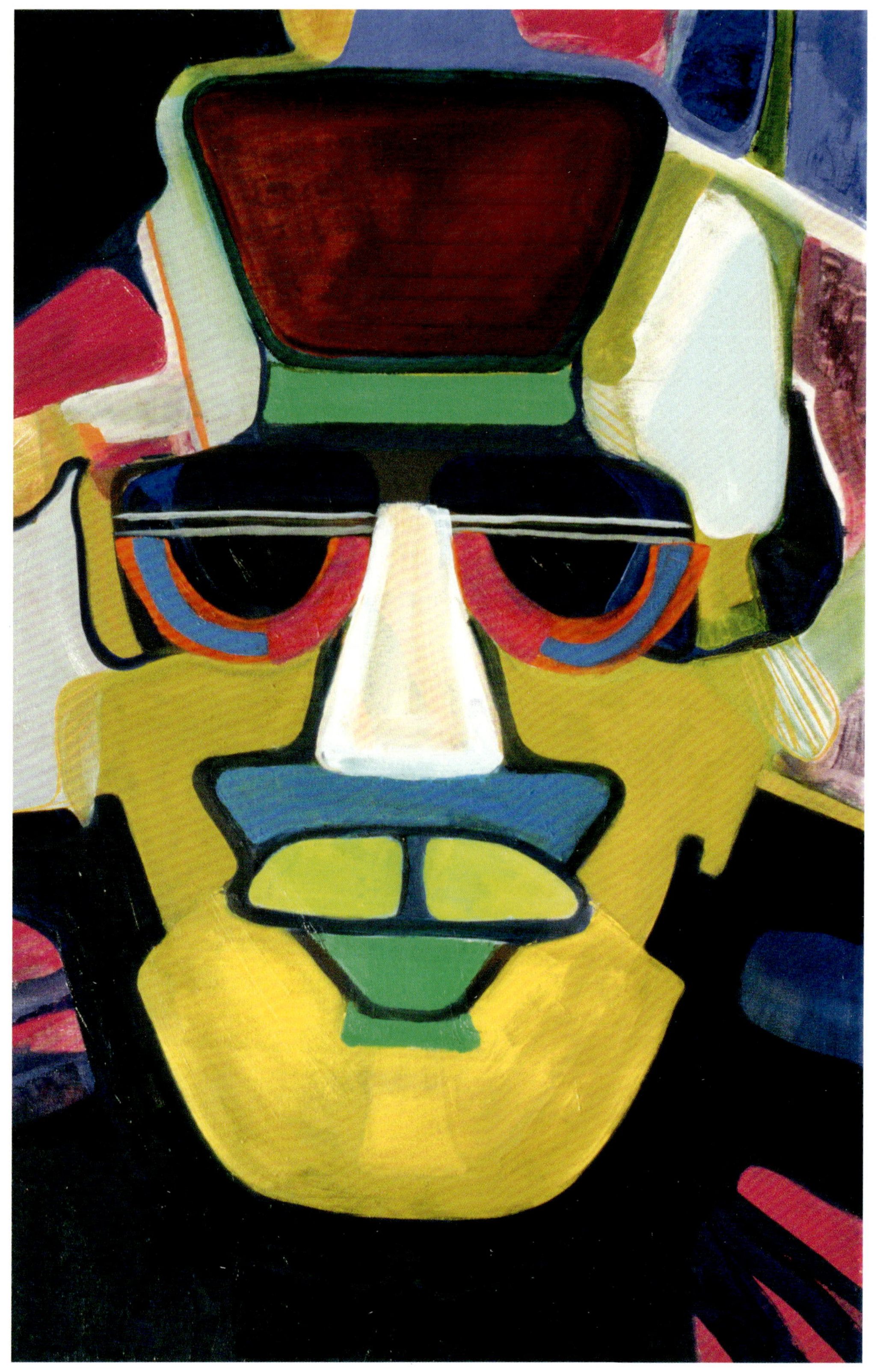

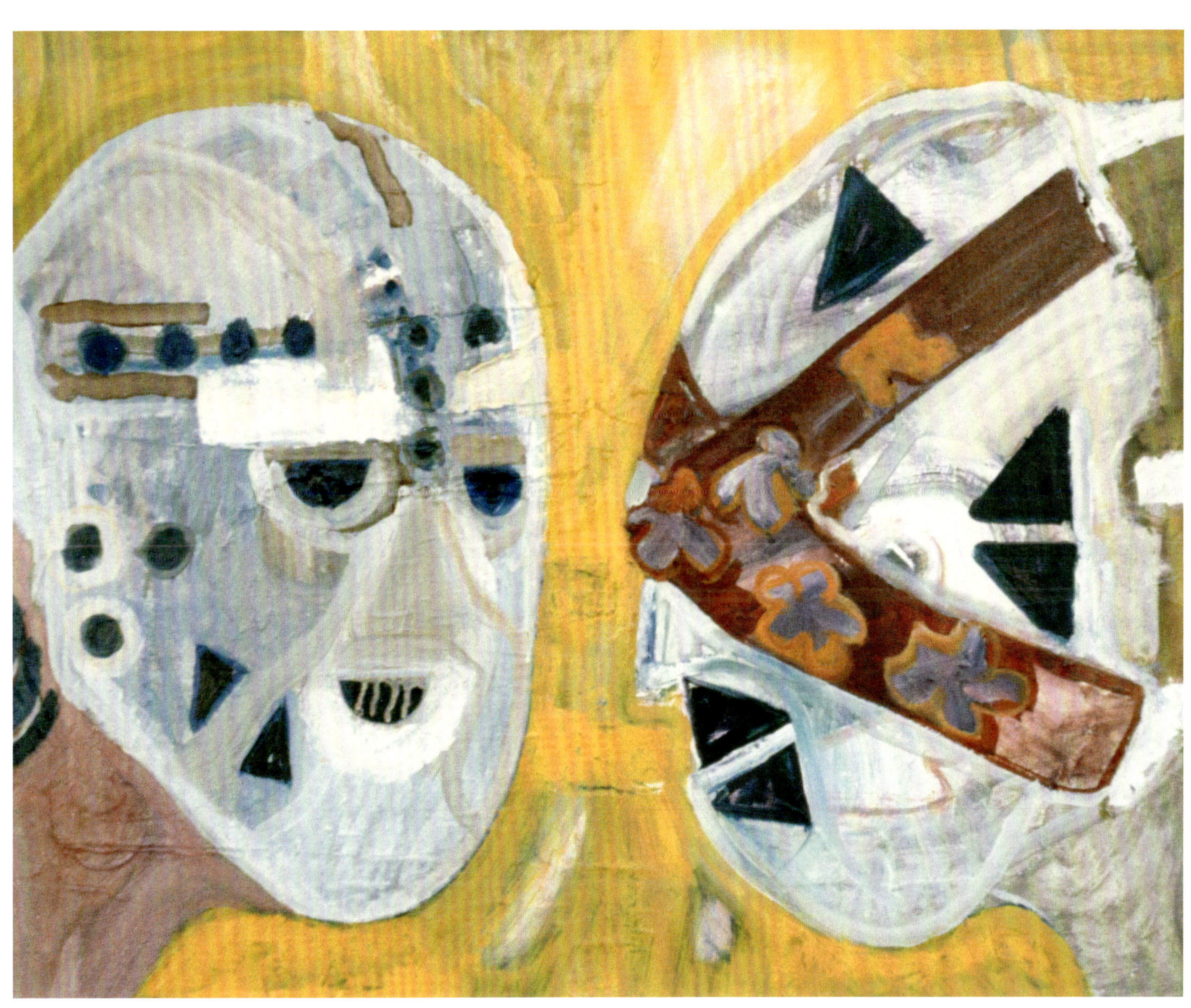

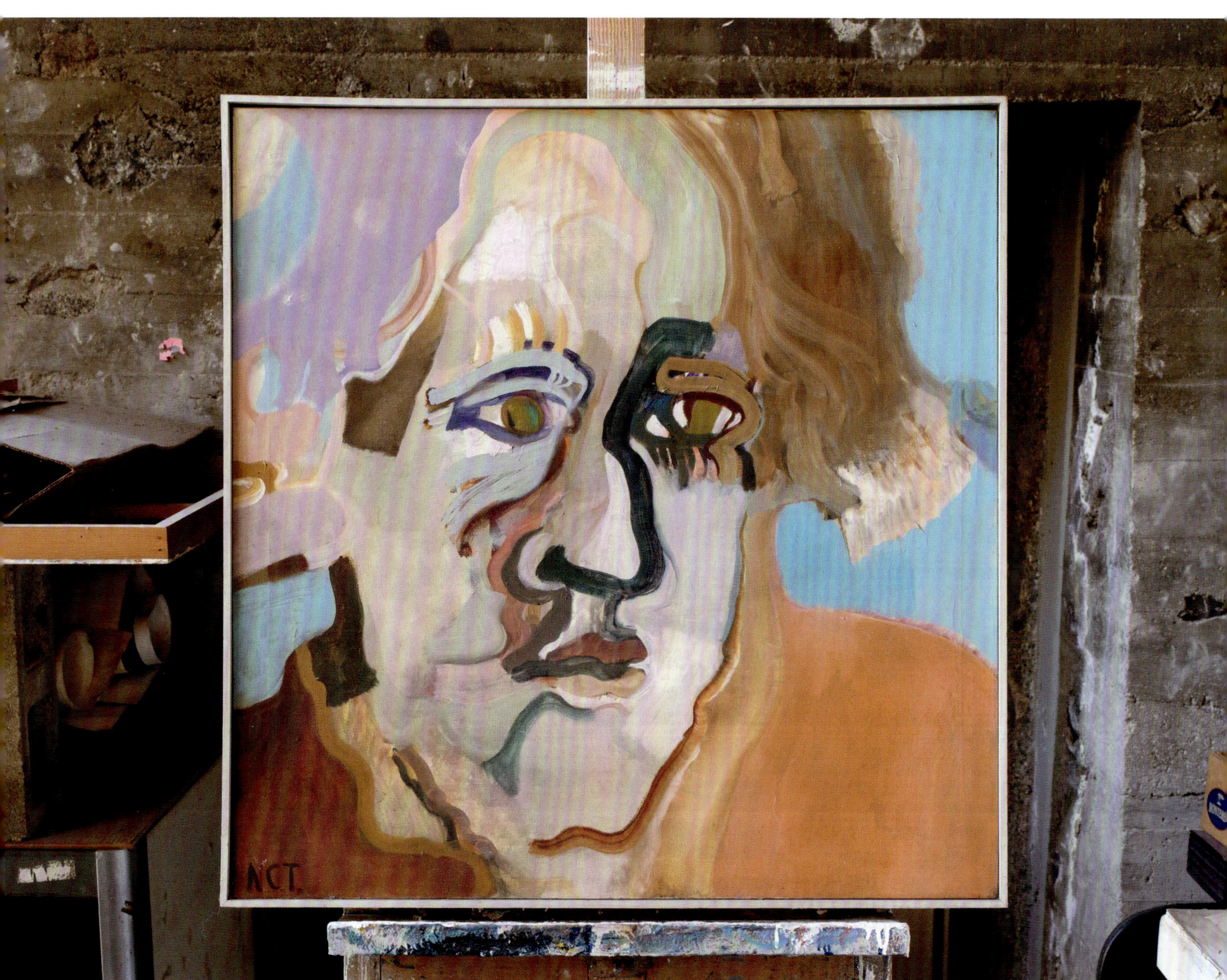

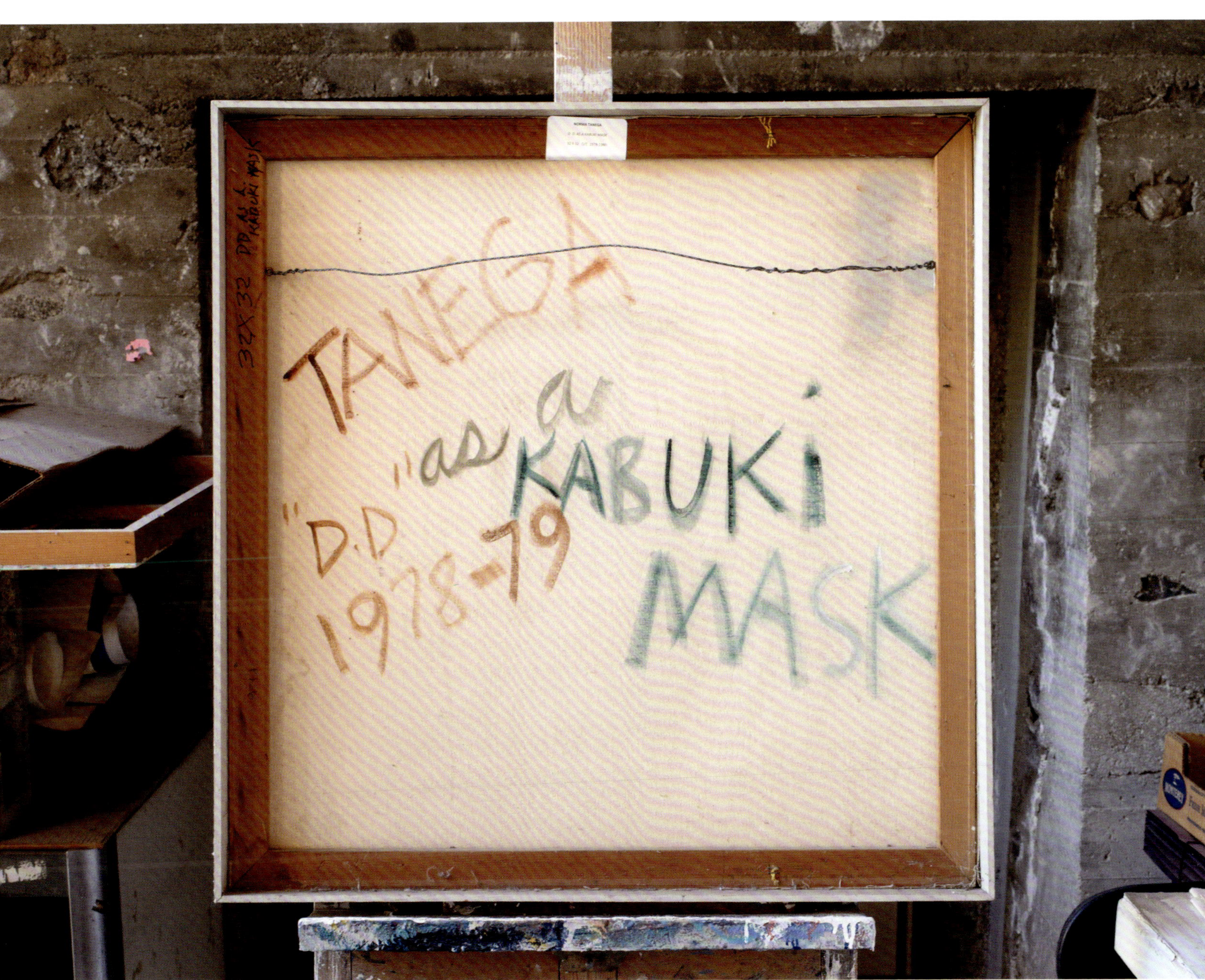

TANEGA
"as a
D.D
1978-79
KABUKI
MASK

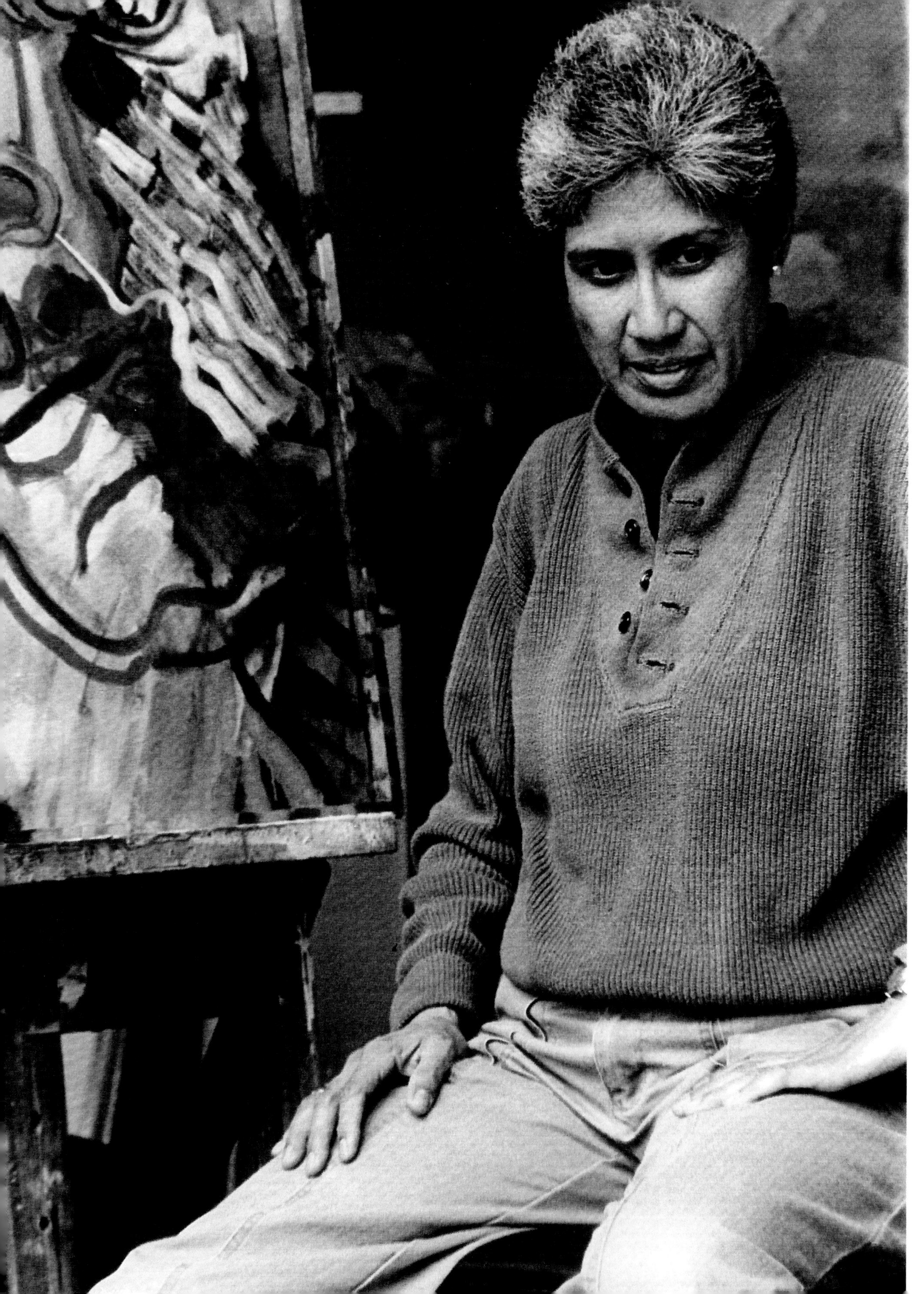

Greetings

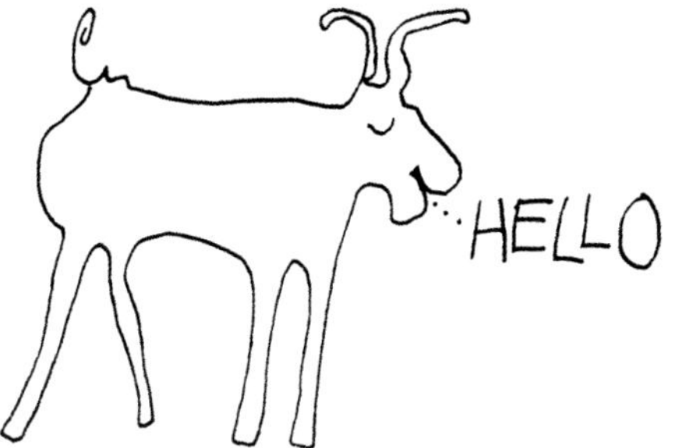

MAXINE BOROWSKY JUNGE (FRIEND, COLLEAGUE): It was clear from the beginning, when I first met Norma, that she was very special and very different. She wasn't an "ordinary person," whatever that is.

MOANA VERCOE (FRIEND, COLLEAGUE): I met Norma during what she referred to as her "third life." I think that the three lives were music, art, and teaching. It is typical of Norma that while other people have stages of their lives, Norma had three lives. She was just too big for one.

AIDA PAVLETICH (ARTIST, POET, MUSICAL COLLABORATOR): Norma had lived across from the La MaMa theater in Greenwich Village before she left for London in the sixties, and we likely crossed paths without meeting there.

STANLEY C. WILSON (ARTIST, COLLEAGUE): I started at Cal Poly University, I think it was September of 1973. I met Norma soon thereafter, when she came in as an adjunct. We kind of struck up a conversation. There was just kind of a natural affinity for Norma and me.

AIDA PAVLETICH: Dusty Springfield introduced us — she said we would be friends. I will forever be grateful to her. So, in 1973, I met the short Filipina woman with the thick wiry hair whose middle name, Cecilia, was the patron saint of music.

ROBERT GRAJEDA (FRIEND, MEMBER OF THE LATIN LIZARDS): I looked in the local newspaper and there was an ad for a school of music. It said, "If you want to play in a rock band, join our school and take lessons." It was an interesting, homebrew kind of school, and it included Norma as one of the teachers; she played drums, and the students that were learning to play their instruments in a band setting participated. That's where I met Norma.

BRIAN RANSOM (FRIEND, CERAMICIST, MUSICAL COLLABORATOR): I was looking for musicians, and I put an ad out in the *Claremont Courier*, the little local rag.

Norma called me up one afternoon and she said, "Hello. You're looking for percussionists?" I said, "Yes. I have a project, and you can come over and kind of see what I'm doing." And she said, "No. I'm in." I'm like, "Do you want to hear about it?" She said, "No. I'm in. I'm the person you're looking for."

CORINNA MÜLLER (LATER LIFE PARTNER): Norma and I were introduced to each other in 2009, so rather late in her life. She was seventy at the time. A mutual friend knew of my love of Norma's music, and decided to put us in touch. Norma and I then started to email and phone each other regularly, and over time, we developed a deep friendship. In 2016, we finally had the opportunity to meet. Norma invited me, her unknown Swedish phone friend, to her California home. When I arrived, we felt an instant soul connection, and for the following years, I spent extensive periods of time with her until her passing. I lovingly think of my time with Norma as our "whirlwind years." We traveled together, and she generously introduced me to her friends and family, and showed me around California.

MOANA VERCOE: I met Norma over ten years ago on campus at the International Festival. Within the crowd, Norma was a presence, and she was in her element—surrounded by music and culture. We figured out that we were both Scrippsies, and it was an instant bond. Norma became my friend—someone I trusted.

ROBERT GRAJEDA: Norma was Filipino and Panamanian. I actually had the honor of meeting her mom, Otilda, before she passed away.

AIDA PAVLETICH: Norma brought her mother, an octogenarian sculptor who loved to drink champagne, to live with her and Diane Divelbess. For Mother's Day, Carol Case brought her an Easter lily plant and I captured her picture with the white trumpet blooms in glorious Tri-X black and white.

MOANA VERCOE: Norma and I both shared what she proudly referred to as "hybrid vigor." She reveled in being able to draw from multiple traditions and cultures. When I took my mother to meet Norma it was as if they had known each other for years. They looked as if they were related; the same gorgeous skin tone, and hair with its own sense of anarchy.

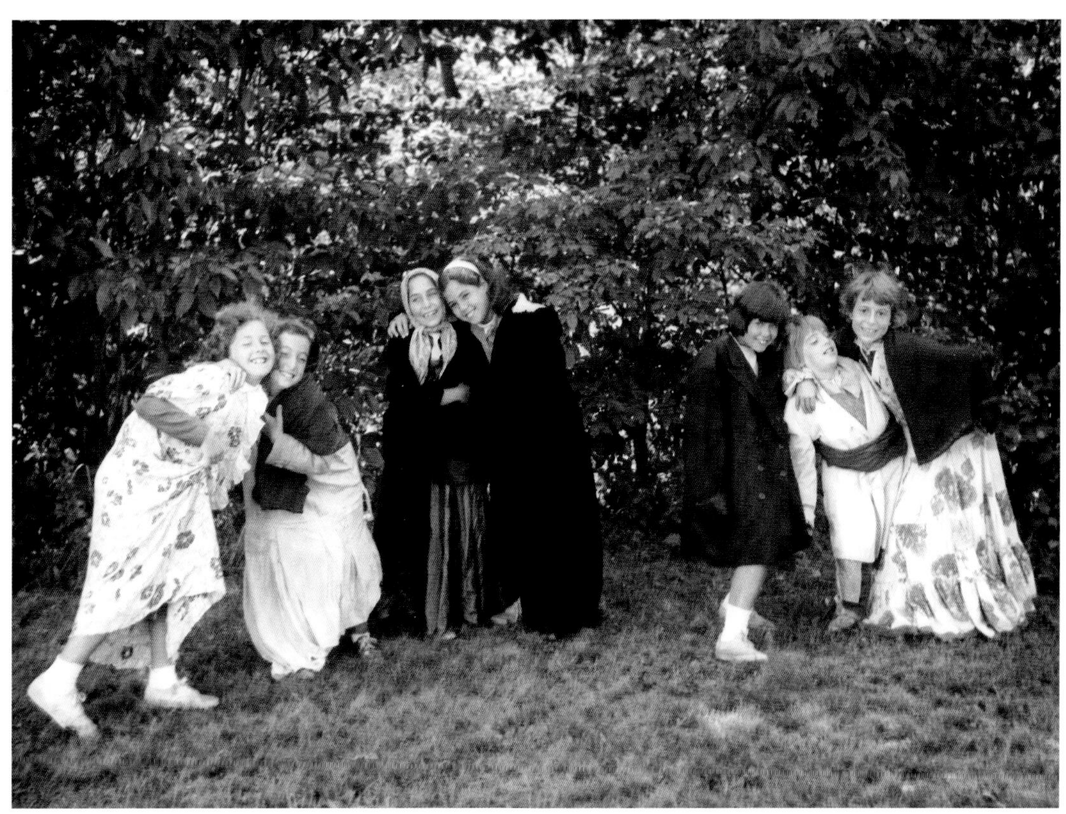

A young NCT, third from right

STANLEY C. WILSON: Norma grew up in Long Beach; I spent a lot of time as a youngster in Long Beach, even though I was born in Los Angeles. And we kind of shared a lot of that territory or the topography. We knew about the land, we knew about the people, we knew about the cultures that were there.

VIRGINIA RIGNEY (ARTIST, LIFELONG FRIEND): I met Norma at Long Beach Polytechnic High School in 1956. Poly was then a high school of approximately three thousand students drawn from diverse neighbors in the central and western neighborhoods of Long Beach. Norma was a senior and student director of the high school art gallery, and I a junior in the gallery arts class led by our art teacher, Elsa Warner. Ms. Warner selected students of artistic merit to create and install art exhibits in this advanced student gallery. Many of us continued a life of art making, and my friendship with Norma continued throughout her life.

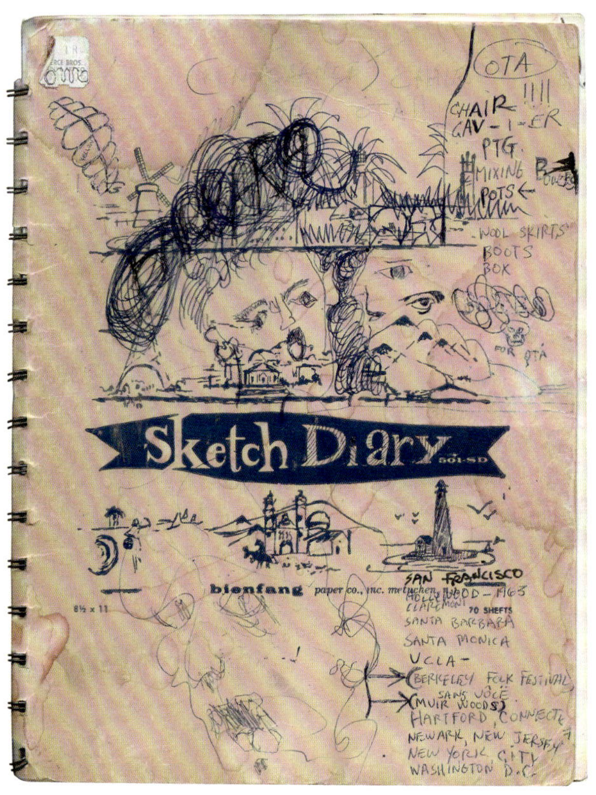

OTA
!!!!
CHAIR
CAV-1-ER
PTG.
MIXING BOWLS
POTS
WOOL SKIRTS
BOOTS
BOX
FOR OTA
Sketch Diary
501-SD
bienfang paper co., inc. metuchen
8½ x 11
SAN FRANCISCO
HOLLYWOOD - 1963
CLAREMONT
70 SHEETS
SANTA BARBARA
SANTA MONICA
UCLA -
BERKELEY FOLK FESTIVAL
SANS JOCE
MUIR WOODS)
HARTFORD, CONNECT.
NEWARK, NEW JERSEY
NEW YORK CITY
WASHINGTON D.C.

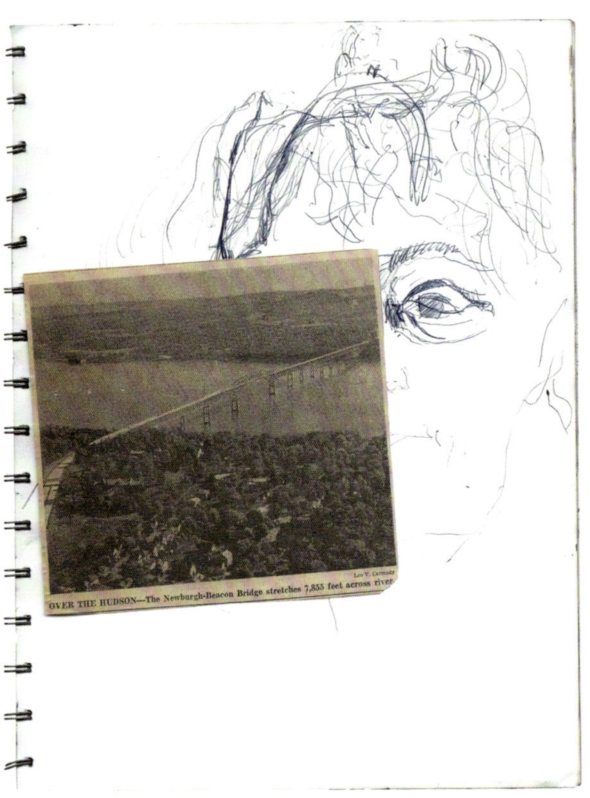

OVER THE HUDSON—The Newburgh-Beacon Bridge stretches 7,855 feet across river.

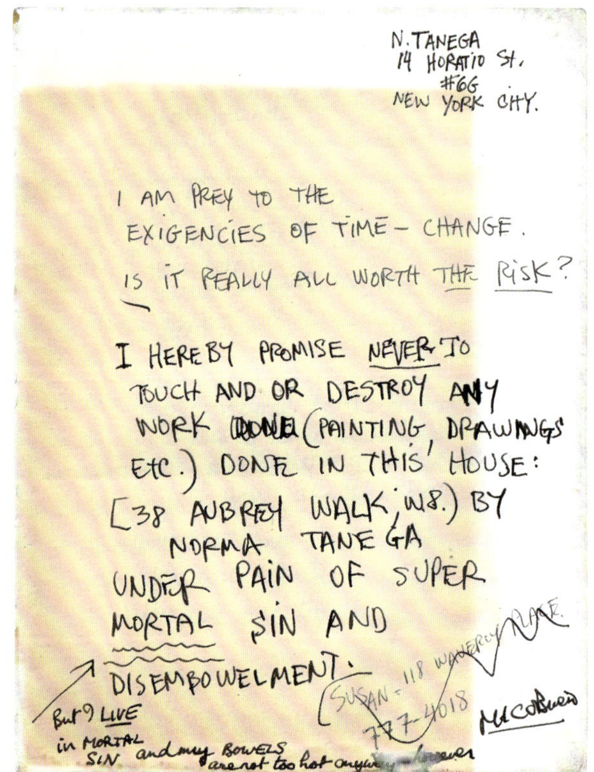

N. TANEGA
14 HORATIO St.
#6G
NEW YORK CITY.

I AM PREY TO THE
EXIGENCIES OF TIME - CHANGE.
IS IT REALLY ALL WORTH THE RISK?

I HEREBY PROMISE NEVER TO
TOUCH AND OR DESTROY ANY
WORK DONE (PAINTING, DRAWINGS
ETC.) DONE IN THIS' HOUSE:
[38 AUBREY WALK, W8.) BY
NORMA TANEGA
UNDER PAIN OF SUPER
MORTAL SIN AND
DISEMBOWELMENT.
But I LIVE
in MORTAL SIN and my BOWELS
are not too hot anymore
SUSAN - 118 WAVERLY PLACE.
777-4018
MCCOWEN

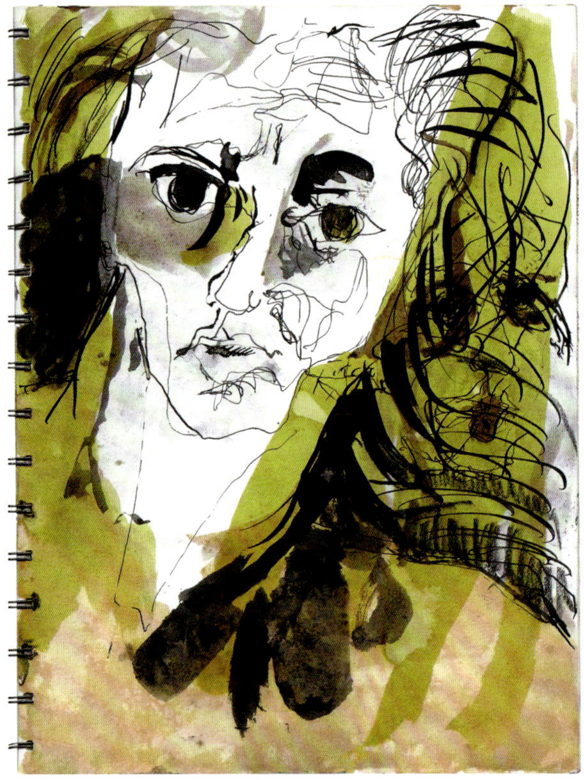

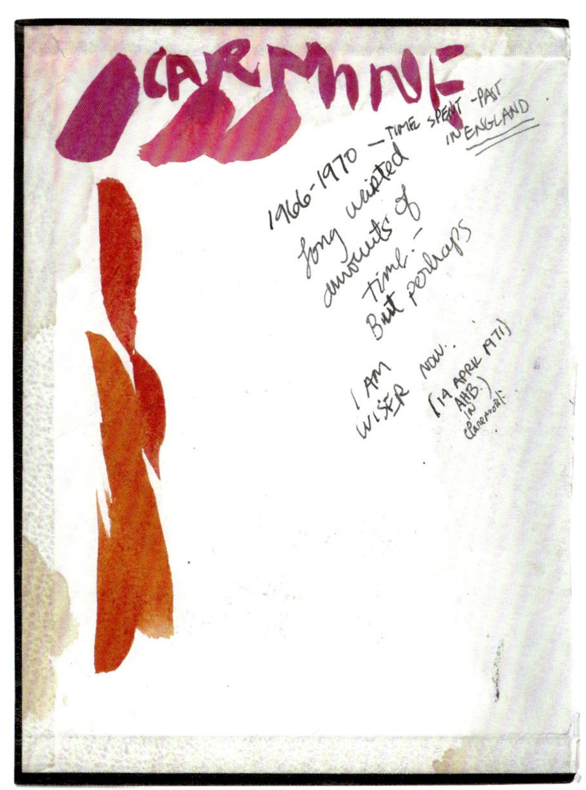
CARMINE
1966–1970 — TIME SPENT — PAST IN ENGLAND
Long wasted amounts of time. — But perhaps
I AM WISER NOW.
(14 APRIL 1971) AHB.)
(a) Claremont.

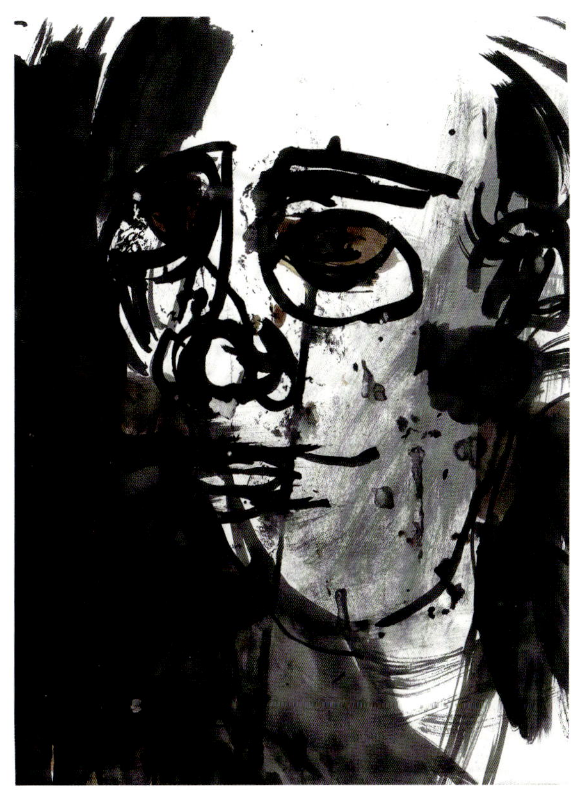

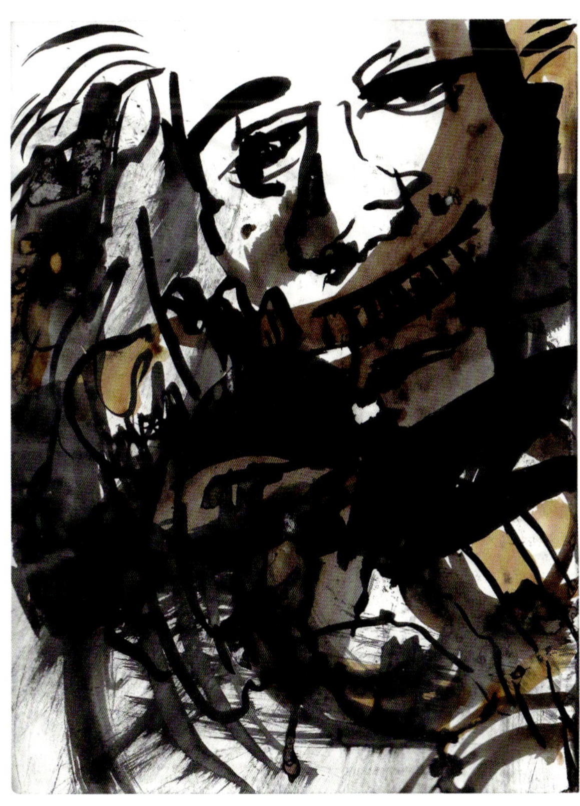

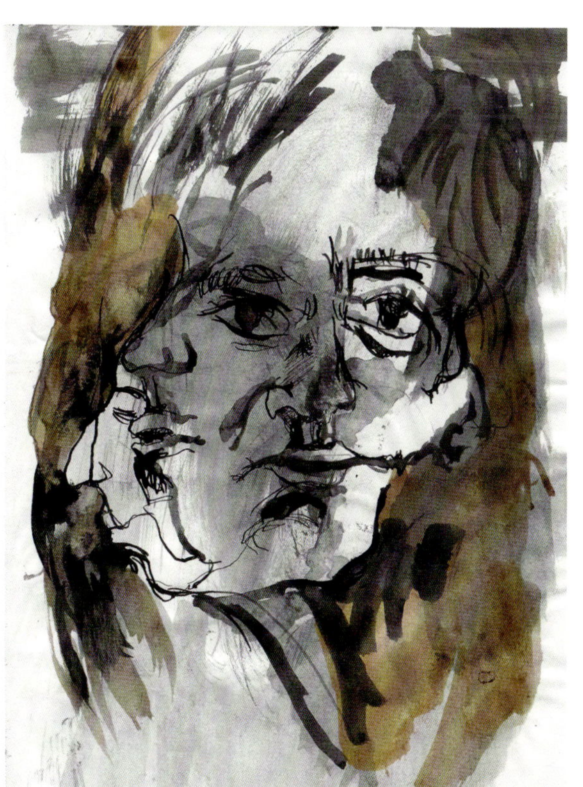

MAXINE BOROWSKY JUNGE: She went to Long Beach Polytechnic High School. There was an extraordinary art teacher there, way back, who must've had a lot of say in both encouraging her and getting her to Scripps College in Claremont, which had a well-thought-of art department at the time.

VIRGINIA RIGNEY: Elsa Warner remained a close friend and mentor to Norma and encouraged her to attend Scripps. Norma's piano teacher, though, encouraged her to become a classical pianist.

DAVID SHEARER (EXECUTIVE DIRECTOR OF CLAREMONT HERITAGE): Claremont is a small college town. We have seven institutions of higher learning: kind of a "Cambridge system" approach—a lot of small, specialized colleges, and then we also have three graduate universities. So that brought a lot of people to Claremont; probably, most notably, the artist Millard Sheets, who actually grew up in this area, but was brought in to teach at Scripps College. He basically formed the art department in 1932, when he was twenty-four years old.

CATHERINE McINTOSH (BOARD MEMBER OF THE CLAREMONT MUSEUM OF ART): Millard Sheets came to Claremont in the thirties and he started hiring at Scripps College. He developed that art department on a model based on Chouinard Art Institute, which was to have working artists be teachers. This was a very different approach. It seems normal now, but it was not normal then. Scripps developed a really strong art department. Sheets also was not into just sculpture and painting and nothing else, which was the norm back then. Scripps was really cutting-edge in terms of a variety of art forms—ceramics, enamel, fiber, mosaics—and not just the classical "painting and sculpture."

DAVID SHEARER: Sheets was just amazing at bringing people together. He hired a lot of really brilliant artists to teach, and he had his own studio where he did artwork. One of his philosophies was that art should be part of everyday living. That was kind of a pivotal point where, suddenly, Claremont became known as this kind of hub of creativity. The music scene in Claremont is phenomenal. We have the Folk Music Center here that has generated—kind of like some of the art departments at the colleges—tons of amazing musicians.

TOM SKELLY (ARTIST, RADIO DJ, MEMBER OF BABOONZ): We claimed residencies as varied as John Cage, Frank Zappa, Claudia Lennear, Vladimir Ussachevsky, David Murray, David Lindley, the Folk Music Center, and many others who were either residents of Claremont or have passed through and left an indelible mark throughout the city's history, from the early twentieth century to the present. Norma became one of the senior music/art staples here.

MARIO VERLANGIERI (STUDENT, MEMBER OF BABOONZ): When we started playing gigs, and people would come out to the gigs to come see Norma play, it became apparent how connected she was with the community. People would show up to come see us play locally, whether they were old friends of Norma's or just fans of the local art scene in general that knew her name. I think a lot of people saw her as a staple from the Folk Music Center, and one of the leaders in the local music scene.

DAVID SHEARER: I mean, I don't know, I tell people there's something in the water or something. There's something special about the place . . . and I think Norma was one of those people that really felt at home here.

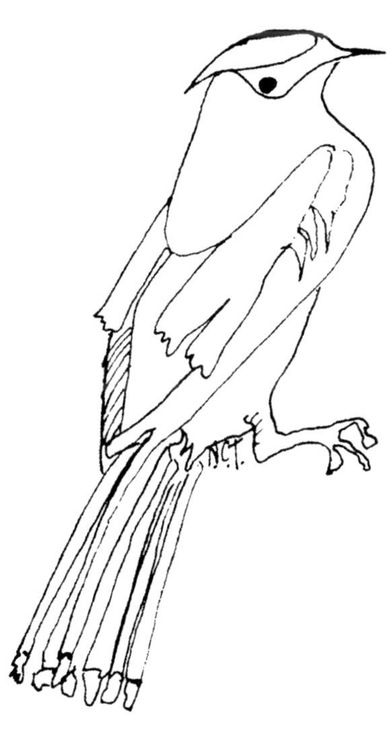

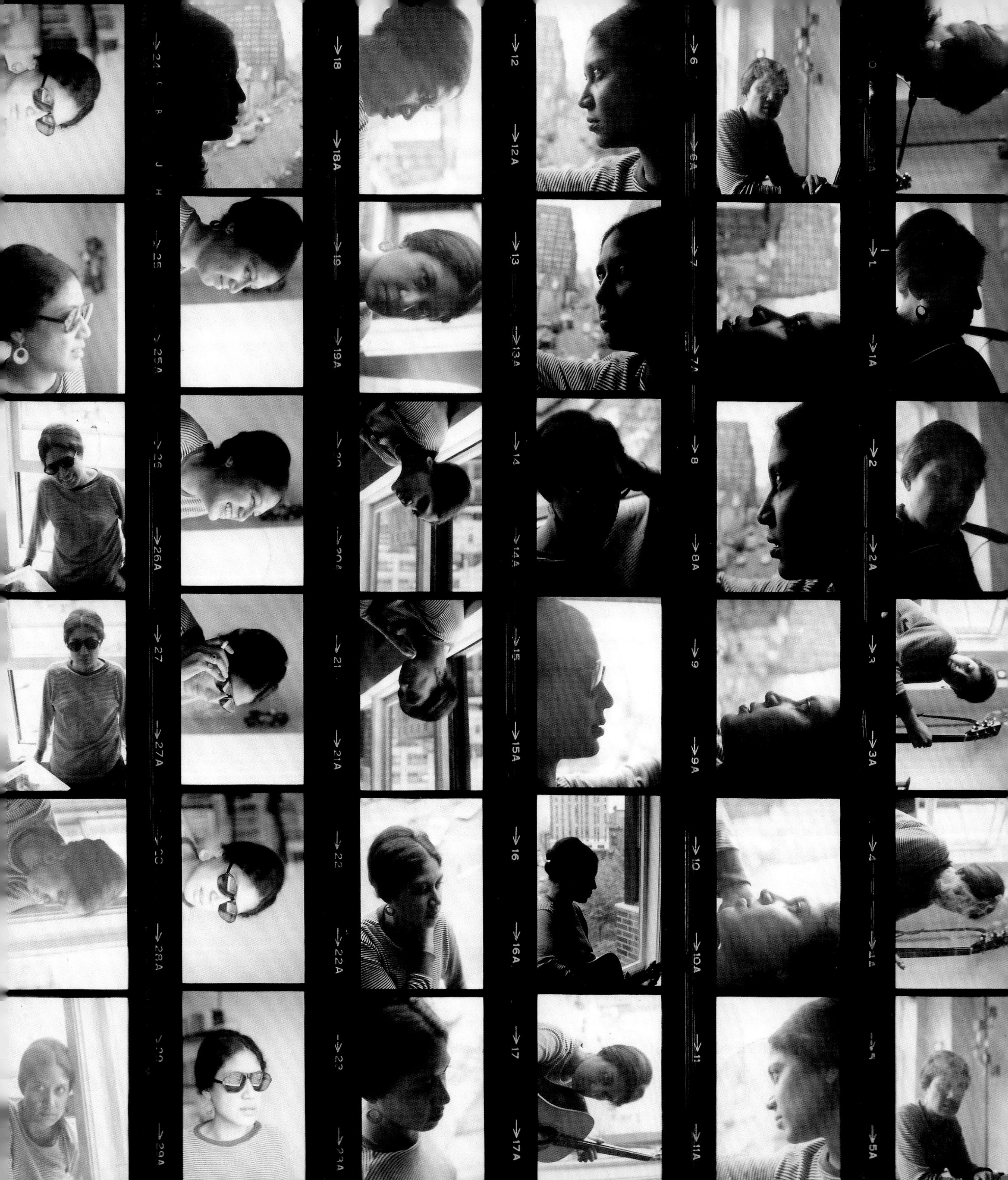

Loves

MAXINE BOROWSKY JUNGE: I was really close with Norma at Scripps. She was in my dorm. I lived in LA, and I would very often take people home to stay with my family. Once, in the early sixties, my parents went to Europe, and I was away riding a motorcycle or something, and my parents asked Norma to housesit. So Norma and Diane Divelbess and two other women came and housesat the house for a few weeks and took care of the dog, and had a fine time in my parents' house. You have to ask Diane that story if you want to know more, because apparently everybody from Scripps turned up. Upon his return, my dad looked at the liquor cabinet and said: "They had a good time."

BRIAN RANSOM: I called Norma "the Legendary Lesbian." I mean, she's in the Legendary Lesbian club. She would have these people come out to Claremont, like really high-stature gay and lesbian figures.

MAXINE BOROWSKY JUNGE: In those days, lesbians and gay folks needed to be very closeted. They certainly weren't out in any kind of direct way. There's always an undercurrent of "this person" or "that person"—some gossip, that kind of thing. It was just people being who they were, and they just didn't announce it.

BRIAN RANSOM: When we recorded with Norma around 2010, she had to be seventy. And we would go downtown to a club to have a drink or something and she would be, like, flirting with all the babes. And the babes, everyone would go, "Whoa! Who's that?" She totally had it, all the way. It was just amazing. I'm like, "Norma, that's some kind of magic juju you got!" "Oh, it's just the teeth."

STANLEY C. WILSON: If you became a friend of Norma's, it was a friend for life. It wasn't something that she used to benefit herself only and then you kind of disappeared. No, you stayed a friend of Norma's, because she had such a warm heart. She was such a giving person. And to be quite honest, she was a person that—I think even though we had different parents who came from different places . . . she gave all that she could. She pulled you in as a family member.

ROBERT GRAJEDA: People gravitated around Norma: students, other artists, members of the community. She attracted a lot of very interesting folks that we'd meet as first being students of hers. Then later on my relationship with Norma progressed to where we were really close friends.

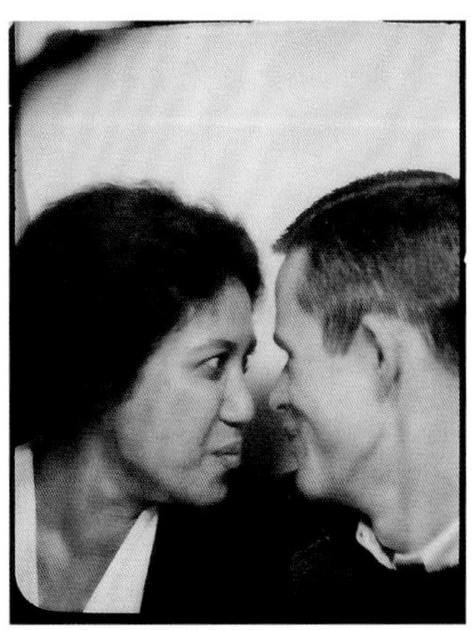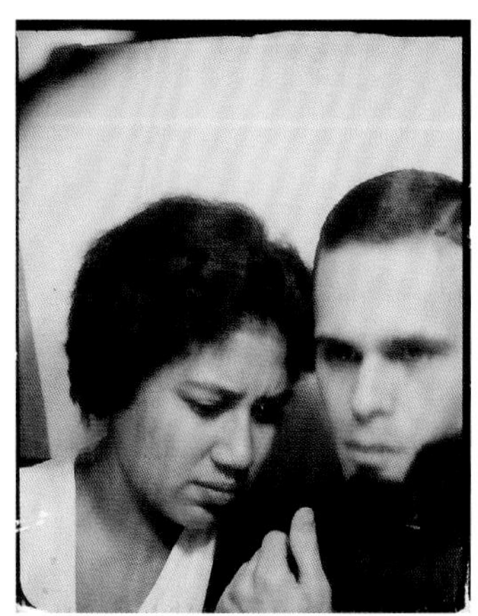

NCT with OTA

DIANE DIVELBESS: David William Authier (OTA) and Norma attended the same high school, Long Beach Poly. I believe that OTA was a year or two older, but am not sure about that. At any rate, Norma and OTA were forever friends from their high school days. David went on to teach for a time at the Portland Art Museum Art School, before I enticed him to teach at Cal Poly Pomona. He hated teaching non-professionally-oriented students, so became our art history slide curator instead. OTA was a true artist. He painted or drew constantly, worked through pages of journals, lived by himself in LA—he said he could only manage to keep a cactus plant alive in his apartment—but did have great friends. He taught me how to really get the most from an art museum visit.

CORINNA MÜLLER: During the times I was back at home in Sweden, Norma and I Skyped twice daily. Once I called in the middle of her dinner, but when I suggested she call me back when she had finished eating, she put down her cutlery and said: "I love you more than food." So this is my advice for you: find someone who loves you more than food!

AIDA PAVLETICH: The eighties, deplorably, lost us many gays, among them Norma's dear friend and fellow painter David Authier. David, who lived near me in Los Feliz, was blindsided by the disease, as were we all, and it left us grieving for our missing friends.

STANLEY C. WILSON: Norma's heart was very wide. And I was impressed by her kindness. I was impressed by her ability to facilitate other individuals that were interested in creating. And so that's who she was. And as I say, I have such a strong and lasting memory of that.

ROBERT GRAJEDA: I met Karin, my wife, through Norma. Norma knew Karin because they were both art professors at Cal Poly.

KARIN SKIBA (FRIEND, COLLEAGUE): I met Diane and Norma in the early eighties when I was teaching art at Cal Poly Pomona. Norma was doing distance ed classes for high schools and Diane was chair of the art department. While I was at Cal Poly, Norma performed music often. It was so wonderful. I knew Norma painted, but it was a real introduction to her innovative live music. Her music and singing were different from the mainstream, and she collaborated with several singers and musicians—I saw her perform several times.

ROBERT GRAJEDA: So, when Karin and I got together and we decided to get married, we got married at Norma's house. There's a big oak tree out in the front of the property; we got married under that oak tree, and it was really cool.

KARIN SKIBA: Norma always welcomed me, and I appreciated it. I am glad you are commemorating her. Please know that she played a part in me finding my wonderful husband, and for that I am incredibly grateful.

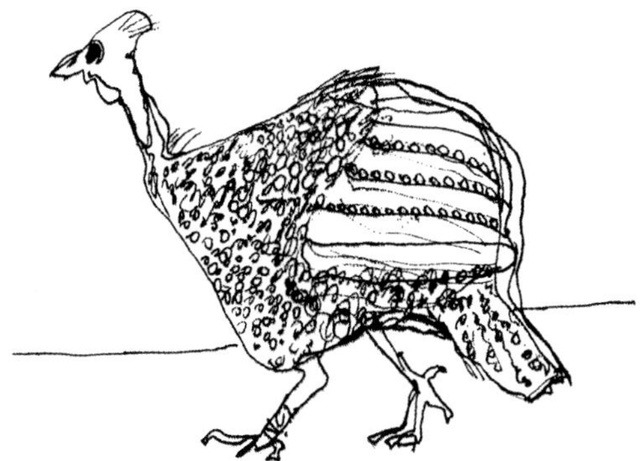

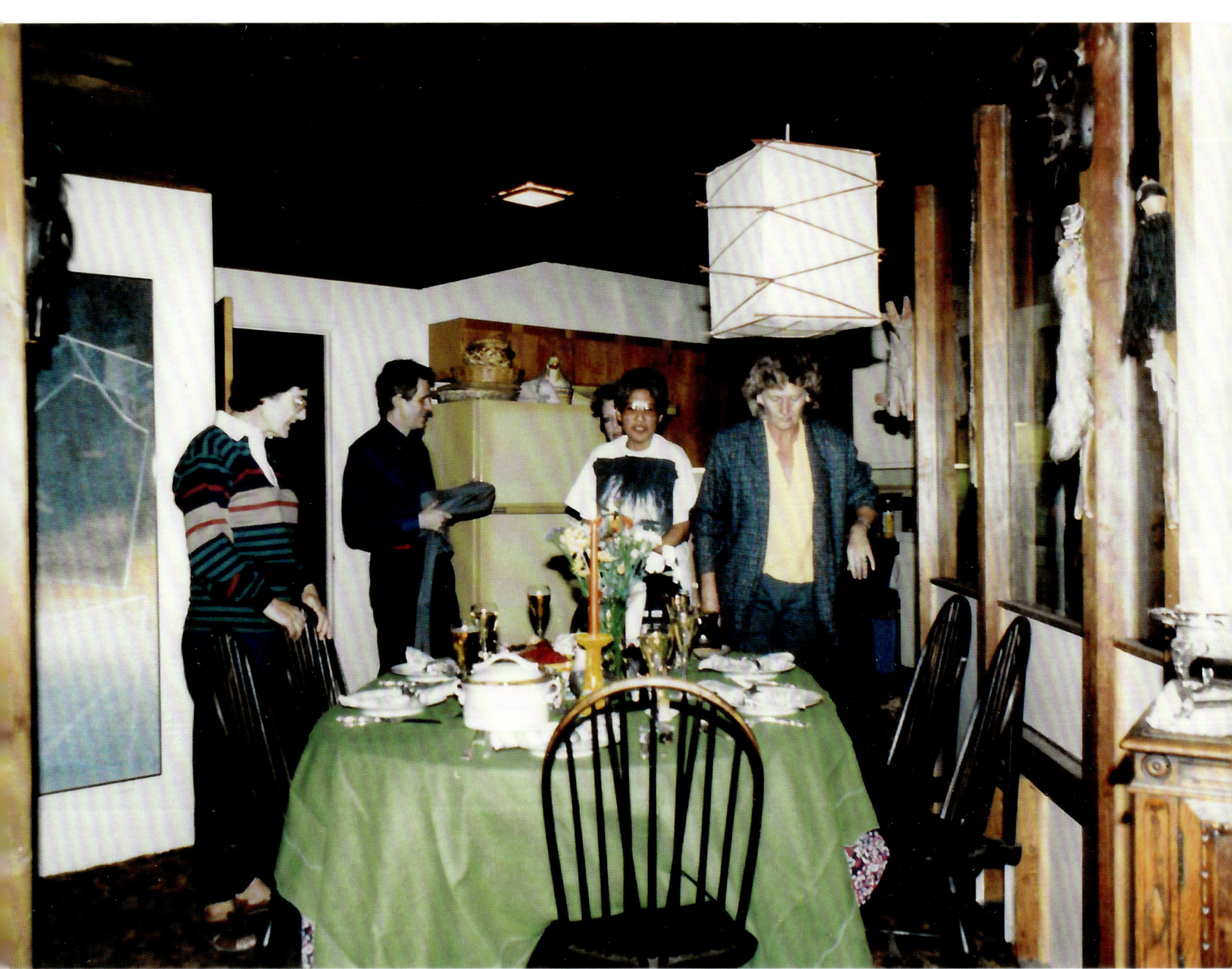

DD, OTA, Diane Schnitzer, NCT, and Bonita Lockwood

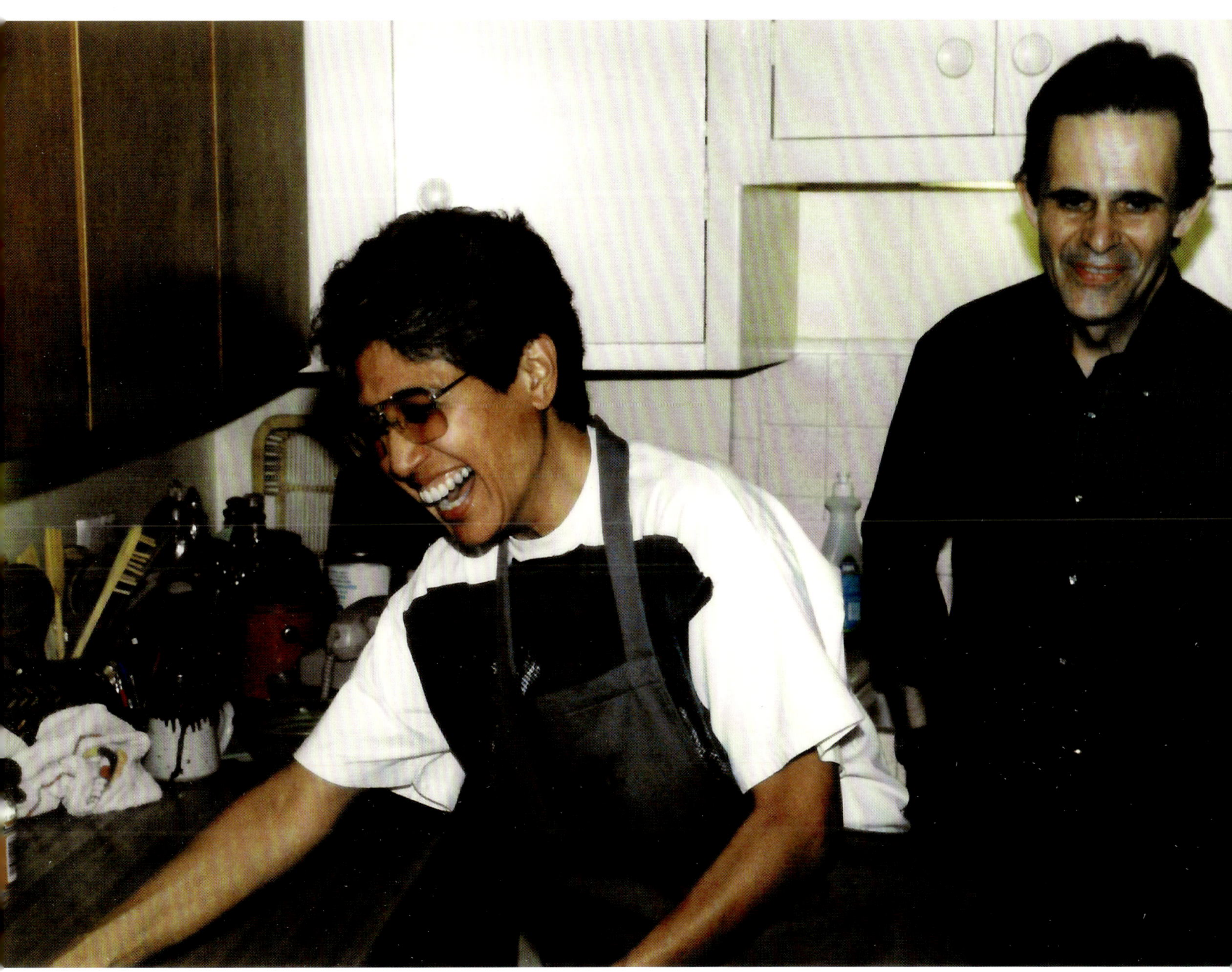

Another joyful meal

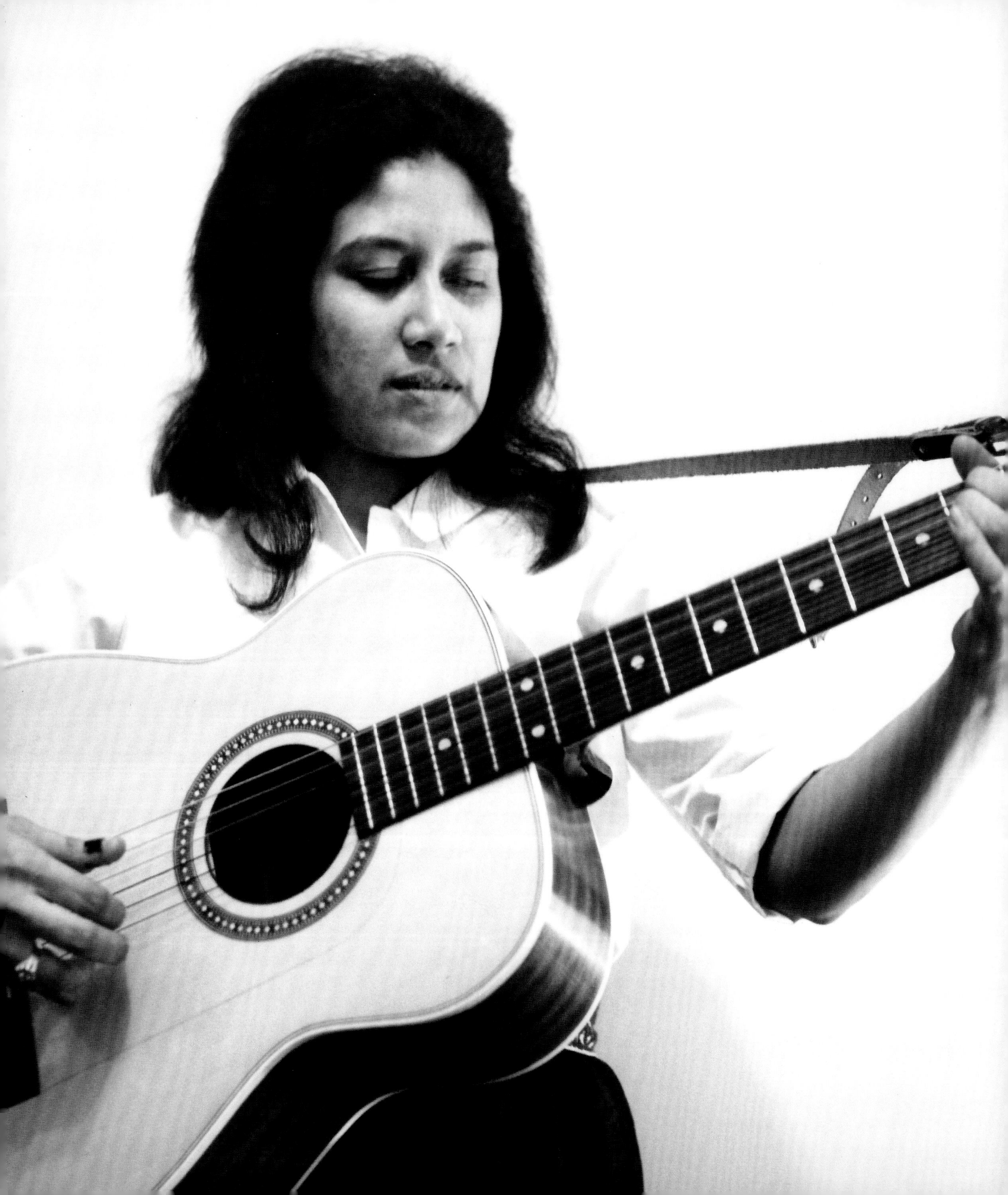

Journeys

CATHERINE McINTOSH: Norma definitely didn't want to be part of the establishment of artists in Claremont that came from the Millard Sheets era. I think it influenced her because of going to Scripps, and because it's just all over Claremont. But I think she always was kind of anti-establishment, which was pretty typical of the sixties. Norma kind of stuck with it.

REBECCA HAMM (FRIEND, MEMBER OF HYBRID VIGOR): Norma always seemed to have a vision. She was eager to work creatively and to push others forward into their own creativity. Her excitement and passion were contagious. I was always learning from being around her: how she saw things, how she shared information she felt was so important for others to consider, her boldness and compassion, and how she lived an artistic life. She was very generous with everything, a true art spirit that recognized the art spirit in others. She also wanted to focus her time and attention in those places where her creativity could flourish. She did not want to spend time where it wasn't welcomed or appreciated. She gave sincere and precious time to those around her.

MOANA VERCOE: During the period I knew Norma, I saw her perform with the band Baboonz and collaborate with Steven Rushingwind, and I got to sit in on jam sessions with Brian Ransom, Mario Verlangieri, and others—playing amazing instruments such as the saxoflute, ceramic instruments built for the Brian Ransom Ceramic Ensemble, and other marvelous music-making creations.

ROBERT GRAJEDA: Norma was a multi-instrumentalist. She played guitar from the folk era, played piano from childhood. She played a drum set as well as hand drums, and she was self-taught. And of course, she sang really beautifully. So, she had all of these assets, all of these things that she brought to bear.

CORINNA MÜLLER: One time, when we Skyped my mom—who's German—Norma burst into a German folk song, "Lieb Nachtigall, wach auf," with a perfectly charming accent! When she had finished, Norma said: "I have no idea where that even came from! I must have learned it in school when I was a kid." Needless to say, my mother was utterly enchanted.

MOANA VERCOE: One of my favorite Norma memories was a road trip up to Whidbey Island in Washington. Somewhere in the middle of the long drive, the Rolling Stones' "Paint It Black" came on the radio and Norma started singing and drumming on the dashboard of the car. It was joyous, pitch-perfect, and she didn't miss a beat. She just radiated. That's what Norma was like when she was creating.

BRIAN RANSOM: Norma played with so many people. I've played with tons of people, too, over the years, but Norma and I had something so incredibly intangible. When I play, even now, with certain people and they hear me making a turn in a performance, they're like, "What?" And you'll hear me hinting that I'm going to come into this new section, but they're like, "How many bars, man?" Norma and I would never have to do that, ever. Norma—I wouldn't have to look at her.

ROBERT GRAJEDA: I saw her do something really cool when we were playing together. I wrote a jazzy blues piece that was an instrumental, it had a nice little melody. I saw what a genius songwriter she was, because I thought, "It'd be really great if we could sing something to this," but the melody was a little bit challenging. She sat down, and in about half an hour she had lyrics. She just knocked out a really cool song.

BRIAN RANSOM: There's nobody else I've ever played with that completely knew where I was going musically. And Norma would lead me the same way, and we would do all these really well-rehearsed-seeming things.

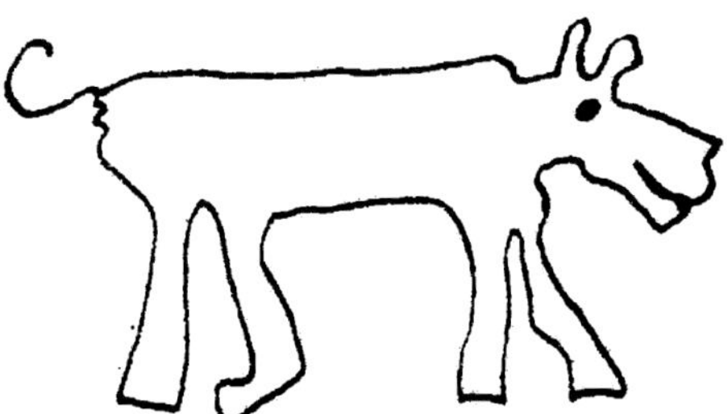 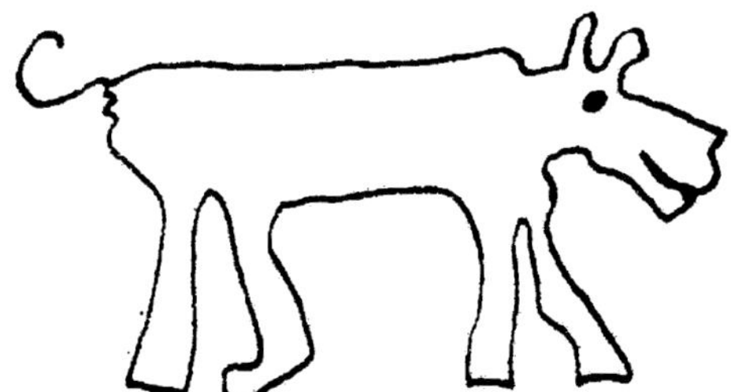

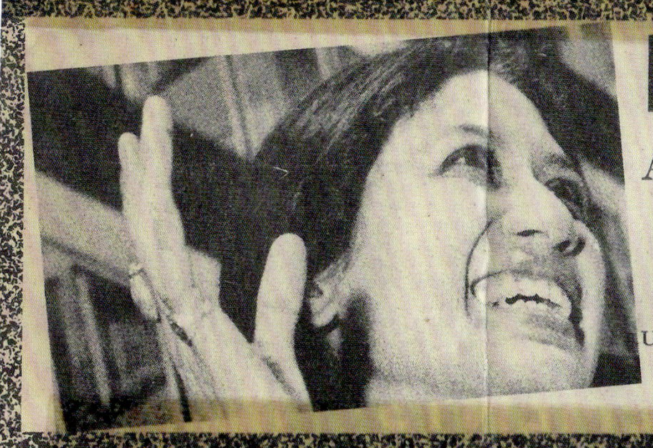

I'm a painter—not a pop singer

says NORMA TANEGA

APART from owning a cat named "Dog" and writing songs about streets that rhyme with 6 a.m., Norma Tanega freely admits that painting—NOT POP—is her first love.

Until success in the unexpected shape of a hit record whisked her away from her little pad on the edge of New York's Greenwich Village, she was quite satisfied to sit and paint.

"Only conservative stuff really," she explained. "Pictorial work and graphic art are what I'm best at.

"I like singing and want to be a good performer—but making a record was one of these pop accidents."

Apparently, she used to sing and play guitar to an English class in New York and was introduced to a physical training instructor who also made records.

"That was odd for a start," she joked. "But before I knew where I was I'd put my song 'Jubilation' on tape.

"People liked my voice and material and I had a hit with 'Cat Named Dog'."

Now she's being feted by all and sundry, has been on tour with people like Len Barry, B. J. Thomas and Britain's Chad and Jeremy—all consistent hit-makers in the States—and is in Britain for a couple of weeks' promotion.

Norma, a delightful and intelligent person (she's gained several academic degrees) is part Philippino-part Panamanian.

She wears enormous rings on her fingers, brightly-coloured smock dresses, attractive chunky ear-rings —and really only needs a feather in her swept-back raven-coloured hair to make her a natural "double" for Minnehaha.

She's still completely unaffected by her elevation to the pop pedestal, too. Money has never meant much to her.

IN FACT, SHE ARRIVED IN BRITAIN LAST WEEK WITH ONLY ONE SILVER DOLLAR IN HER PURSE — A THING SHE FOUND HILARIOUSLY FUNNY.

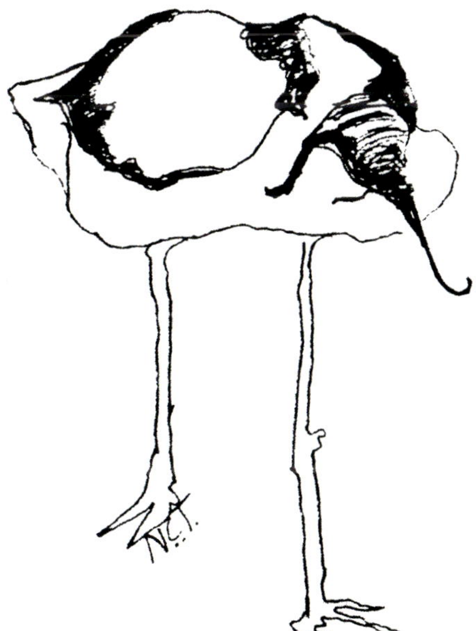

Artist composes music, sings too

By MARGE GROSS
Staff Writer

A paint brush, guitar, records and a singing voice have worked together to shape the life of Norma Tanega.

She not only paints, but composes music, has made a hit record, sung in Carnegie Hall and recently exhibited her art at Ontario City Library's Garden Room.

For the most part, these art works are done in bold, moody shapes using colors of purple, blue-black and dark earth tones. Two paintings showed a definite contrast since they were done in brighter colors — blue, orange, yellows.

"Those (the lighter, happier colors) are a color break for me," Tanega said. "They are my best in five years and I'm very excited about the colors."

She explained that her works have always been bold and moody ... "only more so." Tanega said anyone who thinks of himself as an artist has to deal with emotions.

her name is Elsa Warner. She sent me to Scripps and is the most important person in my life. She's 81 now, and I see her every Thanksgiving ... three of her students are working artists."

Tanega earned her master's degree in fine arts at Claremont Graduate School and now teaches graphics part time at Cal Poly Pomona. She considers herself a working artist, and teaches "so I can eat."

Other facets of Norma Tanega's life are to have been co-owner of an art gallery in Redondo Beach, to have taught art in New York and Los Angeles and now to be a partner in Tanega Toons, publishing her own songs and musical compositions.

Her paintings are in private collections, the Downey Museum of Art and the Brand Library Art Galleries, Glendale.

Norma Tanega may have her times of being moody, but her personality reflects her lastest paintings ... bright and cheerful like the "popcorn faces."

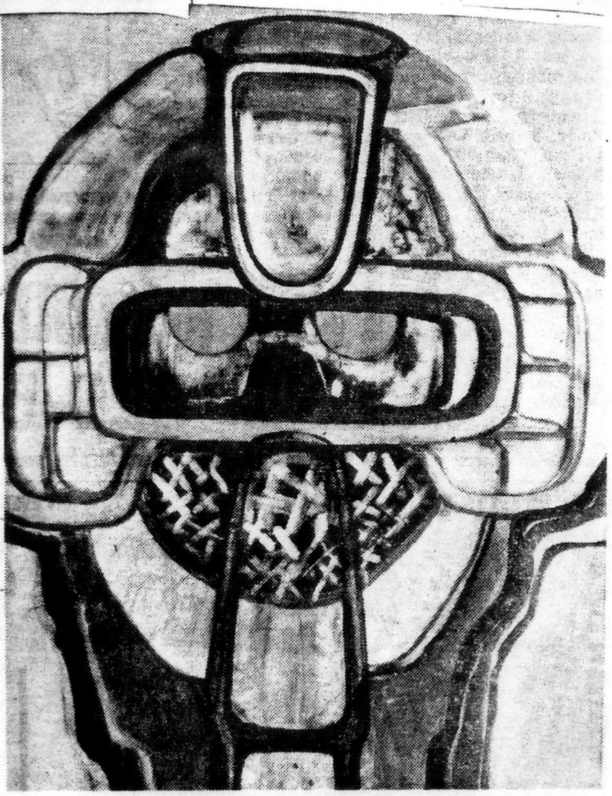

One of Norma Tanega's masks is represented here by this bold painting of wild, brooding colors. The Claremont artist, who also teaches graphics part time at Cal Poly Pomona, has painted a series of masks which she admits are "death masks." Now painting the masks in brighter colors, she calls them "popcorn faces." Tanega is a musician and plays the piano, guitar, banjo, auto-harp and harmonica. She has sung with other artists in Carnegie Hall, New York City.

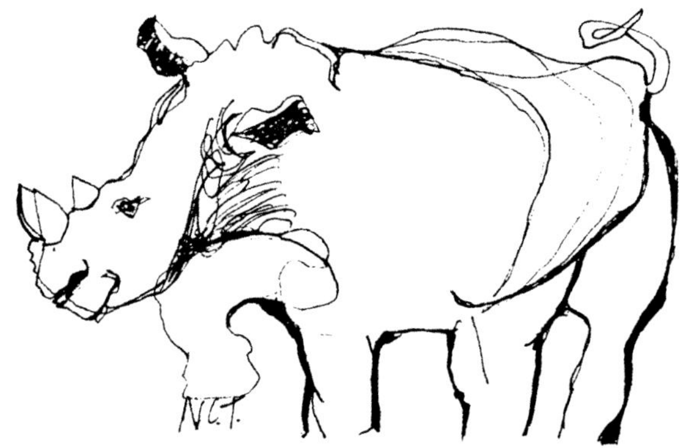

It's our business to be sensitive. We have a corner of that area ... It's hard to be at a high pitch all the time," she said. "When I hit 40, things began to take a change in my acceptance of self."

In the artist's collection are works of strange, wild masks. "Some think they are just masks," she said, "but they are death masks to me. I was dealing with death." There was one brighter, happier mask in the exhibit ... referring to it she said, "Now I call them popcorn faces."

With a shrug, Tanega said, "Most people don't go for my art ... they don't like it." She admitted she can't live with the death masks. A friend has one hanging in a prominent place, and the artist said, "I can't stand going there and seeing it!"

The daughter of a military bandmaster, Tanega grew up in Long Beach and her interest in music came naturally. She studied piano for 10 years and taught herself to play the guitar, banjo, auto-harp and harmonica.

The hit record she cut is called "Walking My Cat Named Dog." It's popularity was primarily in London, where Tanega lived, worked, painted, composed and recorded from 1967 to 1972.

Norma Tanega also was invited to bring her guitar and sing with others such as Pete Seeger, Jose Feliciano and Carolyn Hester in Carnegie Hall, New York City. This was a benefit, and to this day, the fact she sang in the prestigious music hall is "all like a dream" to the artist.

"I like rock 'n roll though I have a total classical background," she said. At one time, Tanega was the only woman with a traveling rock group. "All you hear about rock groups is true," she laughed. "That two months was the biggest part of my education ... I learned more than I did in any university."

"I'm a first generation Panamanian-Philippine," she said. "When I come to fill out statistic forms which ask for race, I'm always 'other,'" she said. "My mother was not going to have me grow up with an accent, and I was fortunate when in high school, the art teacher took an interest in me ...

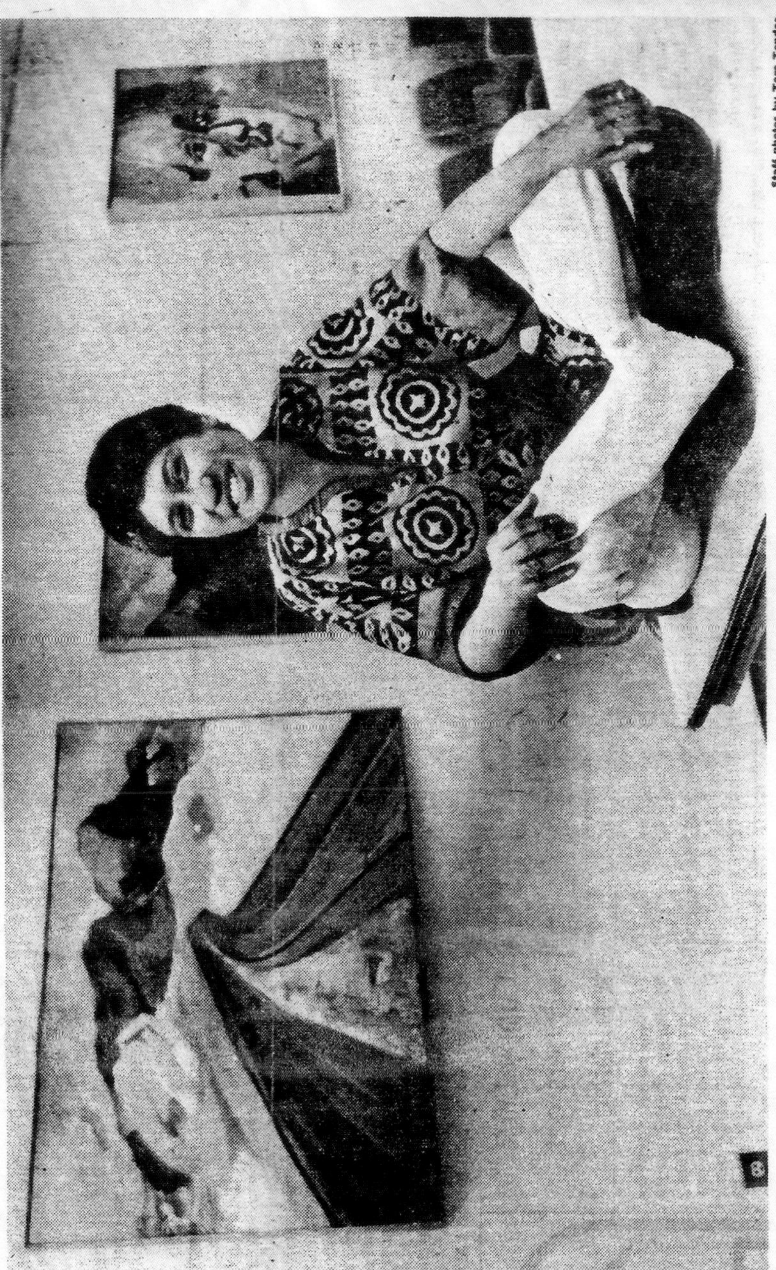

Norma Tanega of Claremont sits amid some of her paintings which were exhibited recently at the Ontario City Library. Tanega's paintings range from dark, brooding colors to her more recent works of brighter tones such as yellows, orange and blue. "Those (lighter paintings) are a color break for me. They are my best in five years and I'm very excited about the colors," she said. Tanega also plays the guitar, sings and has recorded many of her own compositions.

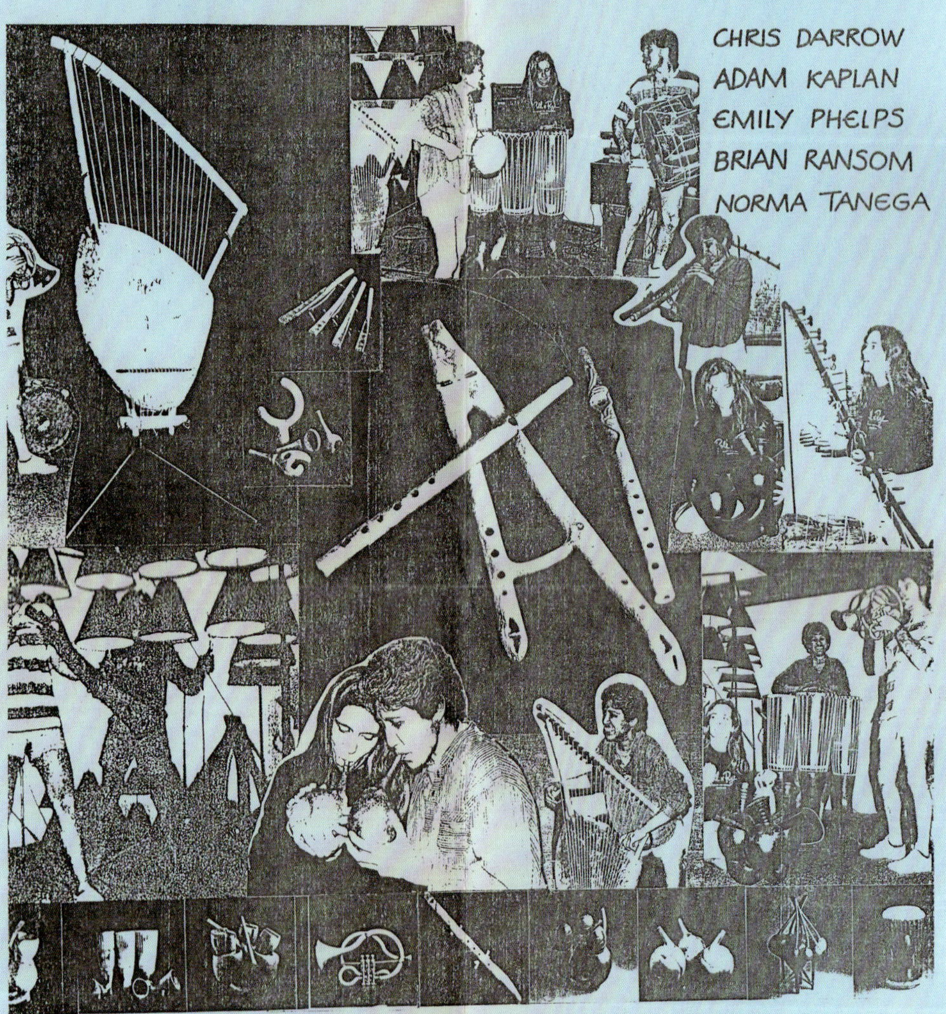

BRIAN RANSOM
CERAMIC ENSEMBLE
CHRIS DARROW
ADAM KAPLAN
EMILY PHELPS
BRIAN RANSOM
NORMA TANEGA
Performing Thursday April 9, 1987
8:00 p.m., Music Bldg., Room 101 Cal Poly Pomona
Reception Following in A.S.I. UU Gallery
Sponsored by the Art Department

MARIO VERLANGIERI: One of our songs from our band Baboonz was called "The Alzheimer's Song." One of Norma's friends left a voice message with just four lines of lyrics. She was like, "Oh, Norma, I've got this idea for a song. Here it is." And it was just these four lines. And Norma had a cassette recording of it from the answering machine and was like, "We need to make a song out of this." We just jammed one day, and she kept saying the words over it, and we had this cool song. It was really cool to experience that process. She was so influenced by the people around her.

BRIAN RANSOM: Norma's favorite thing would be when I would play one of my triple flutes or something, and she'd be on whatever percussion she wanted and we would just . . . it would be like going out for a hike in the hills: we didn't know where we were going, and we didn't know what was going to happen, but we were together on this journey. And she would love it. She'd love doing those duets like that. We would often do them, even when we played with a more complete band—we'd go, "Everybody take a break; Norma and I are just going to play a duet." And there was never any remote fear of . . . there are no wrong notes, because when somebody does something unusual, that's just a door opening to a new musical place. And afterwards I'd say, "How'd you know I was going to do that?" She goes, "Oh, I knew." We had this thing that was really, really very special, and I've never found it with anyone else to that level.

ROBERT GRAJEDA: As an artist, she was open-minded, nonjudgmental. But tough. She could be a diva, in a sense.

KARIN SKIBA: We were aware of Norma's early success and life in England. It was always very impressive and exciting.

MARIO VERLANGIERI: Norma was always so humble about her early career. I mean, she was a mentor to me, and she acted how you'd imagine a mentor would act; she would hint at things, give you little bits and pieces. "Oh yeah, this one time with Bob Dylan . . ." and I'd be like, "What? Hang on. Tell me more about that."

ROBERT GRAJEDA: She had toured the world, played with Bob Dylan, José Feliciano at Carnegie Hall, worked with Dusty Springfield in London in the sixties, of course. So she always had that: "I've been there and done that, so I have a lot to offer." But she also was very supportive and nonjudgmental about what you were doing; in other words, she supported your ability to be successful with whatever your musical capabilities were.

MARIO VERLANGIERI: She didn't brag about it. She wanted to share her experience with me, a young musician with dreams of being a rock star, getting signed, or whatever. She was very supportive, but also very realistic: when it came to the business or record labels, she would talk about the good things and the bad things. Her whole [career] arc gave a real perspective on what it's like to be an artist. When you're young, you have this idea of what it is to be a musician, and it was great to see her, this great artist who had achieved success, and what is that really like? Because she was always Norma, my music teacher, my mentor, and my friend.

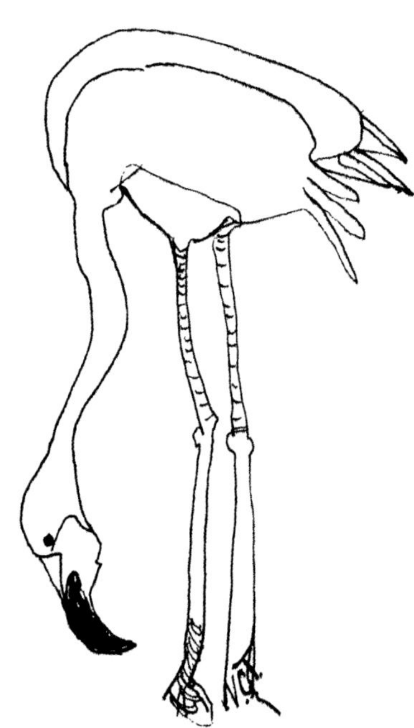

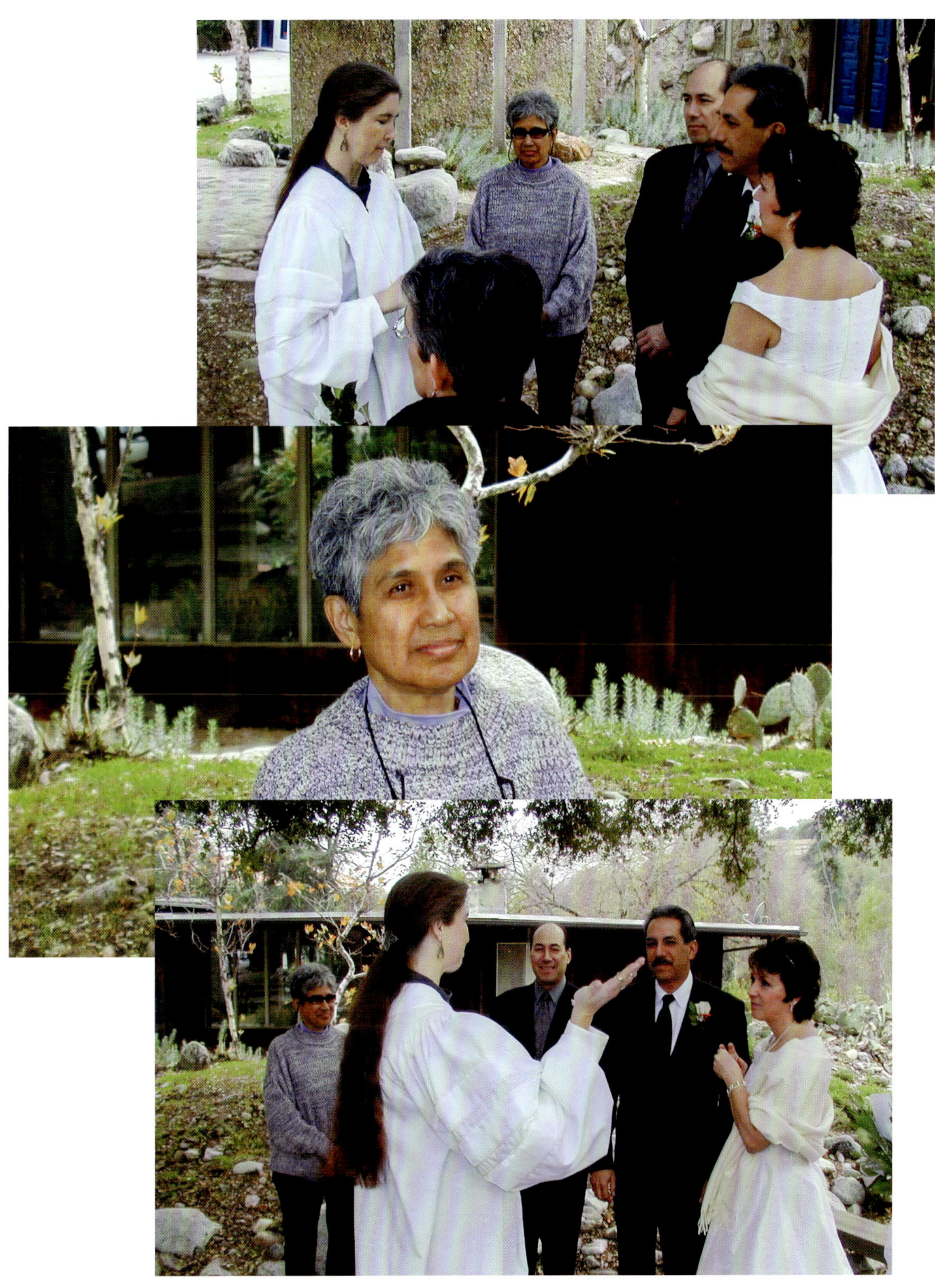

Robert Grajeda and Karin Skiba's wedding

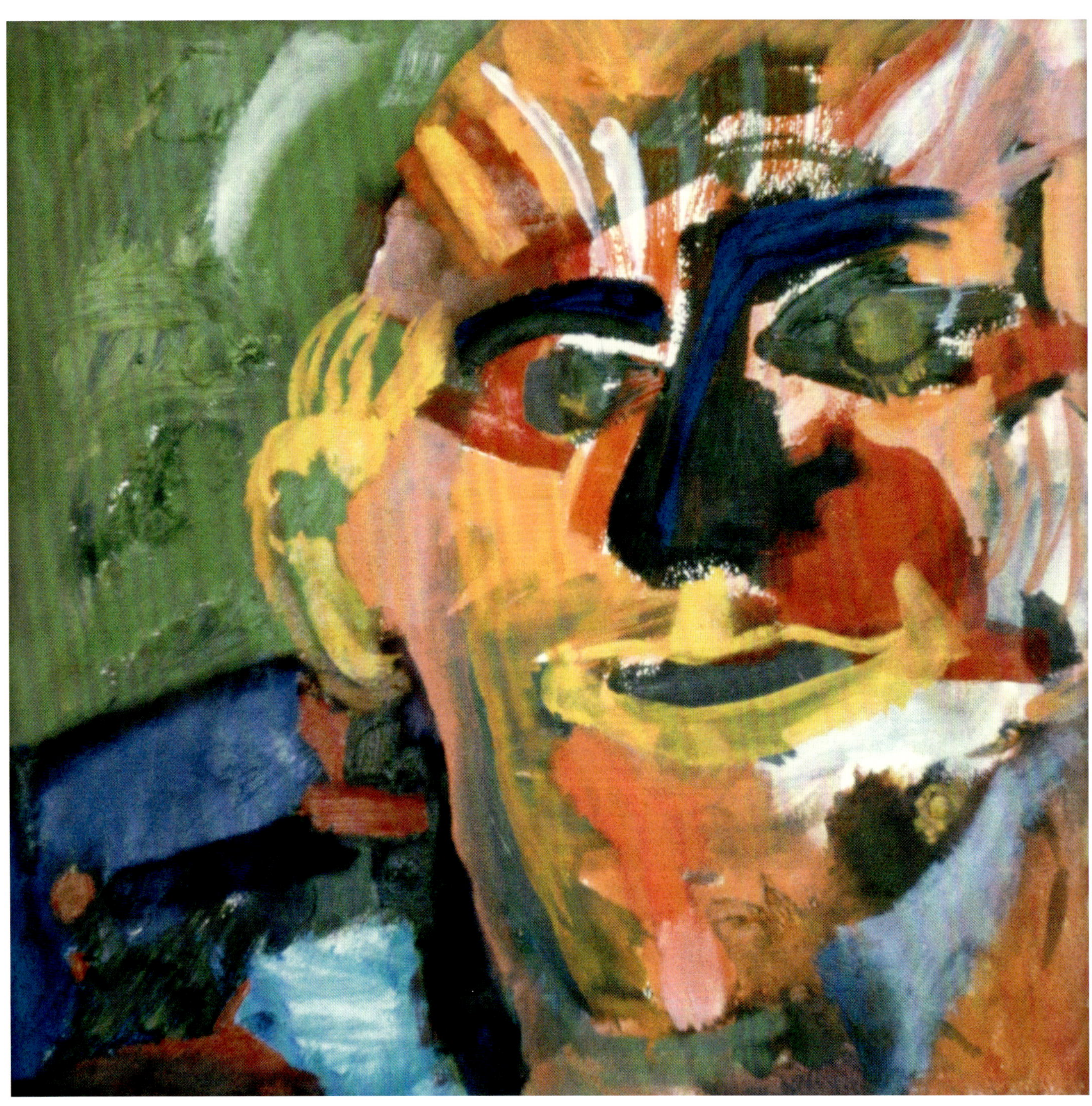

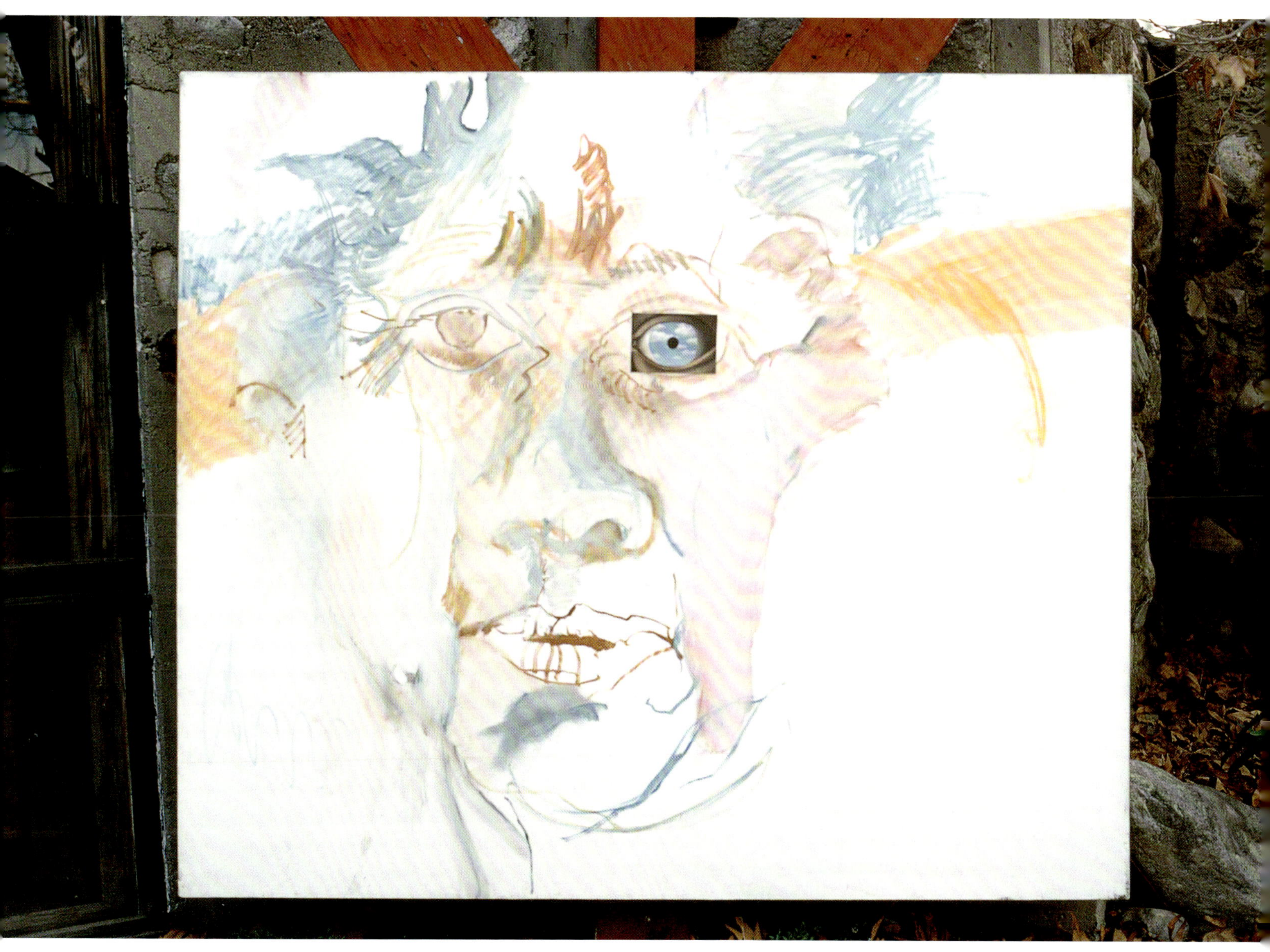

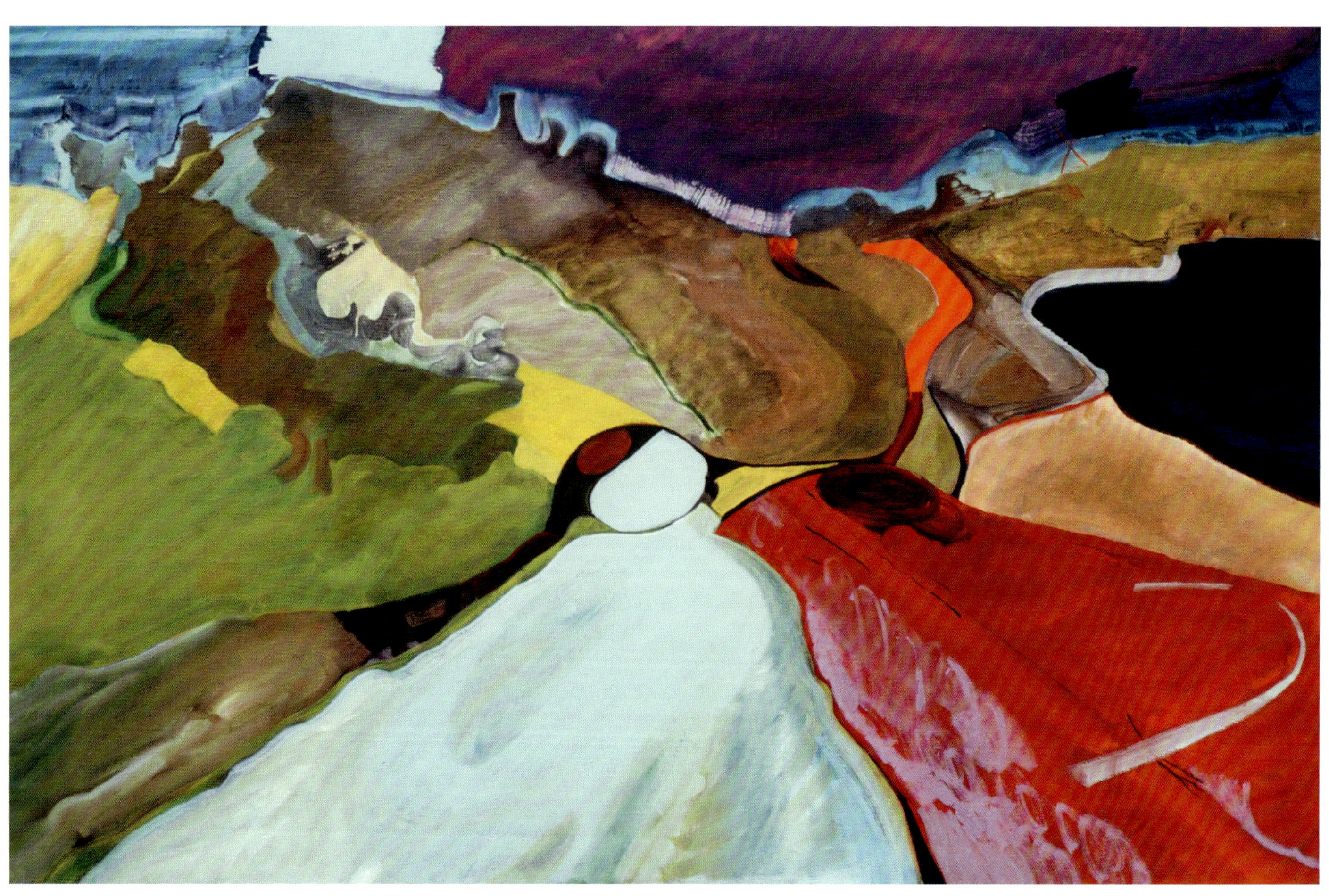

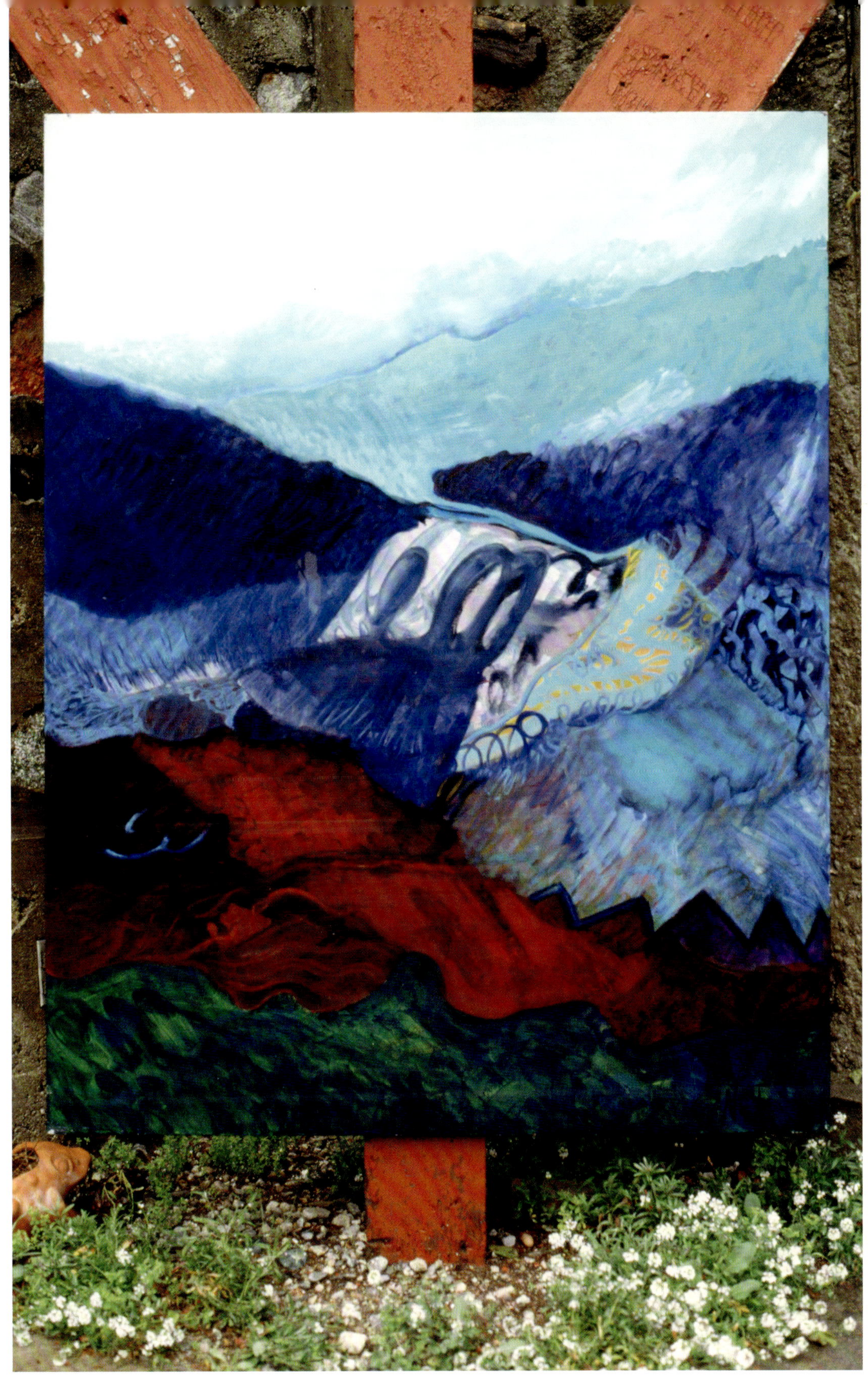

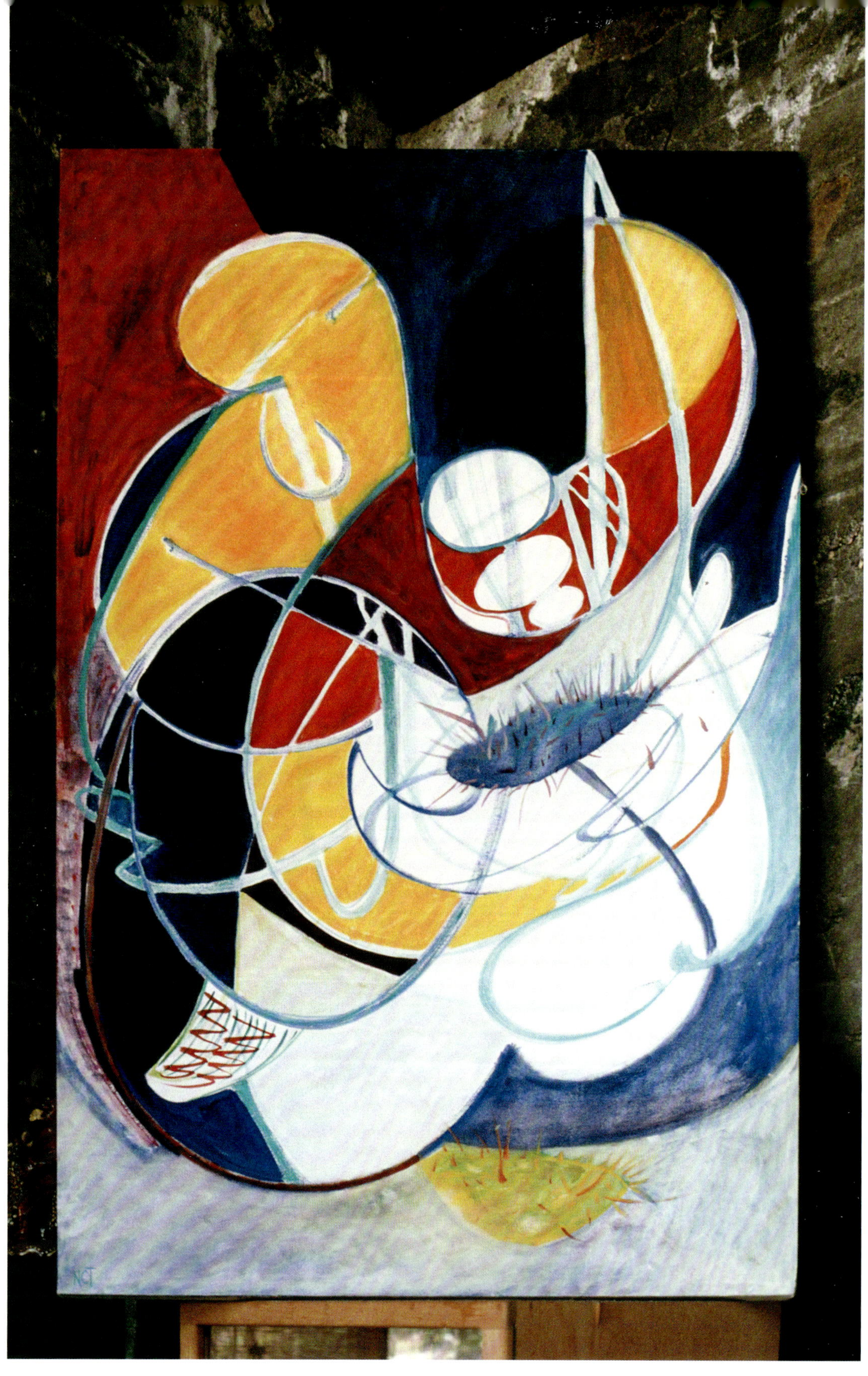

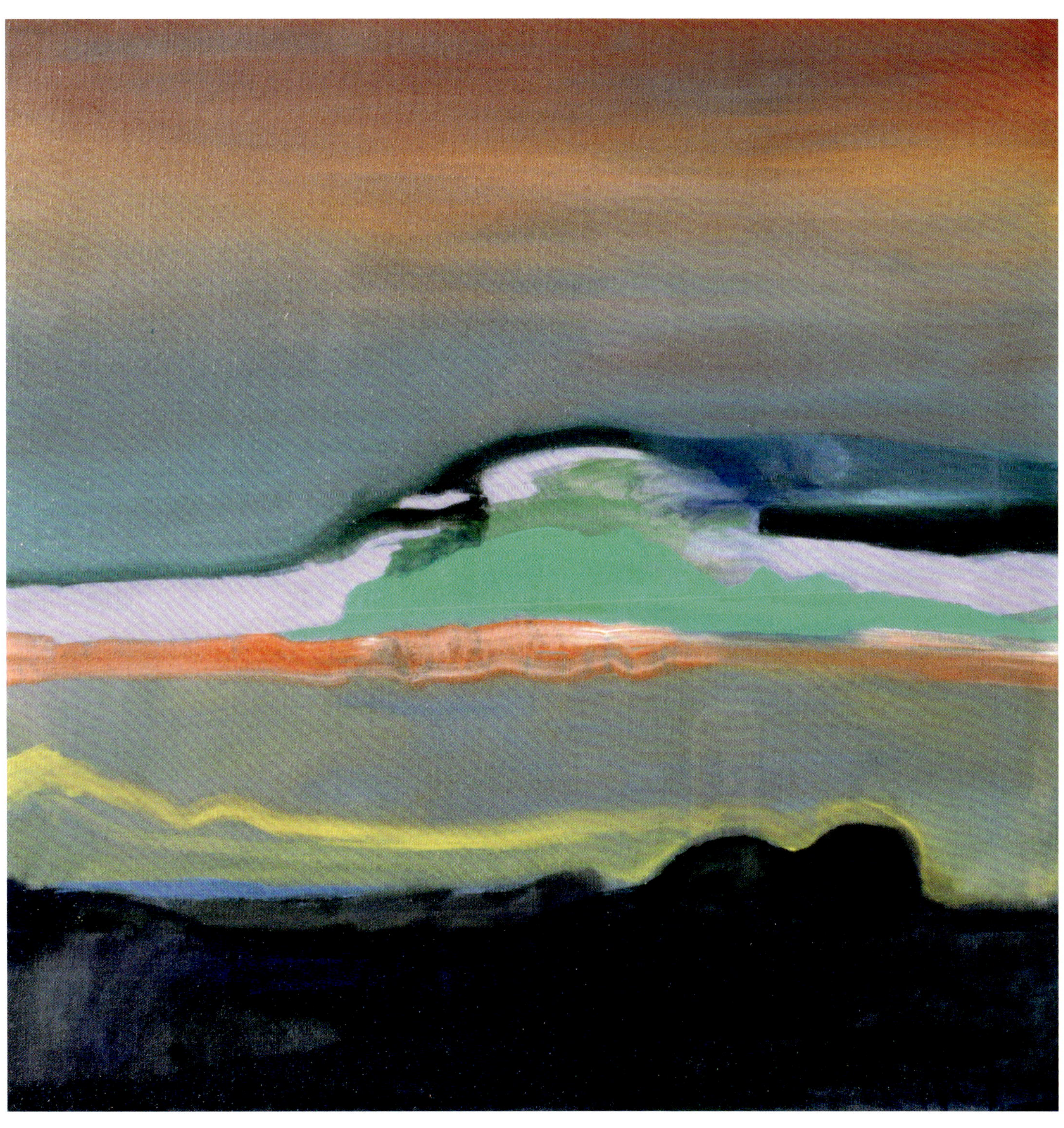

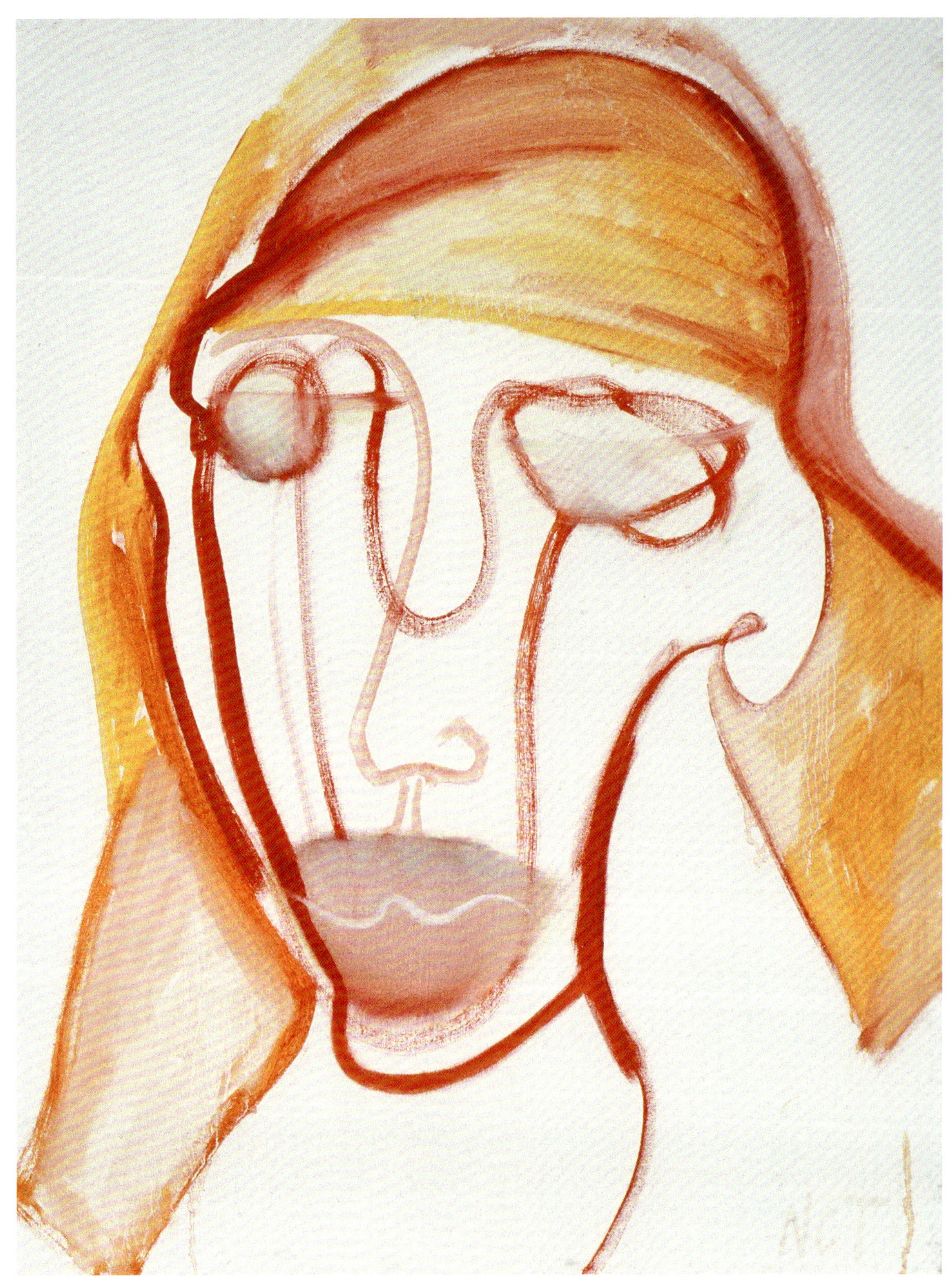

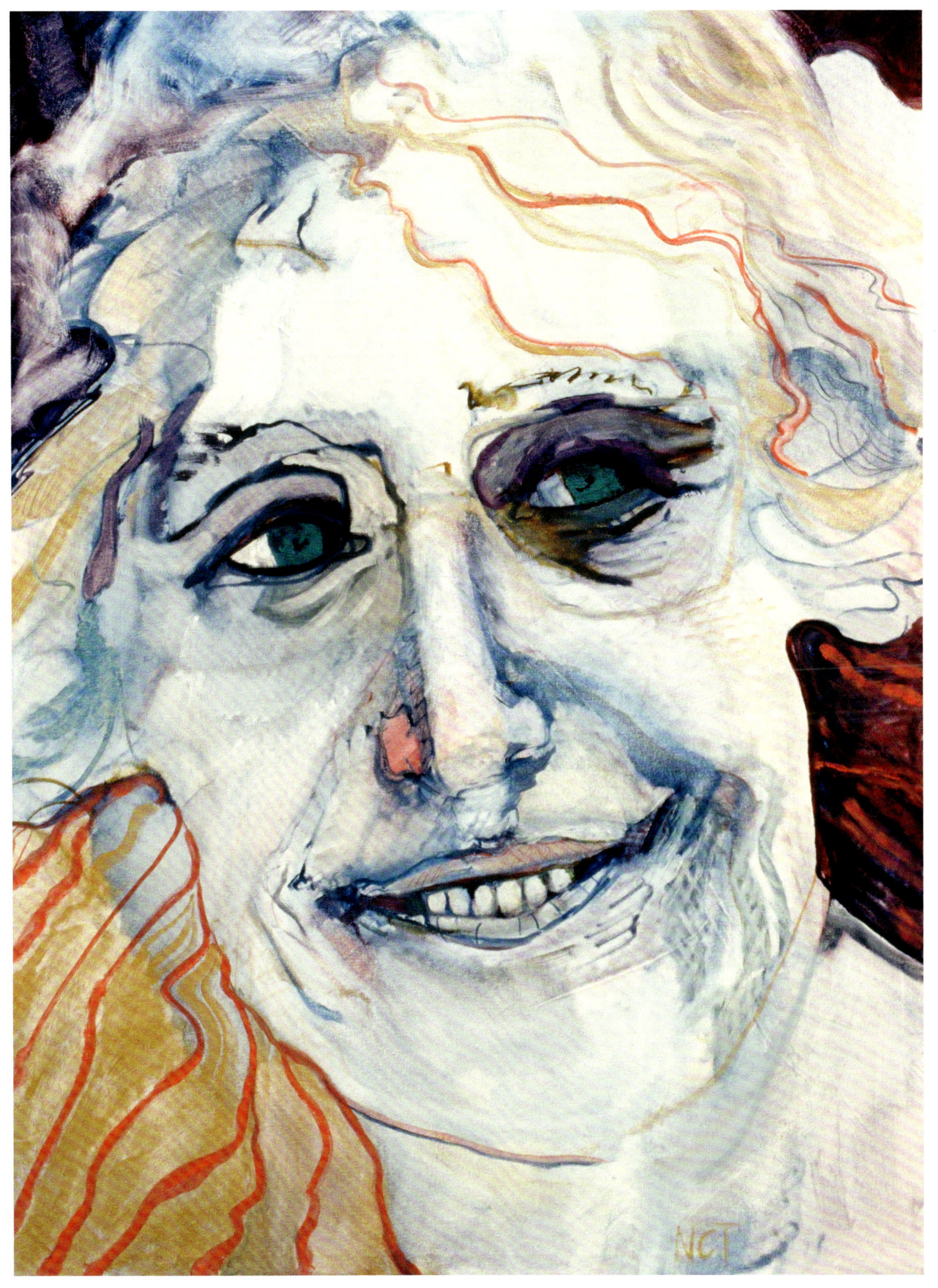

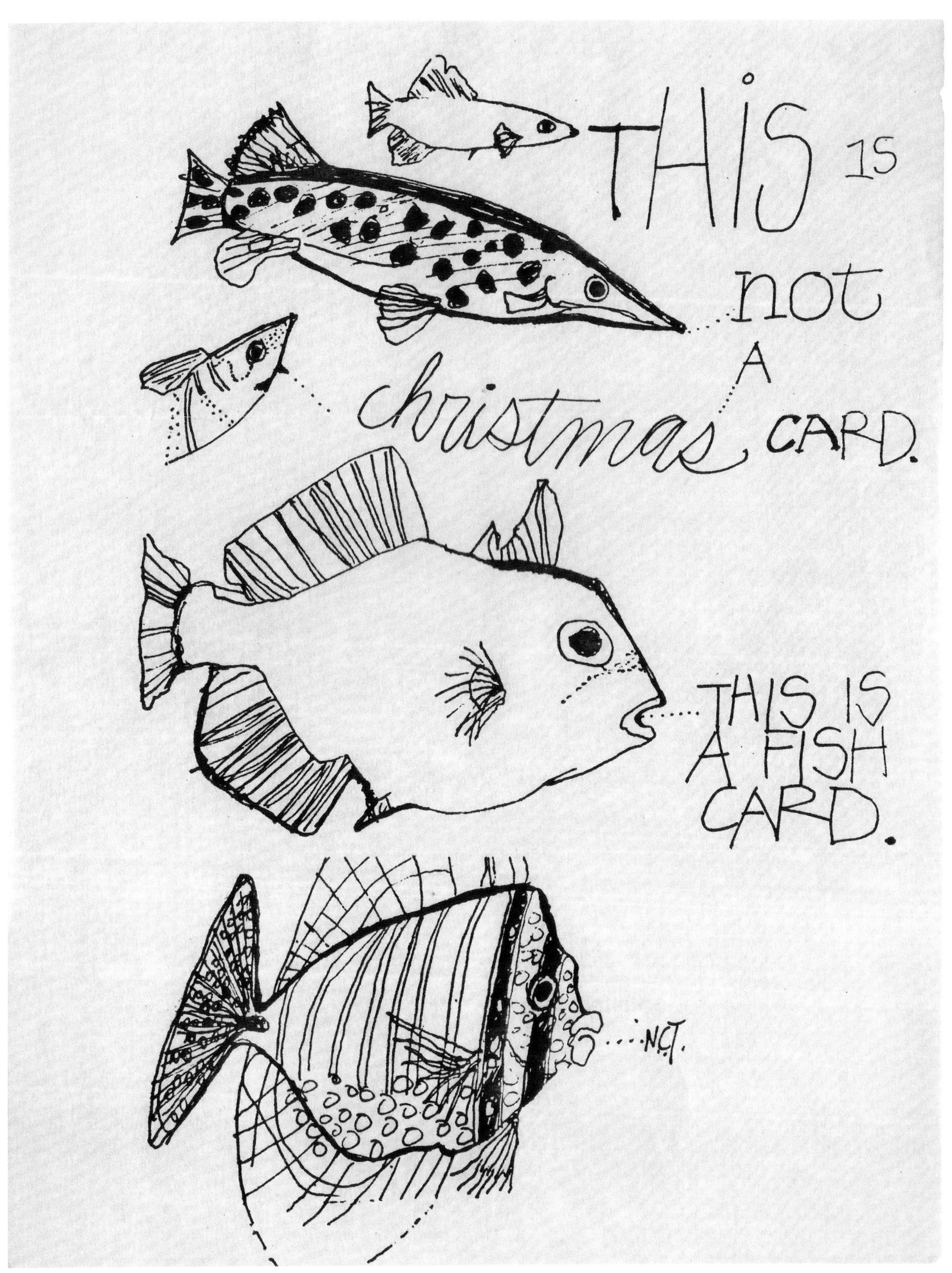

THiS iS not A christmas CARD.
THIS IS A FISH CARD.
N.T.

Spaces

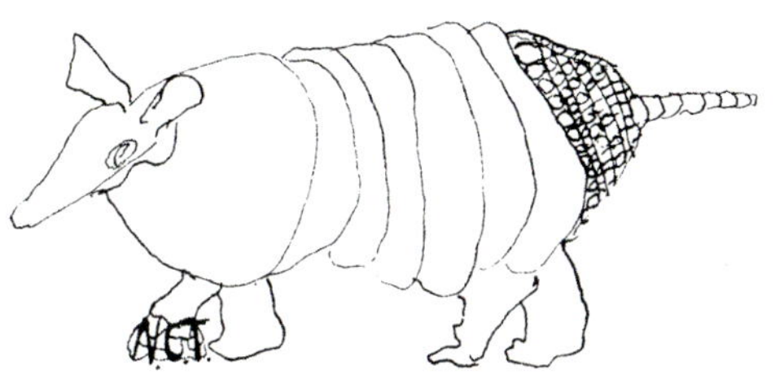

AIDA PAVLETICH: Norma lived in Claremont with the artist Diane Divelbess, near the edge of the Los Angeles and San Bernardino County border.

STANLEY C. WILSON: Diane was a dear friend and actually a mentor of mine; I had had her as a teacher when I was a student many, many years prior to teaching in Pomona.

BRIAN RANSOM: Diane is like a saint among humans. I mean, she is the most beautiful soul ever. I can't say enough about Diane.

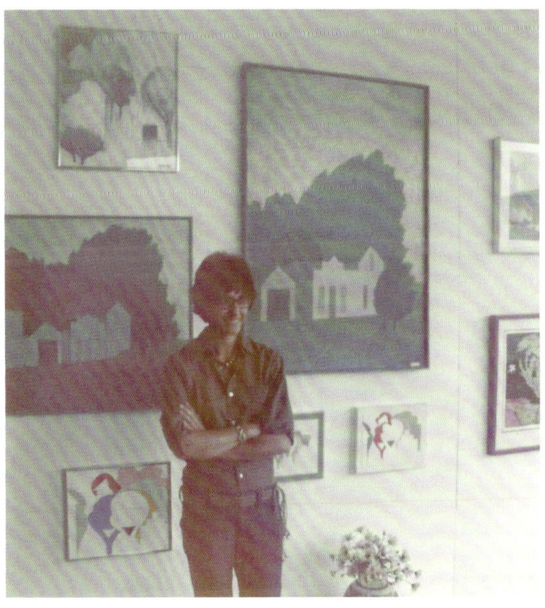

DD at the Tanega-Maher Gallery, 1973

STANLEY C. WILSON: When Norma first lived with Diane on Mount Baldy, their house had been an artist studio. Over the years they converted it to a working space, living quarters, and music studio. So that became a place where Norma had all of her instruments, all of her drums and gongs and guitars and all that, and was where she started to teach people music.

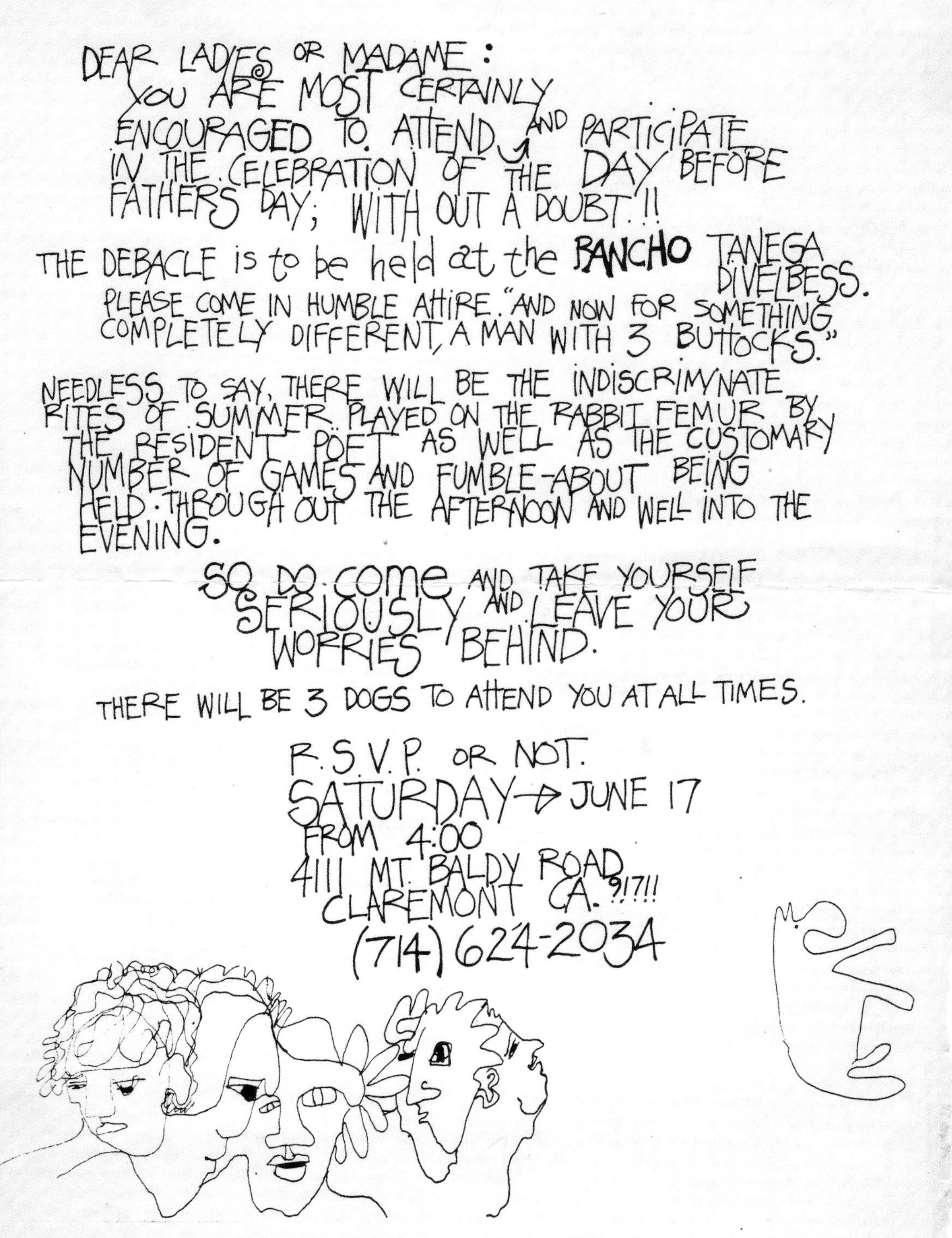

DEAR LADYES OR MADAME:
YOU ARE MOST CERTAINLY
ENCOURAGED TO ATTEND AND PARTICIPATE
IN THE CELEBRATION OF THE DAY BEFORE
FATHERS DAY; WITH OUT A DOUBT!!

THE DEBACLE is to be held at the RANCHO TANEGA
DIVELBESS.
PLEASE COME IN HUMBLE ATTIRE "AND NOW FOR SOMETHING
COMPLETELY DIFFERENT, A MAN WITH 3 BUTTOCKS."

NEEDLESS TO SAY, THERE WILL BE THE INDISCRIMINATE
RITES OF SUMMER PLAYED ON THE RABBIT FEMUR BY
THE RESIDENT POET AS WELL AS THE CUSTOMARY
NUMBER OF GAMES AND FUMBLE-ABOUT BEING
HELD THROUGHOUT THE AFTERNOON AND WELL INTO THE
EVENING.

SO DO COME AND TAKE YOURSELF
SERIOUSLY AND LEAVE YOUR
WORRIES BEHIND.

THERE WILL BE 3 DOGS TO ATTEND YOU AT ALL TIMES.

R.S.V.P. OR NOT.
SATURDAY → JUNE 17
FROM 4:00
4111 MT. BALDY ROAD
CLAREMONT CA. 91711
(714) 624-2034

Paris, Musée du Louvre

Portrait funéraire
destiné à être place sur une momie
Antinoé? Égypte

Peinture sur bois
Époque romaine (fin du règne de Trajan)

GR. 129

ALSO MY FIRST POST-
CARD OF A PRISON
(IN MANILA)

9 MAR 85
SAT 9AM

DEAR FRIENDS,
WHAT A NICE VISIT and
DINNER! DON'T YOU THINK
THAT WE THREE HAVE ELE-
VATED BEING SILLY TO THE
LEVEL OF AT LEAST A MINOR
ART? AND THE POSTCARDS!
I'm LOOKING AT THEM SLOWLY,
THEY ARE SO WONDERFUL -
LIKE THE HAND COLORED ONE
OF THE LAVA BEDS IN HAWAII.
AND THE SEPIATONE PHOTO OF
AN ICE FLOW UPON WHICH SOME
PHOTOGRAPHER SUPERIMPOSED THE
NUDE GIRL FROM "SEPTEMBER MORN"
SHIVERING AS SHE WADES INTO THE
ICE FILLED WATER. ITS TITLED:
'TAKU MAID'. A DELIGHT!

DIANE   NORMA
DIVELBESS   TANEGA
4111 MT BALDY RD
CLAREMONT CA
91711

and THE PICTURE BOOK of VENICE
HAS BROUGHT BACK A FLOOD OF
MEMORIES - I WAS THERE EXACTLY
3 MONTHS AGO! THANK YOU, THANK
YOU! ALL MY LOVE, O.T.A.
+ O-TA!   (BILL-DAVID)

Paris-Grand Palais
Exposition Le Douanier ROUSSEAU
15 septembre 1984 - 7 janvier 1985

Henri ROUSSEAU, dit Le Douanier (1844-1910)
La liberté invitant les artistes à prendre part à la
22e exposition de la Société des Artistes Indépendants
(1905-1906)

Tokyo, Musée national d'art moderne

EX 2548

Dear DD & NCT & MET -
we're having a great
time! The Rousseau
Show was dynamite and Deux is giving me
a wonderful
cruise in
our honors!

5 DEC. EARLY MORN
(I.E. 10 AM) HAVING COFFEE W/ ANN
DEAR FRIENDS MON DIEU! AM
HAVING A GREAT TIME! WINDY
CITY, BEAUTIFUL (NO RAIN) WEATHER,
and THIS CITY. LAST NITE WENT TO
A CHAMBER MUSIC CONCERT AT ST.
GERMAIN des PRÉS CHURCH. THEN TO
CAFÉ WHERE WE MET JOHN + JEAN, THEY
DRANK WINE, ME I HAD TO FUDGE SUN-
DAE! THE FOOD IS WONDERUL! THE
ART AMAZING. SAW THIS ROUSSEAU RET-
ROSPECTIVE also WATTEAU RETRO, LIKE
NEW YORKERS, PARISEANS ARE PASSIONATEL
CONCERNED ABOUT ART. TODAY TO
THE BEAUBOURG FOR KANDINSKY
RETRO ET AL. TOMORROW LOUVRE,
SAT. TO CHARTRES. SUNDAY
ON TO VENICE IF I
CAN BEAR

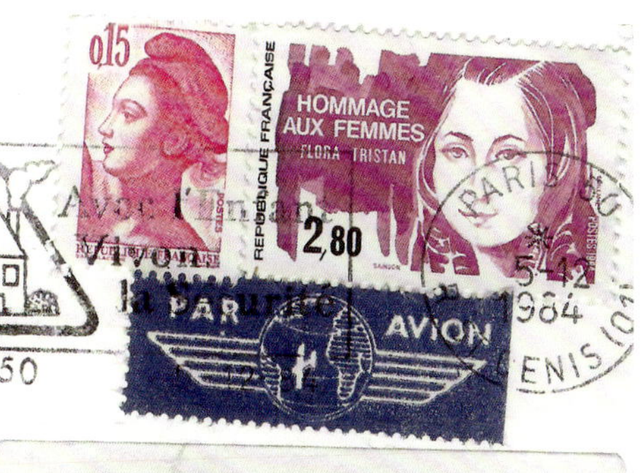

Divelbess-Tanega
Diane   Norma
4111 Mt Baldy Road
Claremont, CA 91711   USA

TO LEAVE THIS LOVELY PLACE
and MY FRIENDS. NIRMA, DIANE
I AM VERY HAPPY. ALL O.T.A's
LOVE TO YOU and OUR FRIENDS.
Bill David.
P.S. THE EIFFEL TOWER HAS GOT
TO BE ONE OF THE MASTERPIECES
OF SCULPTURE du MONDE.

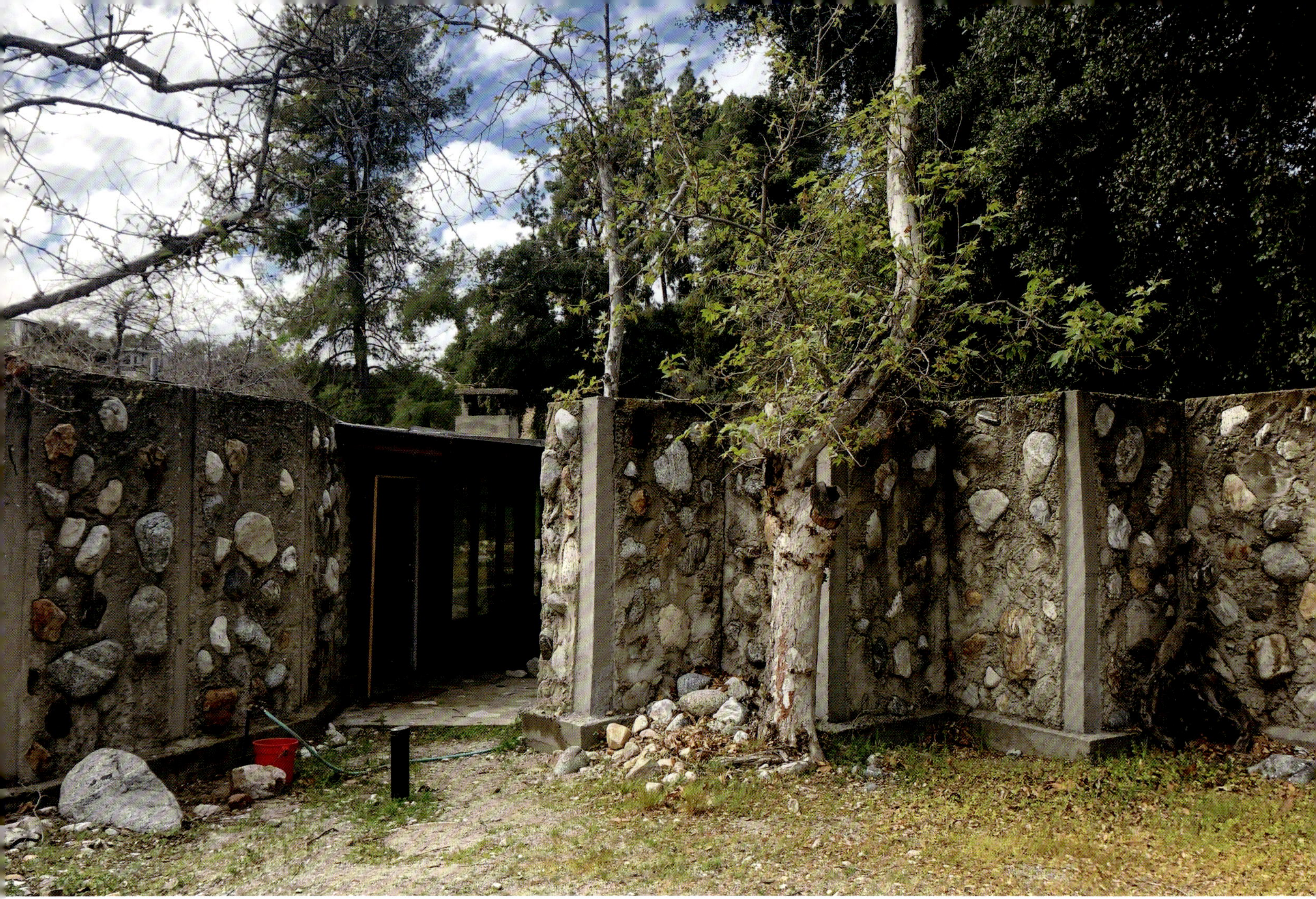

CATHERINE McINTOSH: I grew up in Padua Hills, and we could literally see Norma's house from our backyard. Or we could, until they built this big mansion next to it. Actually, when I was growing up, it wasn't her house; it belonged to Lindley Mixon, the ceramist. He had hired Foster Rhodes Jackson to design his house and studio.

CORINNA MÜLLER: Norma's house was not only an architectural dream designed by Foster Rhodes Jackson (a student of Frank Lloyd Wright); it was an extension of Norma herself, and everything vibrated with artistic and musical energy. The house was filled to the brim with music instruments and works of art; both her own and those of artist friends. It must have been immensely inspiring, but it also took a lot of maintenance. Her friends suggested she should move to something that wasn't in constant need of repair. Of course,

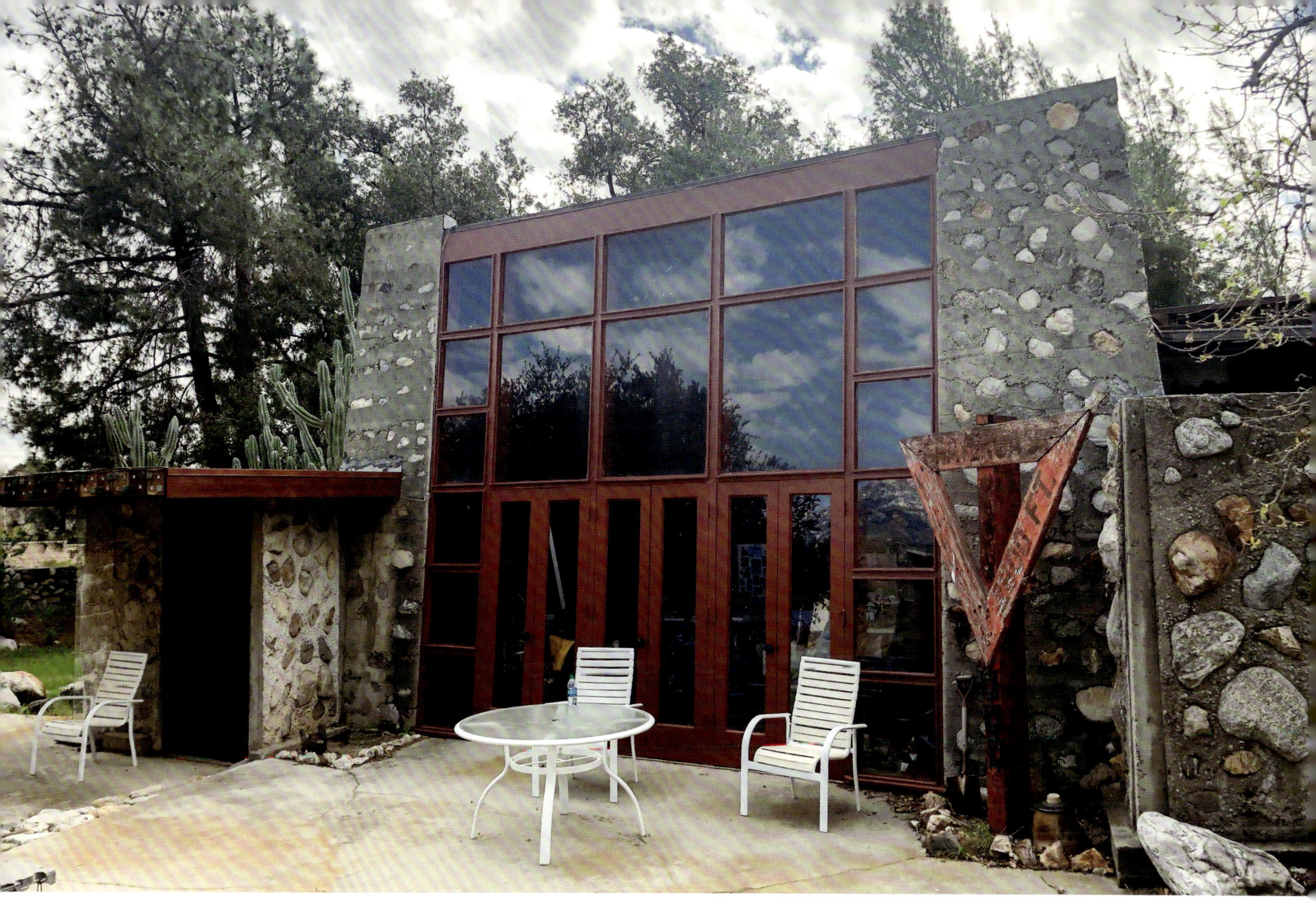

that would have been a rational decision, but Norma was so inseparable from the house that it was hard to even imagine her in a different setting. So with help from friends, she managed to stay.

BRIAN RANSOM: I have three sons who are all musicians; they all knew Norma very well, and they just loved Norma and Norma loved them. I kept so many of my instruments at the house, and they would come up there all the time. And I recently asked my middle son, Stefan, "What do you remember about Norma?" And Stef's like, "I don't know, man, I just remember the smell of the house." He goes, "I would touch a painting and my finger would come back with blue paint on it. We would hear the coyotes wailing in the distance, Norma would bring us all some kind of sour bread sandwiches with butter on them, and we would all sit out in the courtyard and eat them."

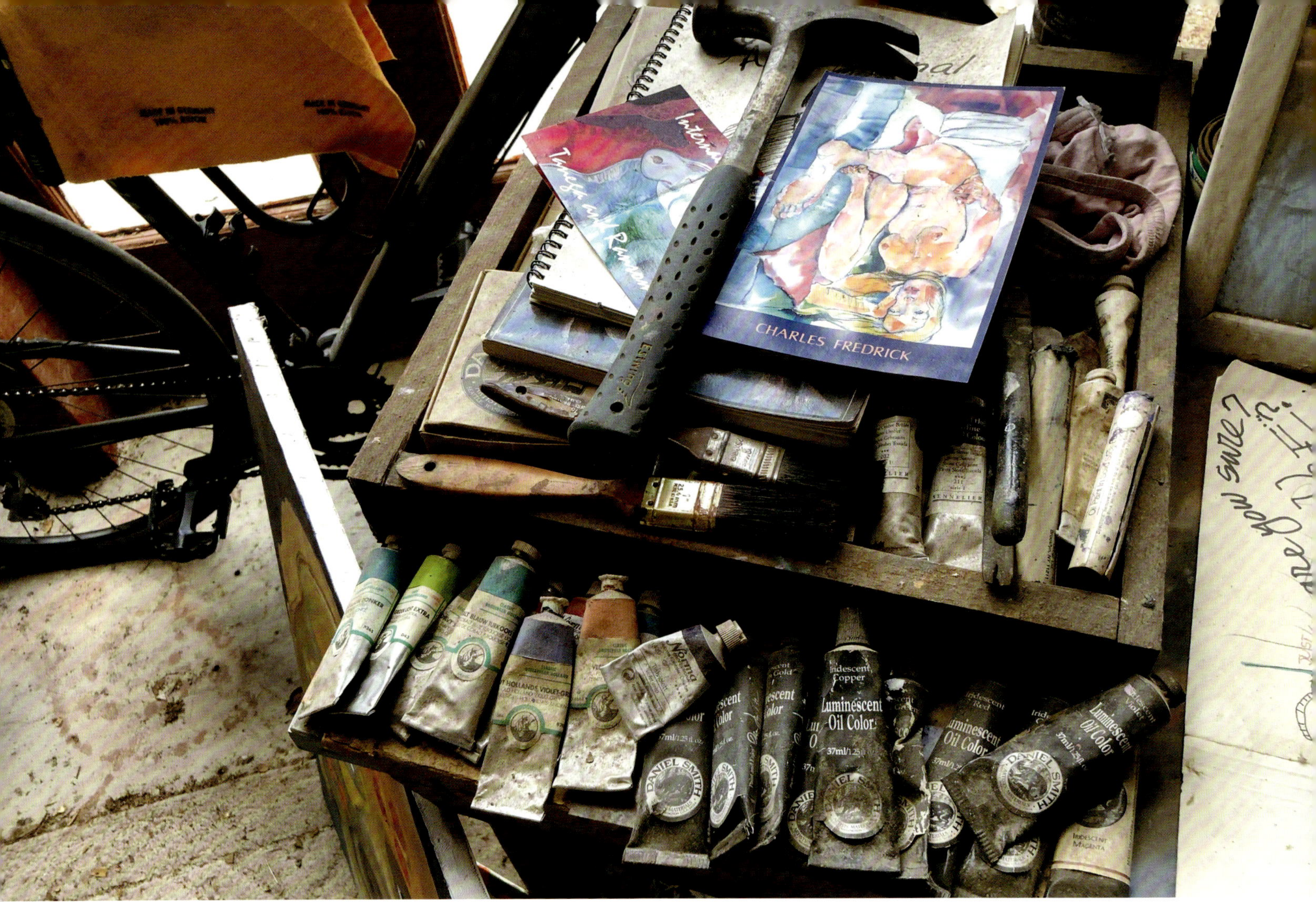

STANLEY C. WILSON: The house was a wonderful place. It was just north of the Claremont village and it was set at the base of the Baldy Mountains. So it had a kind of open-air quality to it.

MARIO VERLANGIERI: The house was, I mean, "magical," I guess, is the word. You'd walk in, and open those big, glass doors, and be in Norma's painting studio. You'd just be inspired, because it was her creative space, and it just had this artist vibe that it gave off. It had this awesome view of the mountains. Some of her paintings are of the mountains from that view, because she would look out the window at the view and paint it.

MOANA VERCOE: Norma kept "memory boards" in the studio. Some were pictures from her different collaborations. By the powder room, she kept

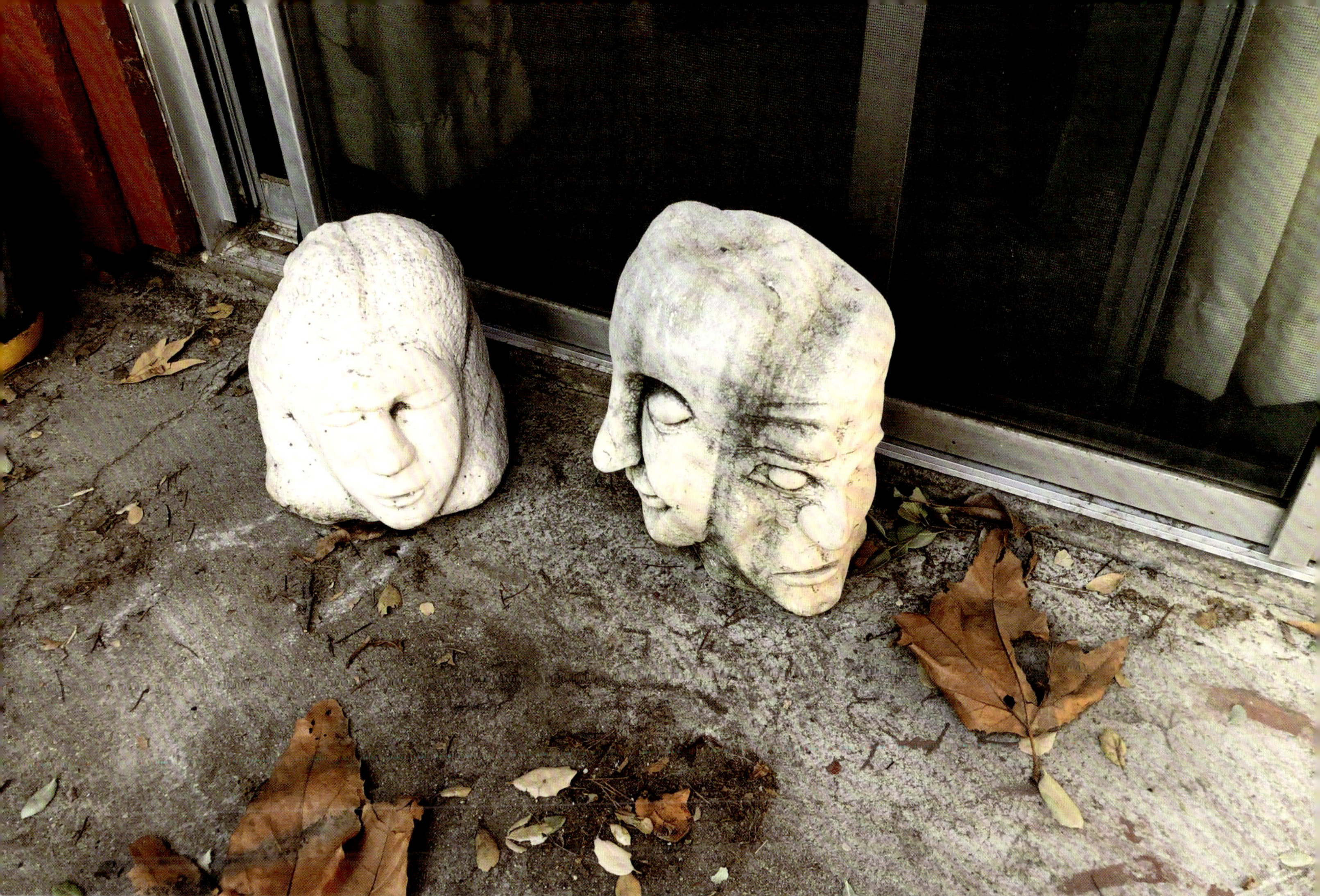

a corkboard with important things like the Wi-Fi password, a couple of business cards, and images that she liked of people who were important to her, including the Queen. That board made her happy.

BRIAN RANSOM: I wish you could have seen her house the way it used to be. That music room was pristine, with her beautiful grand piano back there, and then the room that looks out onto the patio was her painting studio, and light streams would just flood into that room. Her paintings were just everywhere. The rest of the house was just a quiet kind of living zone, but the studio and the music room were these really engaging spaces with two or three paintings in progress at a time.

MARIO VERLANGIERI: I mean, Norma loved that house so much. She would always talk about how much he loved it. And then to play in that room—

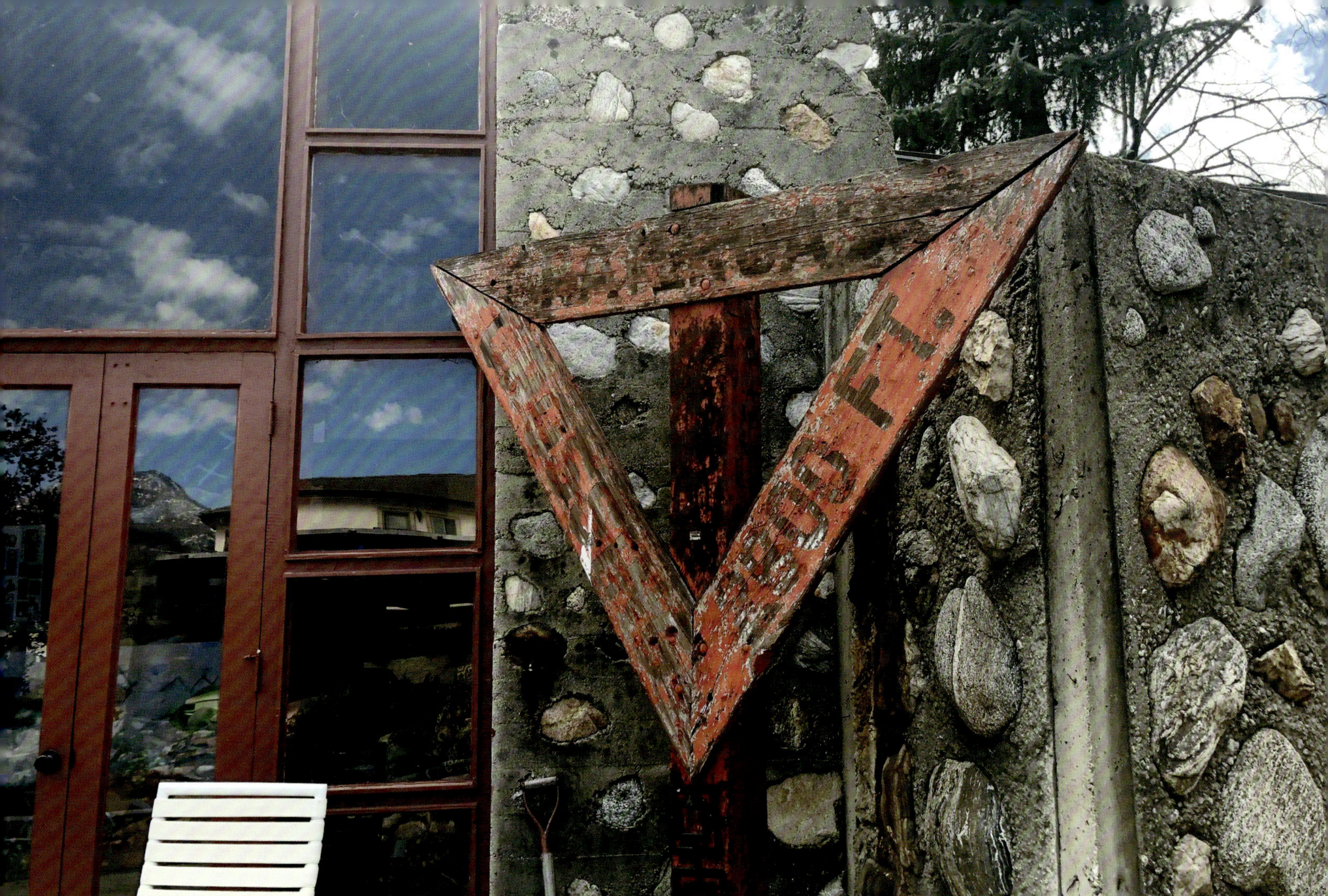

I mean, all of her projects were done in that house, for the most part. She would always insist on recording there, because the room had a vibe, and all the instruments were right there, so that if you were inspired, you could pick something up. And that's what we would do with Baboonz. A lot of times we would experiment around with stuff and just like, "Oh, let's try this here. Oh yeah. Grab this off the wall and let's try it," you know?

KARIN SKIBA: When Norma was first working with Robert Grajeda in the band Latin Lizards, I saw their poster on her bulletin board. I told her Robert needed to meet me. Norma was not real encouraging, but finally gave me his phone number. After a series of calls, he gave me a surprise visit at the end of the year in 2000, and we eventually decided to collaborate, which led to several performances of music and spoken word, a lovely romance, and we were

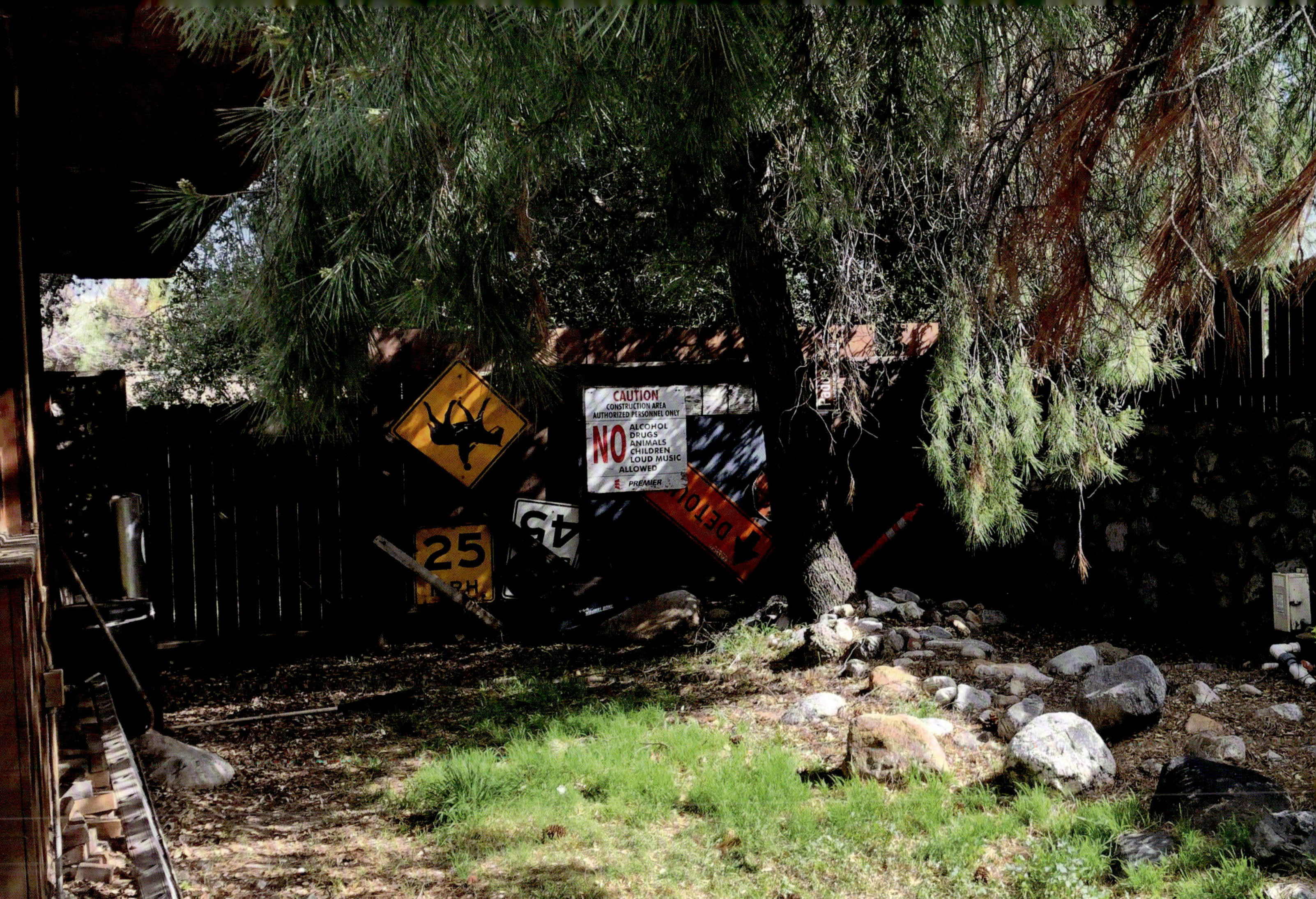

married in 2002! After comparing histories, we realized we were crossing paths at Norma's and probably were at the same parties at the Claremont house without knowing each other. Norma had brought us together despite initially giving me a hard time!

STANLEY C. WILSON: Oh, there were parties all the time.

AIDA PAVLETICH: We got together on Thanksgiving, along with "orphan" friends whose families were gone or far away. Usually, Norma's dear friend the teacher Anne Bages came by, and Diane Schnitzer often brought delicious homemade apple pies. I came with baked kabocha squashes from a Koreatown market. Virginia Rigney and others made long trips from the mountains to join Norma.

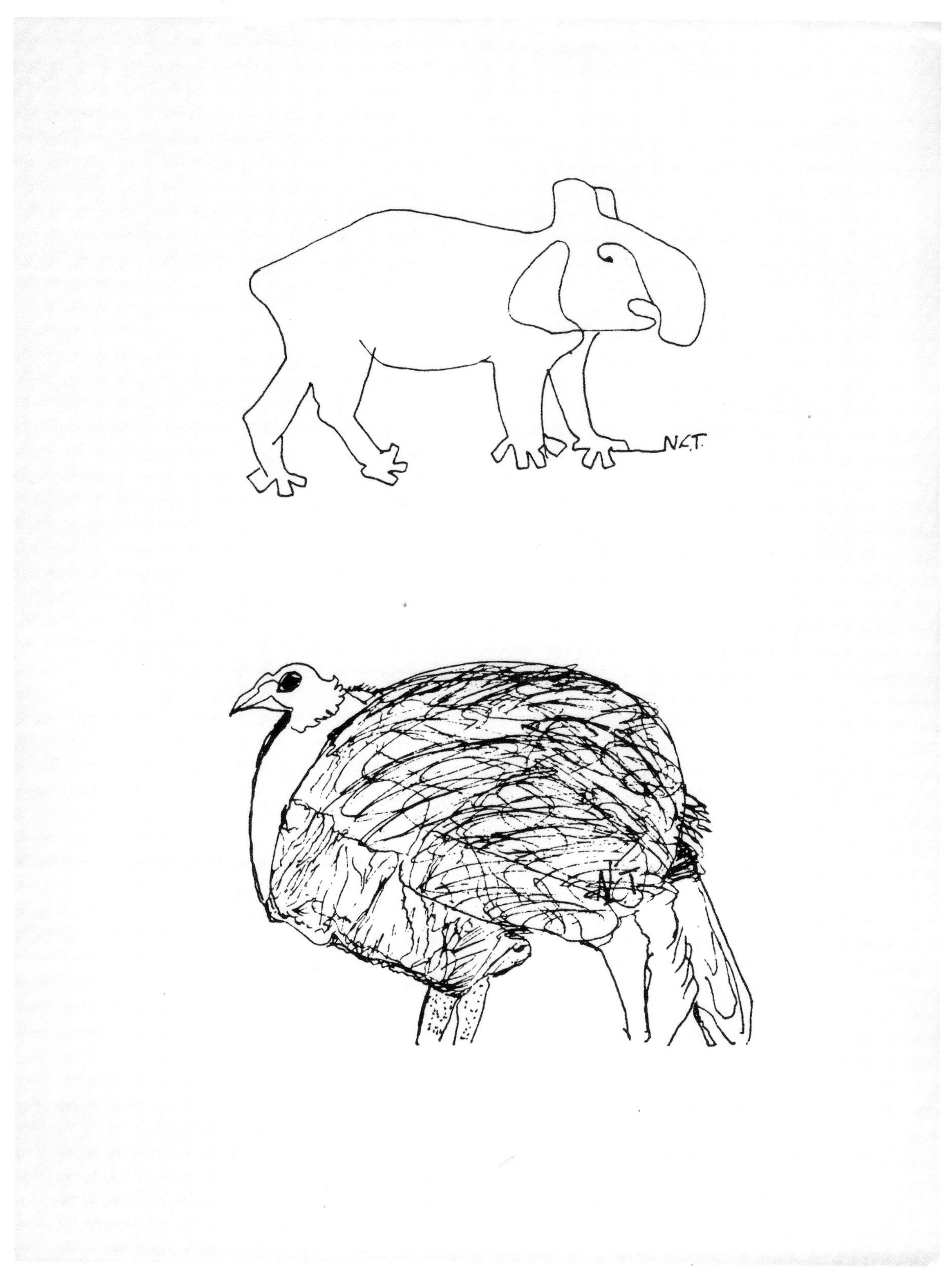

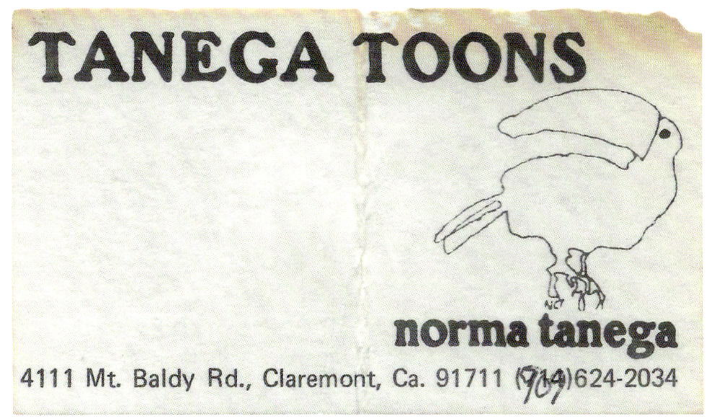

BRIAN RANSOM: I remember, I went to my first Thanksgiving dinner at Norma's house, and realized it was okay to throw food. I'm like, "Wow! Now, this is cool. This is the best Thanksgiving I've ever been to." It was just such a fantastic, phantasmagorical kind of world with endless amounts of the best wine you've ever had in your life and just the most amazing people.

AIDA PAVLETICH: More friends joined Norma at her weekend parties and holiday events; Mary Barnes, a teacher from Claremont; Ellen Brouse, a graphic designer from Azusa; as well as students from her English as a second language classes, including Aki Shamsabadi, a Persian electrical engineer from Pasadena, where she worked for Parsons; Bonita Lockwood, athlete and teacher from Long Beach; Diane Schnitzer, artist from Laguna Beach; Vida Ratzlaff Hackman, a painter who had a rustic adobe studio in North Hollywood. In the spring, the excellent writer Michelle Kort and gifted songwriter Miriam Cutler came by and made a great International Women's Day party.

STANLEY C. WILSON: And then, of course, at the memorial service for Norma, the same thing happened again; it was like Norma was there; the same people that had been part of her life—including her family and friends and artists— all showed up, and people are walking around with drinks and hors d'oeuvres inside and outside. It was just like a normal party. It was a real celebration of life. That's one of the things that I miss most about my time with Norma: she celebrated.

ROBERT GRAJEDA: A lot of interesting souls passed through my life when I was hanging around with Norma. People that you would meet and see, and you'd realize that they were trying to get a grip on things in terms of their own journeys through life, and Norma was a really great supporter of that.

DAVID SHEARER: Norma's own gallery had been a little bit like that, where she would focus on other people's work more than her own.

AIDA PAVLETICH: In the seventies, Norma shared a gallery in Redondo Beach with Daniel Maher, where they showed their own paintings and provided framing services. Dan, an ex-priest, lived aboard a sailboat at the marina and shared the gallery work. Norma drove down from Claremont.

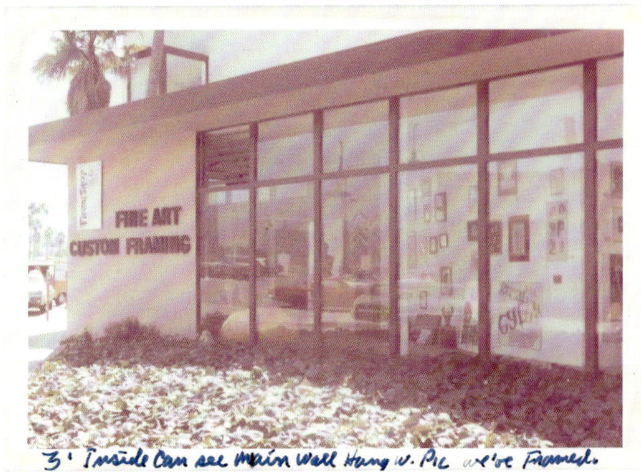

3' Inside can see main wall hung w. pic we've framed.

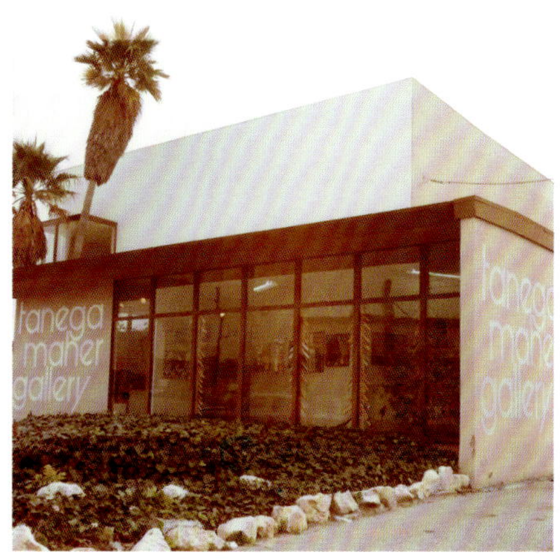

STANLEY C. WILSON: For Norma to drive back and forth from Claremont to Redondo Beach was quite a feat in itself—that's like fifty miles. But the Tanega-Maher Gallery down in Redondo Beach was in a prime spot: the South Bay Area in Southern California is a lot different than, let's say, downtown Los Angeles or West LA, which is the gallery area. It's different in the sense that it is a beach community, and so it would be middle- to upper-income people that would be in the Tanega-Maher Gallery. A lot of people that lived in the beach communities had money to buy art, so that was good for Norma and Dan. And then also on the other side, Dan Maher was a framer, and his framing work brought a constant income in—people that would either buy things in the gallery or bring things by which Dan would matte and frame. Norma could see the potential in many of us that were teaching at Cal Poly. And based upon our friendship and, I guess, her encouragement, she asked me if I would be interested in a show, and I said, "Definitely, yes."

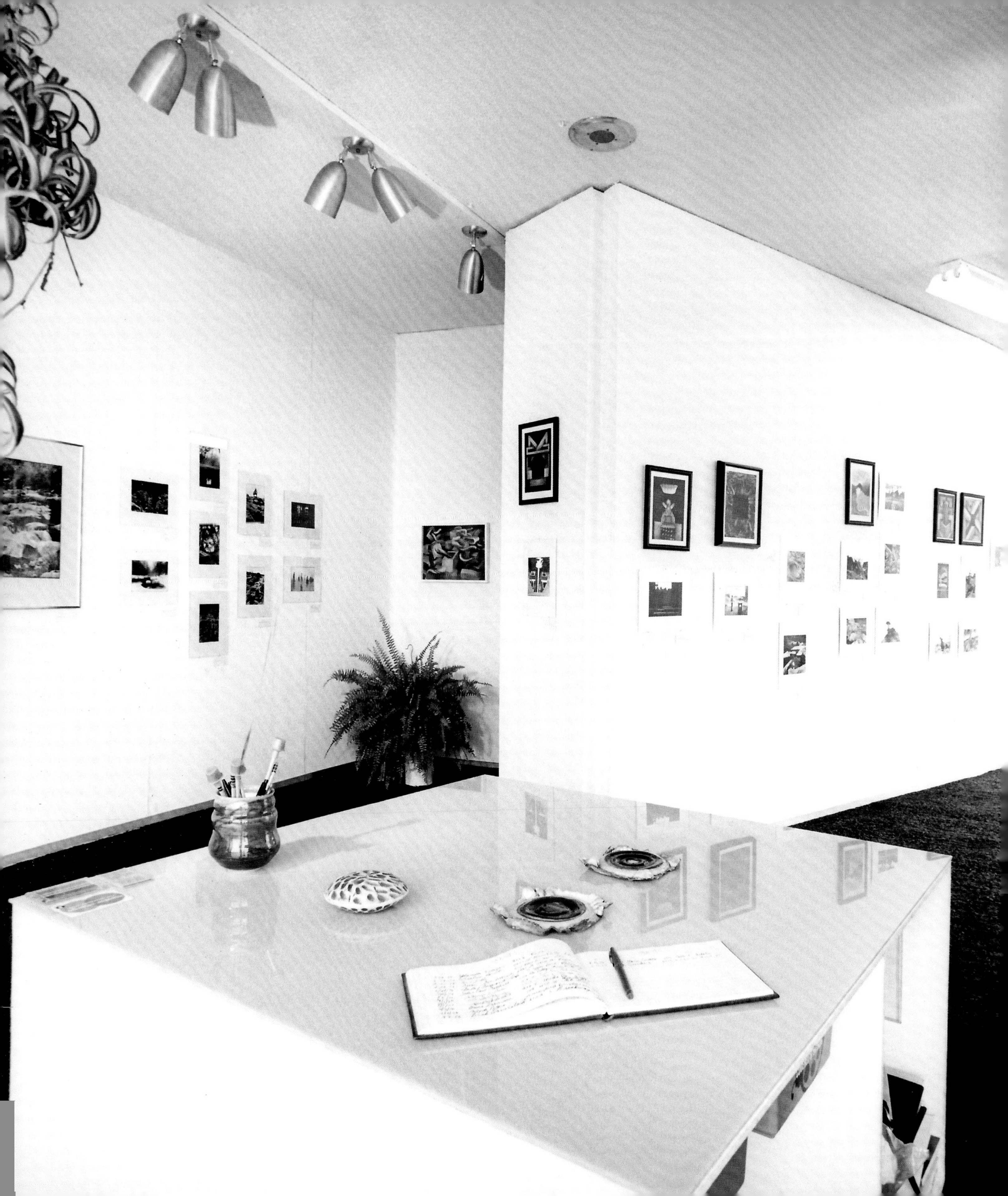

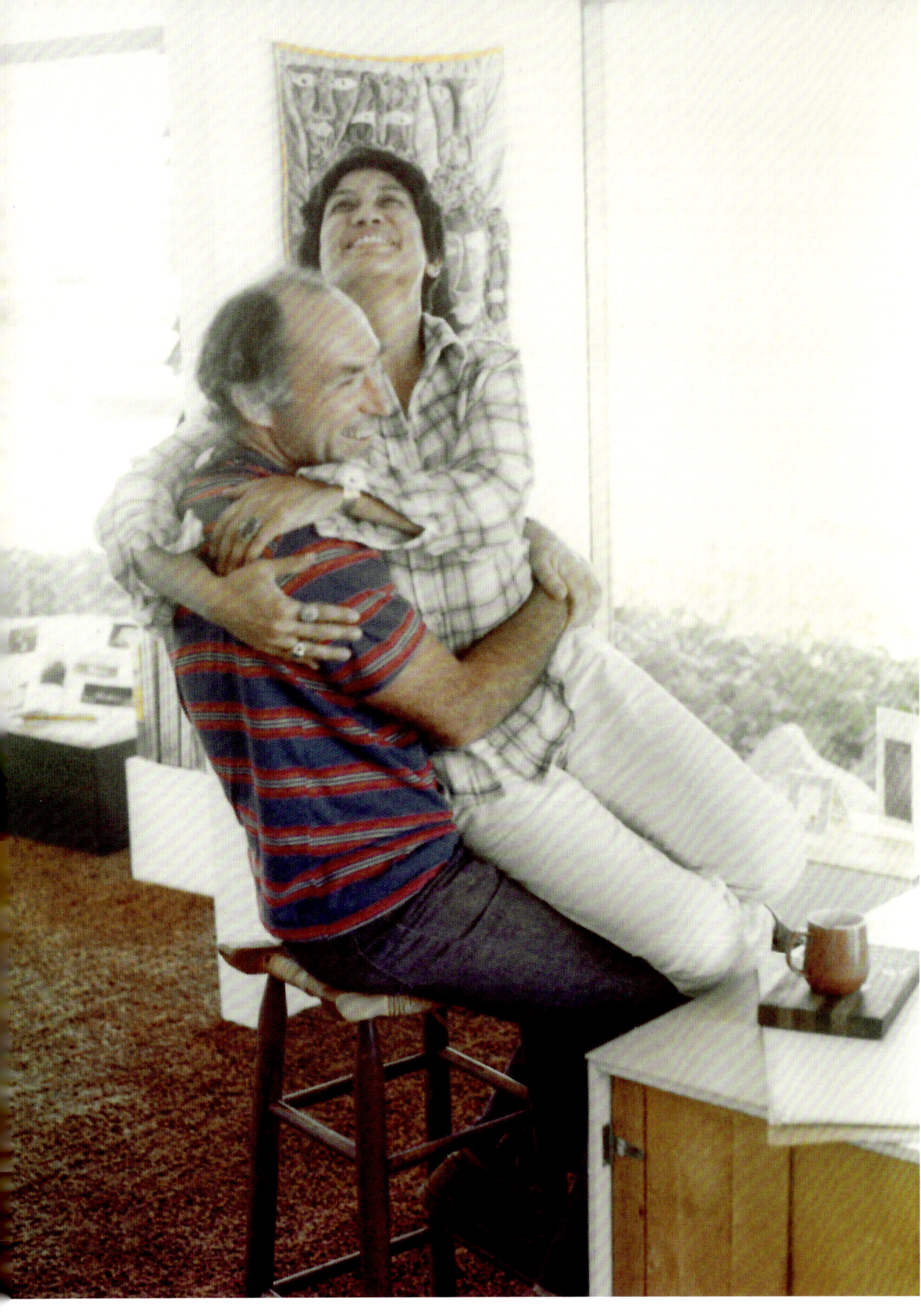

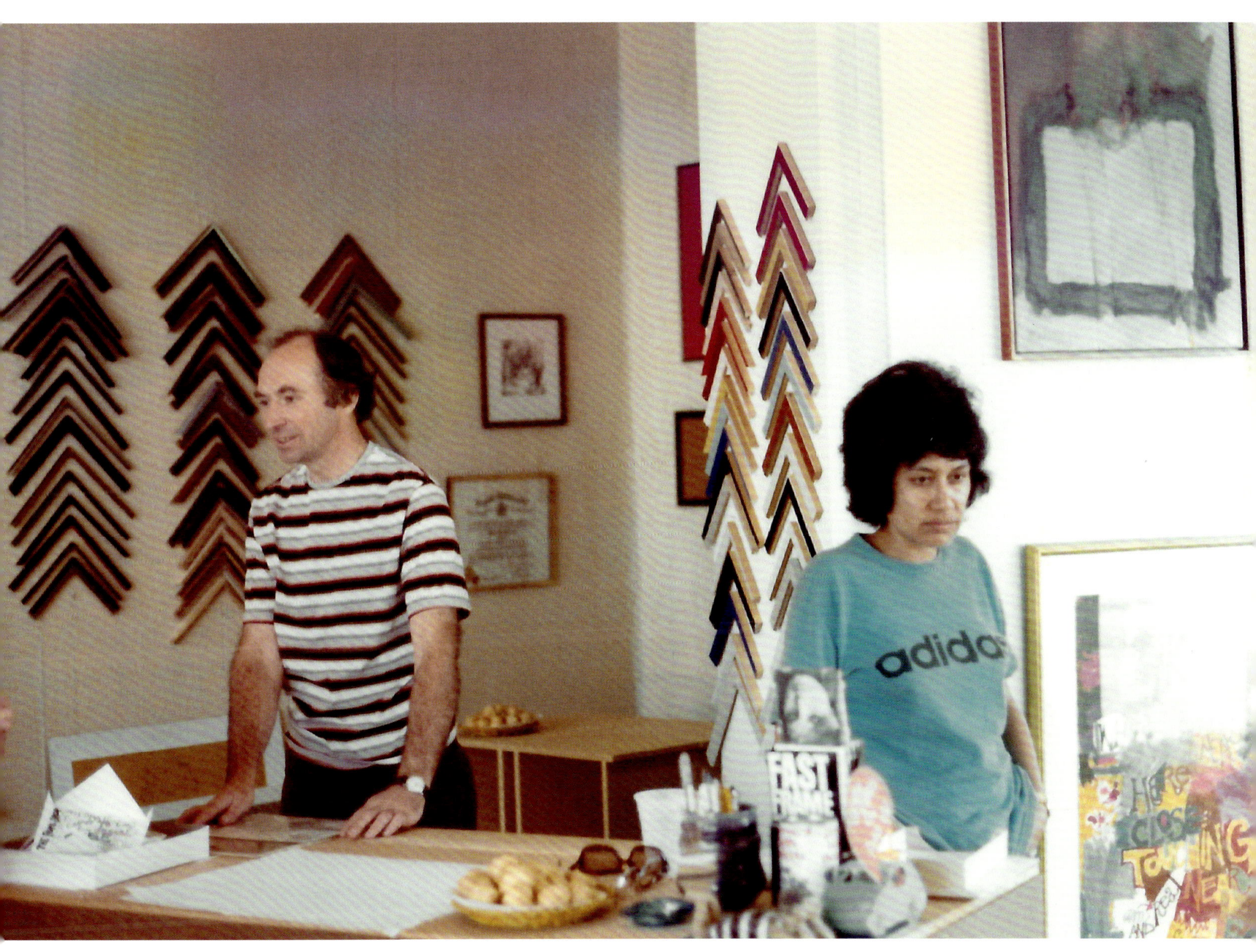

Dan Maher and NCT

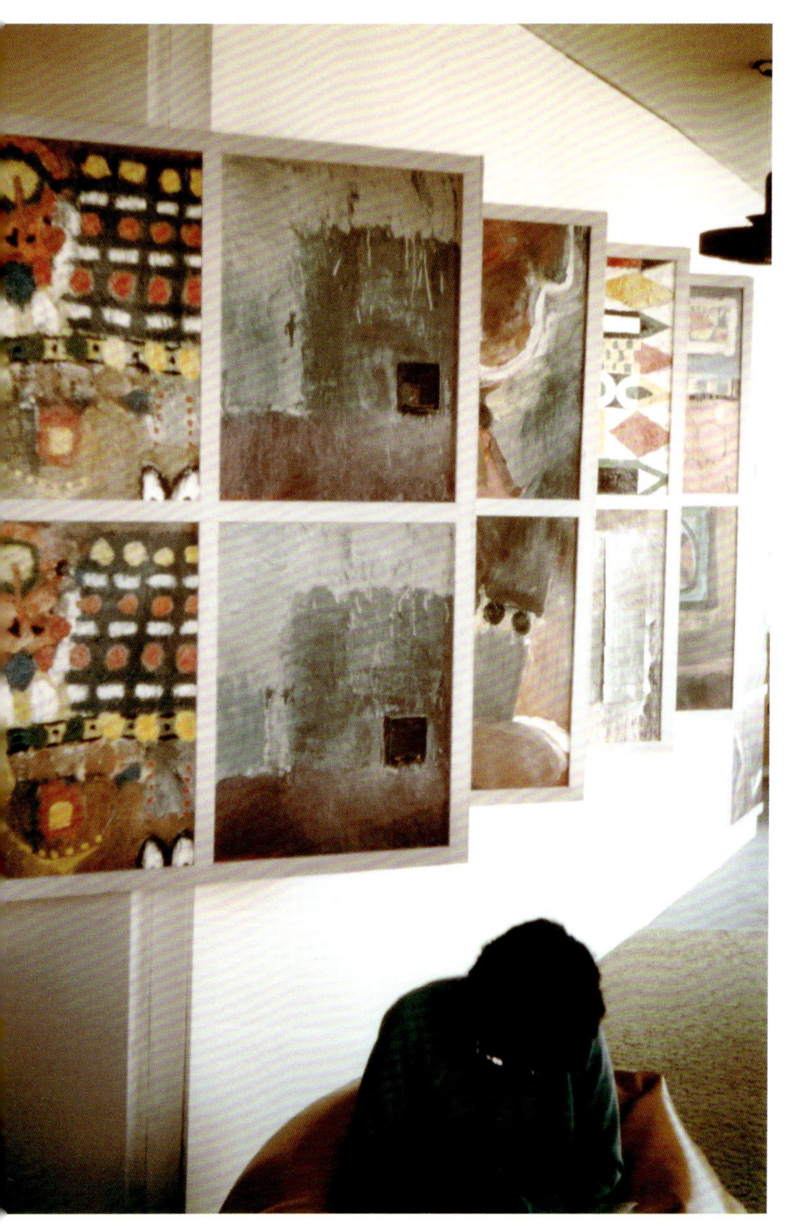
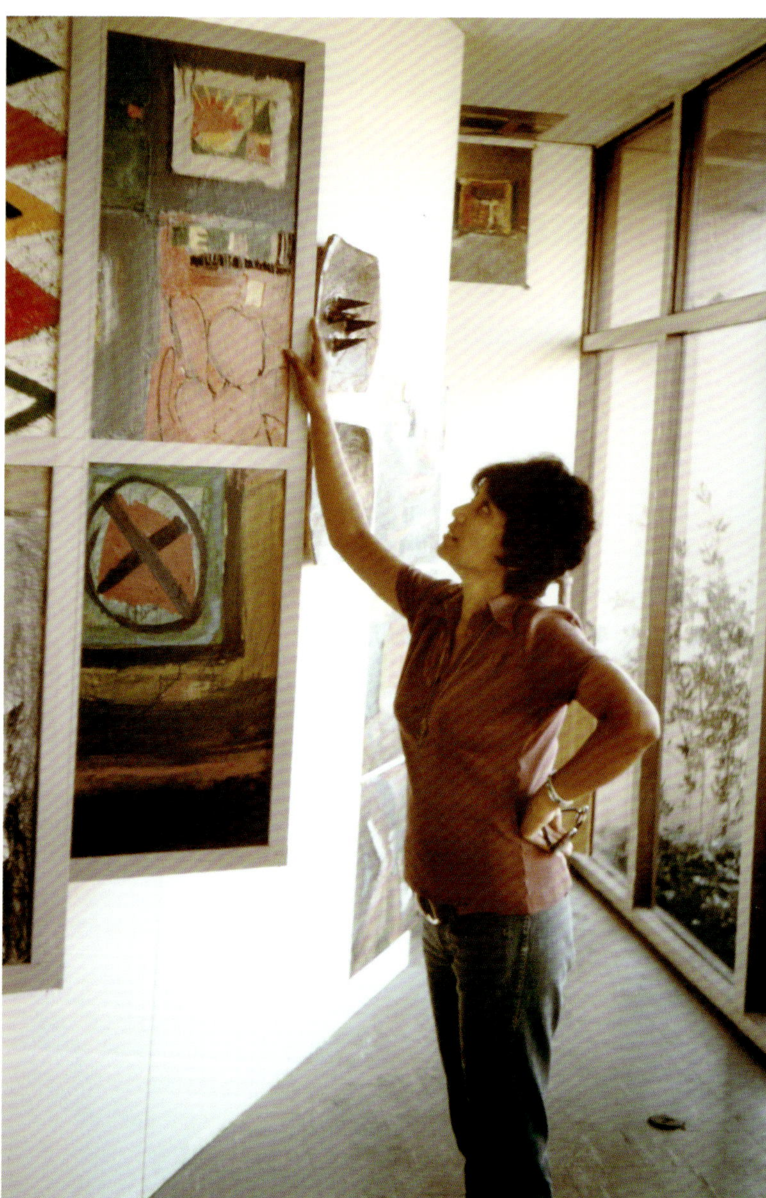

KARIN SKIBA: The creative scene was exciting at that time, since downtown LA was the hot spot for art. And it seemed as if we were moving ahead to compete with New York as an art center. Loft spaces were being developed and there was a genuine population of artists.

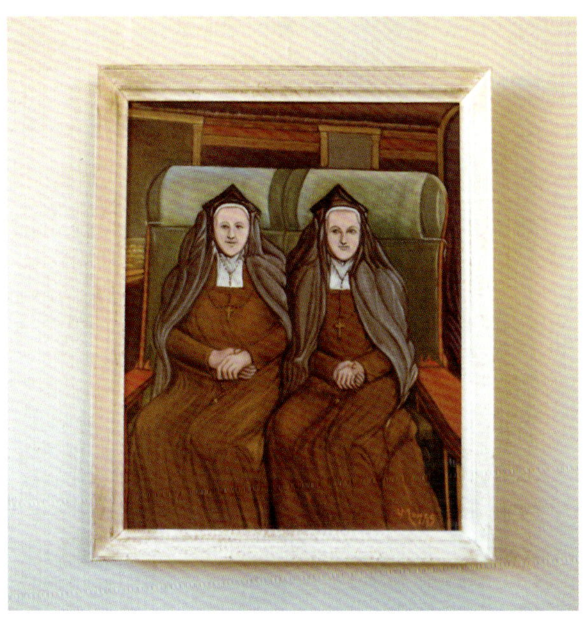 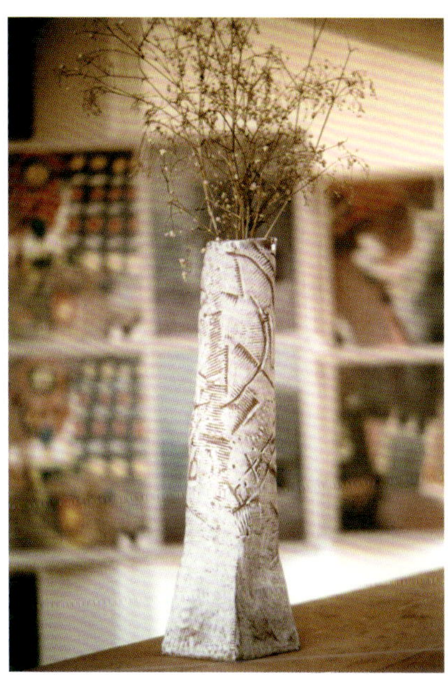

STANLEY C. WILSON: The word for the gallery was "diverse." There was a large cross section of imagery that Norman and Dan selected to show, and it was everything from a two-dimensional work, to some three-dimensional artists to some who, like me, were kind of caught in between two-dimensional and three-dimensional—wall reliefs, those kinds of things. It was kind of an organized chaos. The thing that I liked most about the Tanega-Maher Gallery, and the thing that I liked most about Norma, is that Norma would be completely involved with each artist. She would design the exhibition mailers. She would really get into the head of the artist and really think about imagery that she would lay out in the mailers to deal with the ideas and concepts that would be exhibited. And that would be really important to introduce your work to the community, so that the gallery became a place where artists met, a place where you felt a real strong sense of community and felt a real strong sense of support. In some ways I thought it was kind of chaotic, but in other ways it was their plan and they were successful; sometimes they would sell out a large majority of the work in the show, and I've dealt with other gallery dealers that were more cut and dry: "OK, this is the percentage, this is what you get. This is what I get," and then there's no room for change. No, Norma and Dan, they were always negotiating, and it was always with the advantage of the artist in mind. They celebrated the creator. They celebrated the creative process and they did everything they could to really make that happen.

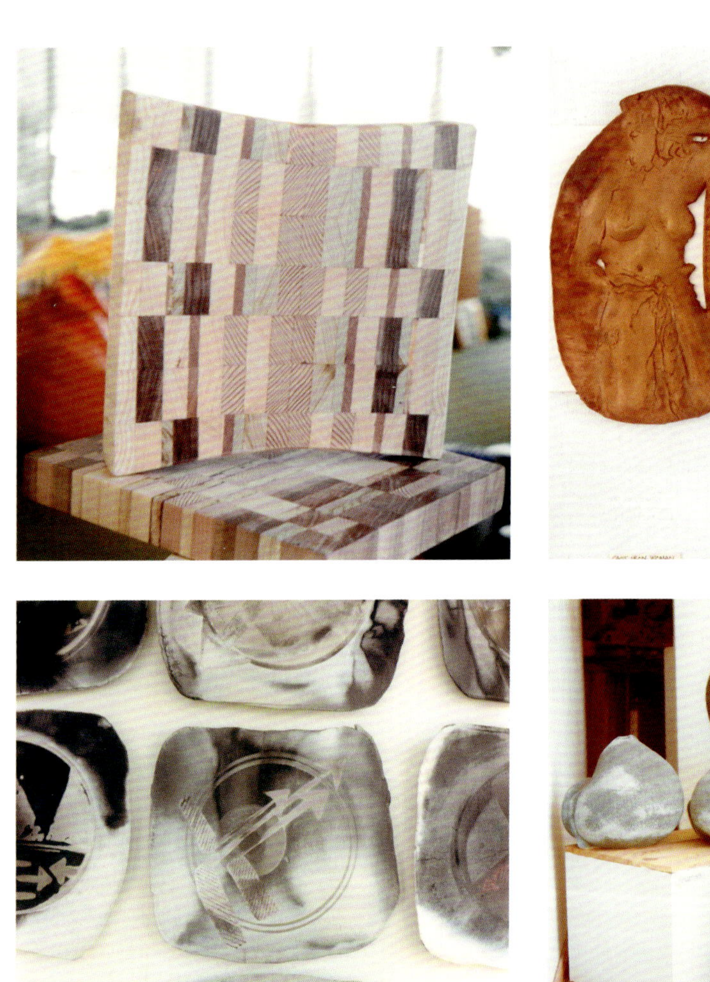

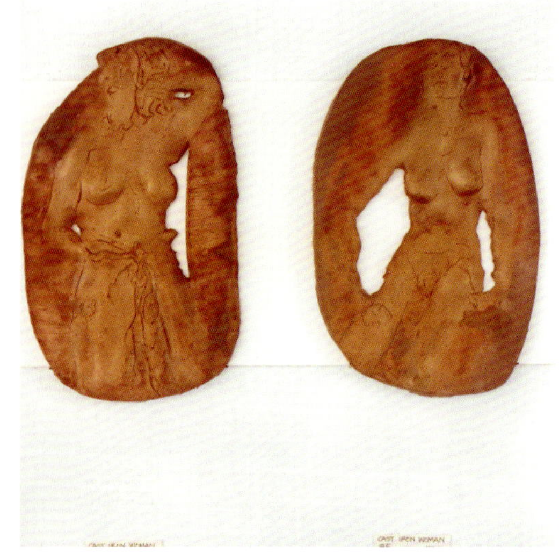

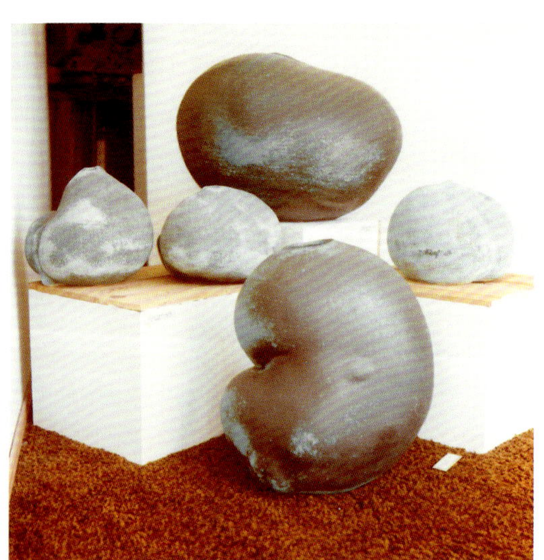

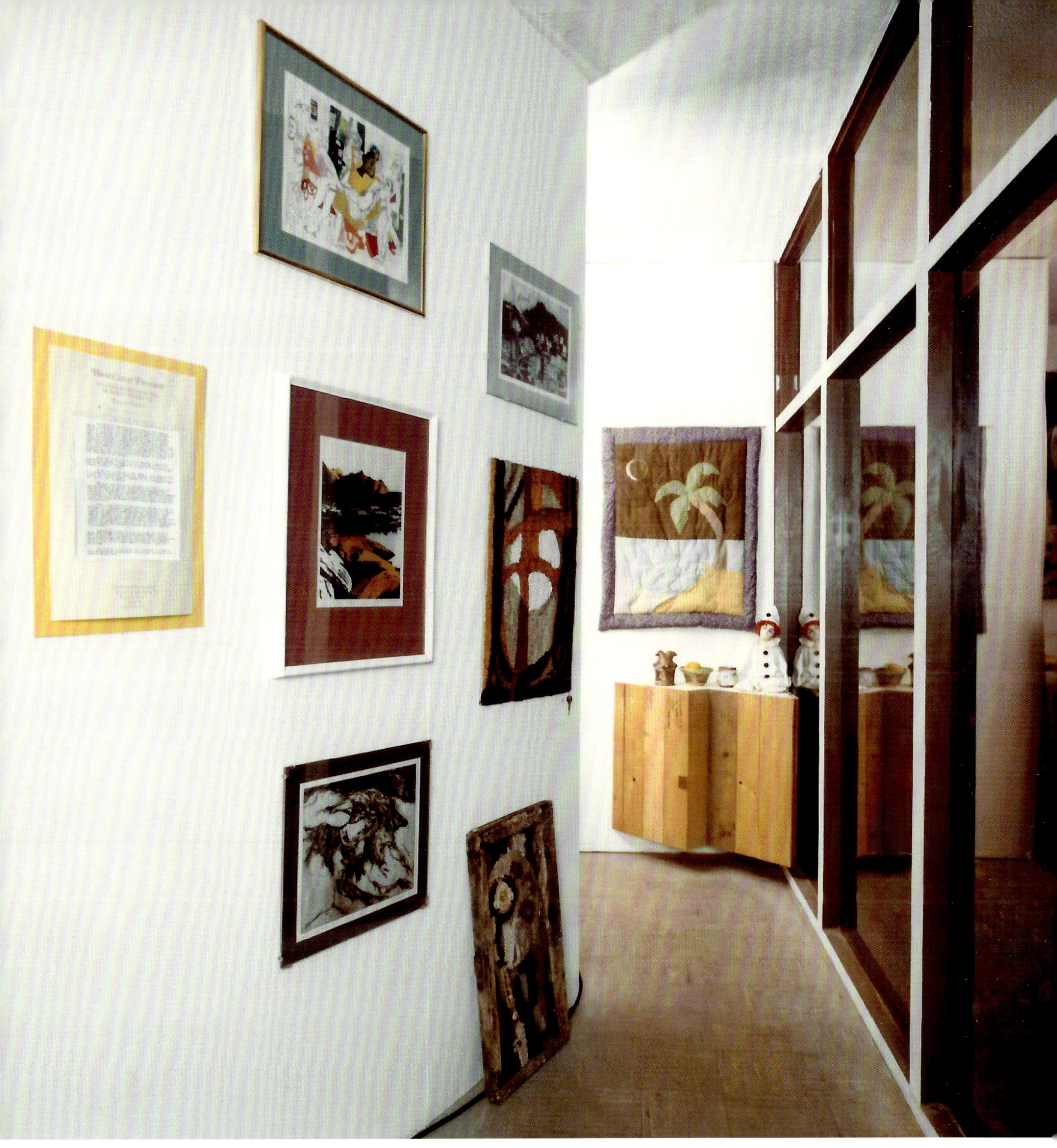

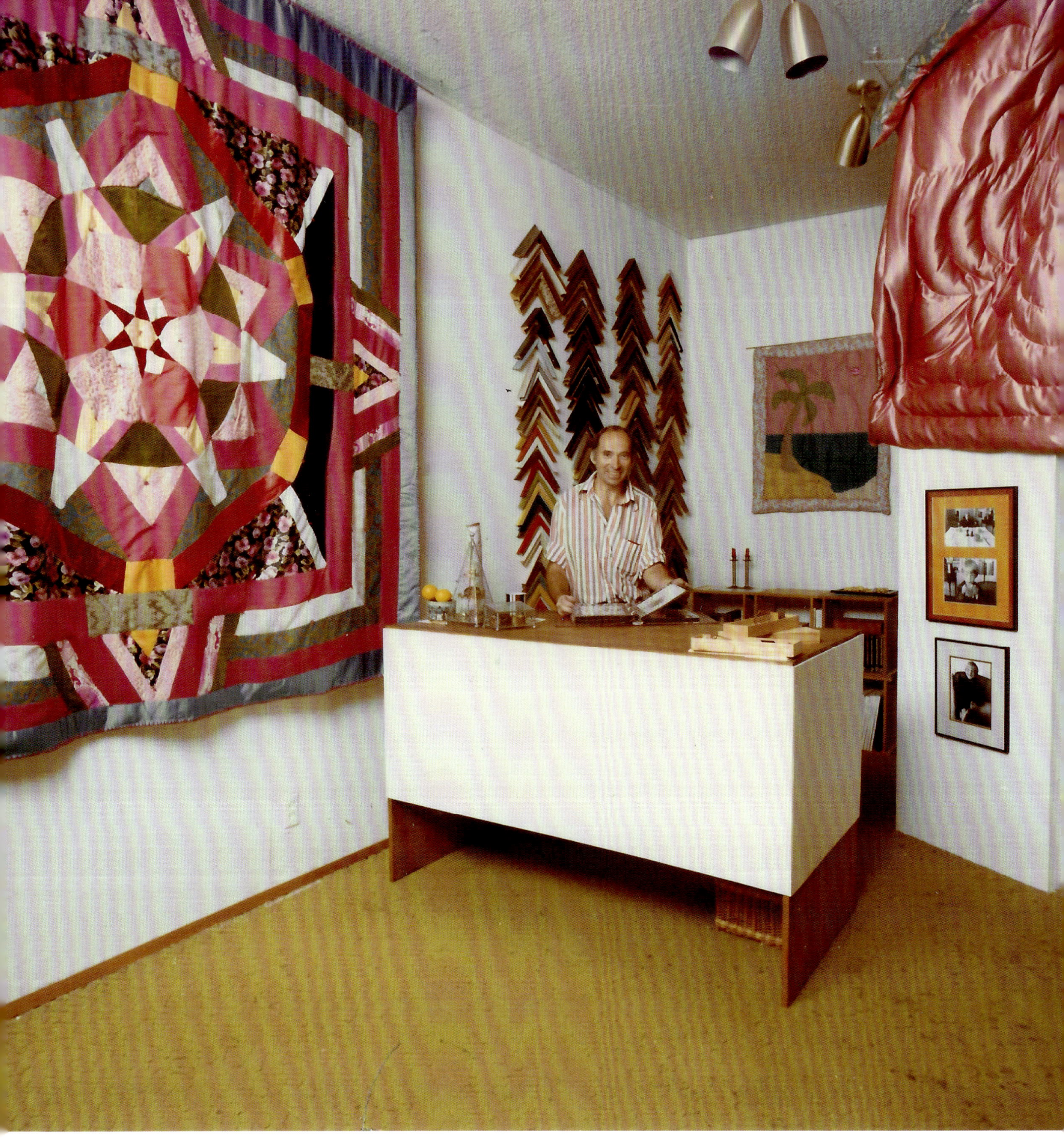

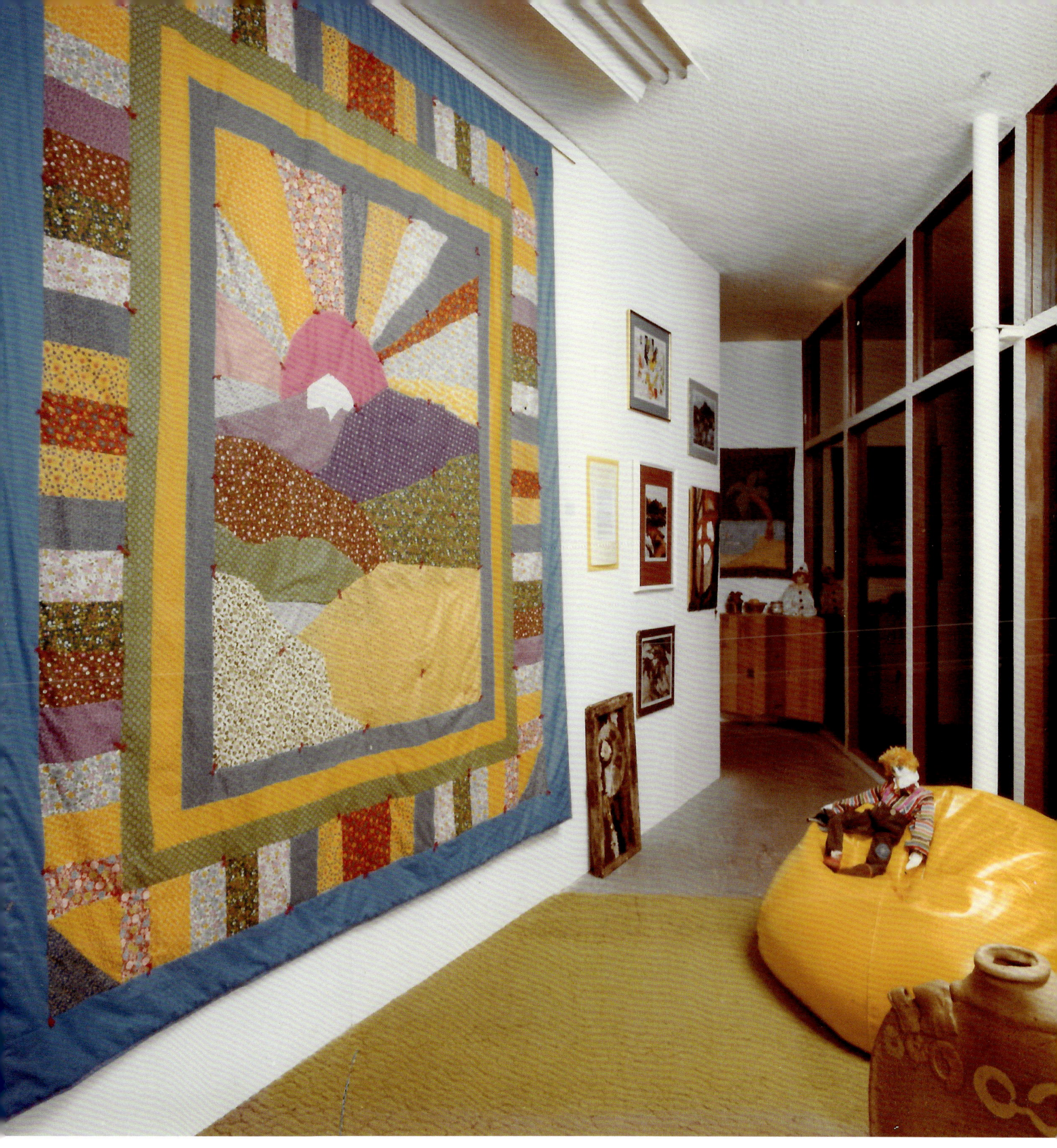

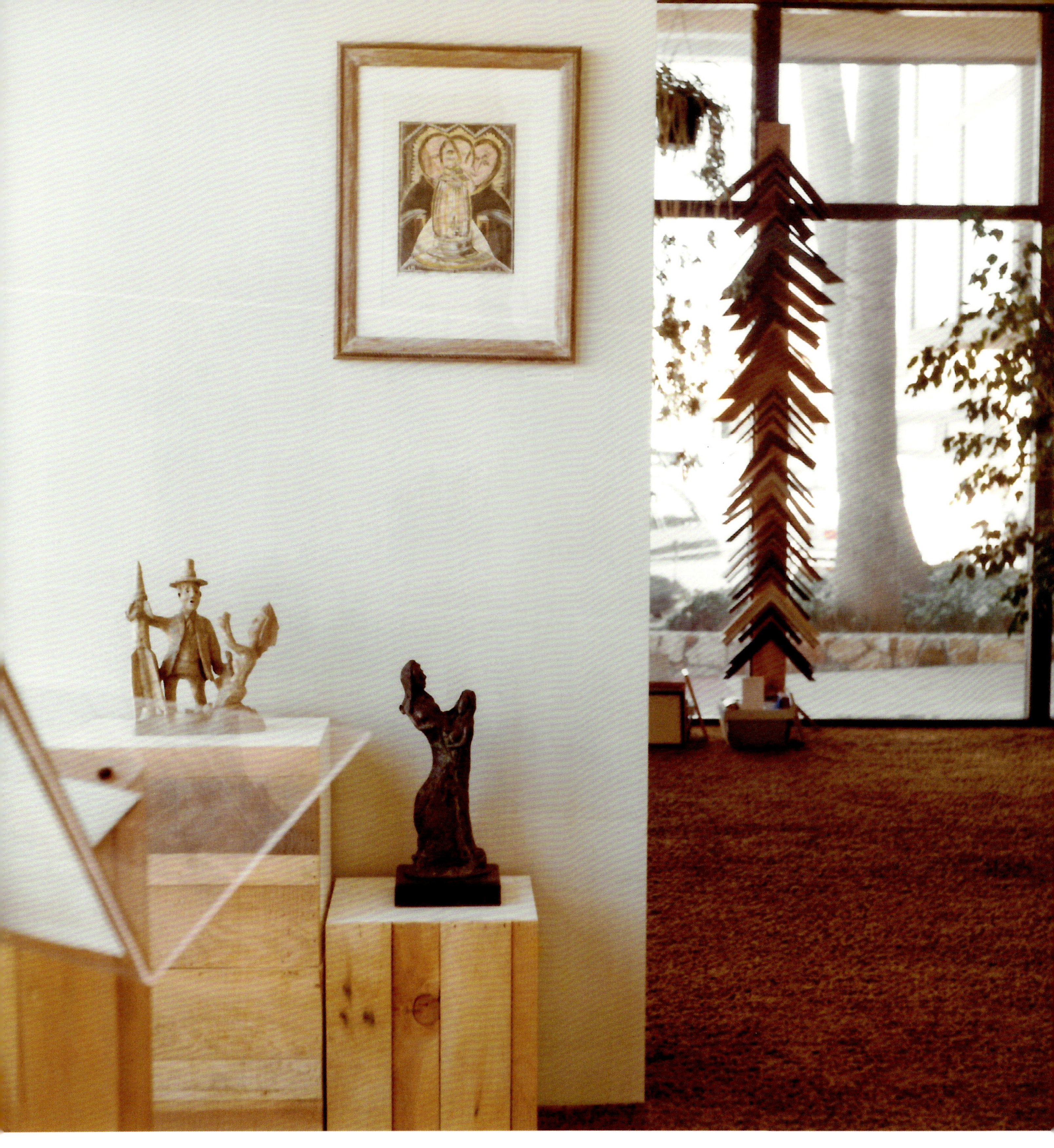

REDONDO BEACH
THE FRAME SHOP GALLERY
KING HARBOR MARINA
HERMOSA BEACH MUNICIPAL PIER
CITY OF HERMOSA BEACH
CITY OF REDONDO BEACH
REDONDO BEACH STATE BEACH
CITY OF REDONDO BEACH
CITY OF TORRANCE
TORRANCE COUNTY BEACH
ESTATES

TANEGA MAHER GALLERY
NORMA TANEGA
DANIEL MAHER
214 AVENIDA DEL NORTE
REDONDO BEACH
CALIFORNIA 90277
(213) 375-8777

Esplanade
Knob Hill
Ave A
Ave B
Ave C
Ave D
Ave E
Ave F
Ave G
Ave H
Ave I
Catalina Ave
Pacific Coast Hwy
Avenida Del Norte
Vista Del Mar
Via el Prado
Elena
Blvd
Prospect
Palos Verdes
Via Valencia
Calle Mayor

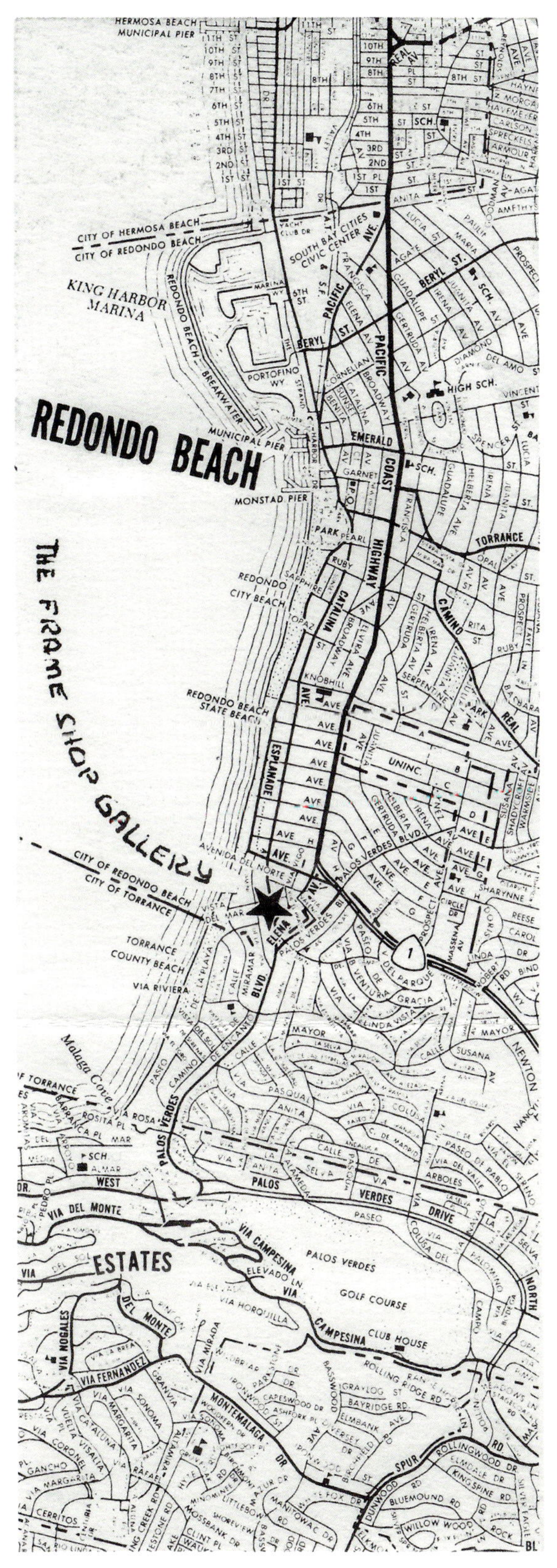

69

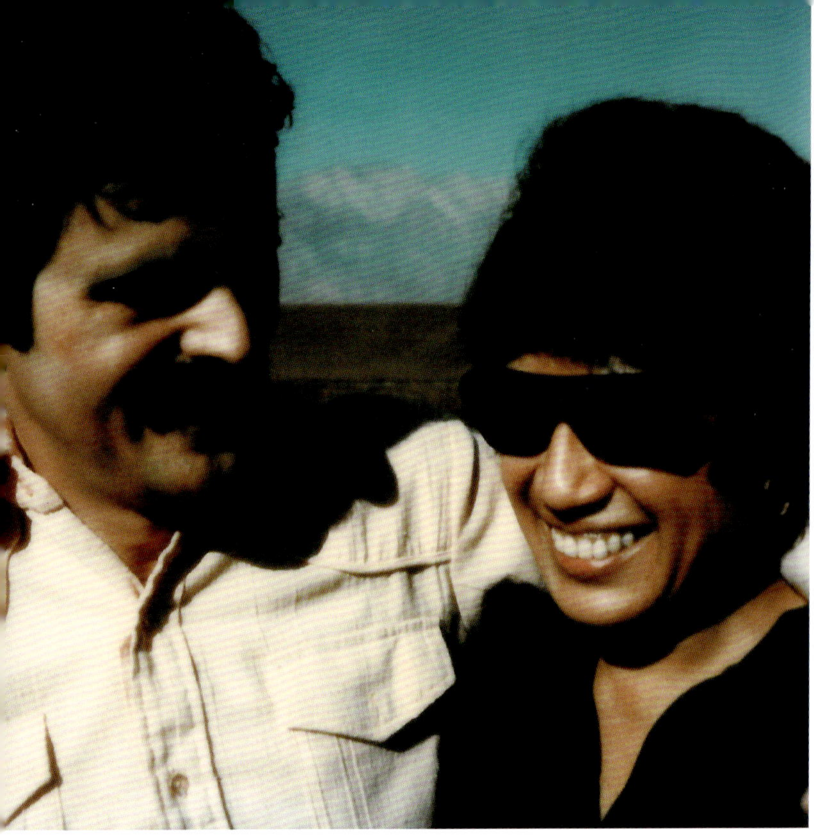

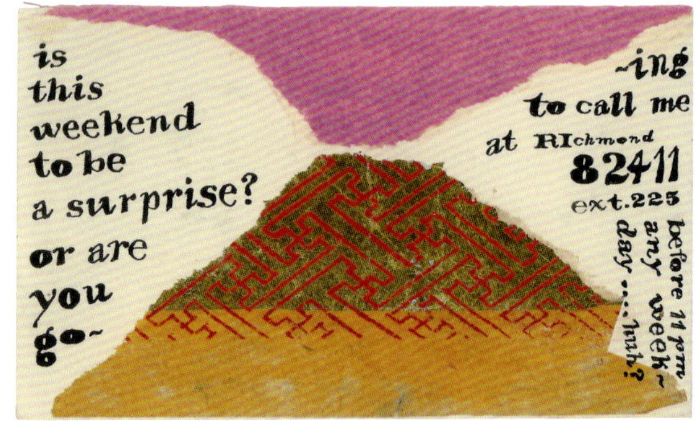
is
this
weekend
to be
a surprise?
or are
you
go~
~ing
to call me
at RIchmond
82411
ext.225
before 11pm
any week~
day ...huh?

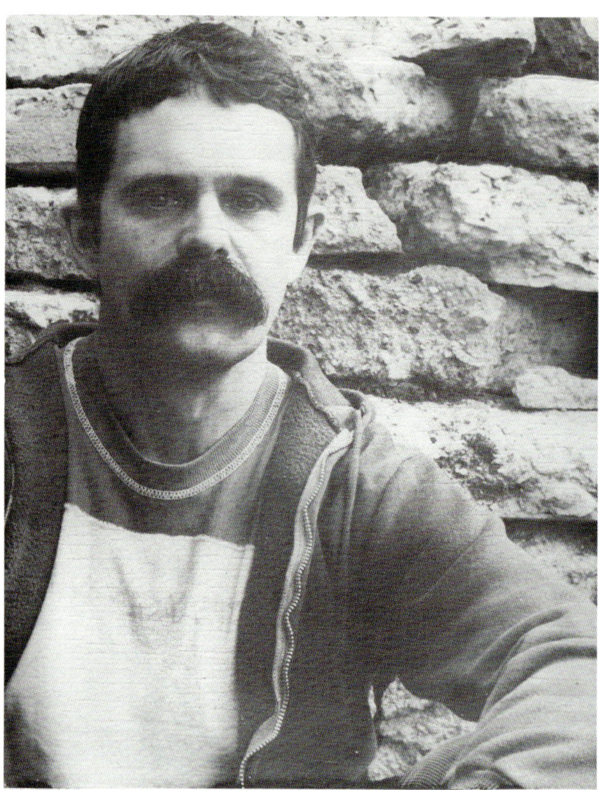
Photo by Richard Kline
W.C.C.D. AUTHIER
an exhibition
1958-1977:Drawings frm. 20 yrs.
Mar. 5-25,1977
come to the
reception, Sat. Mar. 5, 6-9pm
TANEGA MAHER GALLERY
214 Avenida del Norte
Redondo Beach, Calif.
(213) 540-8887

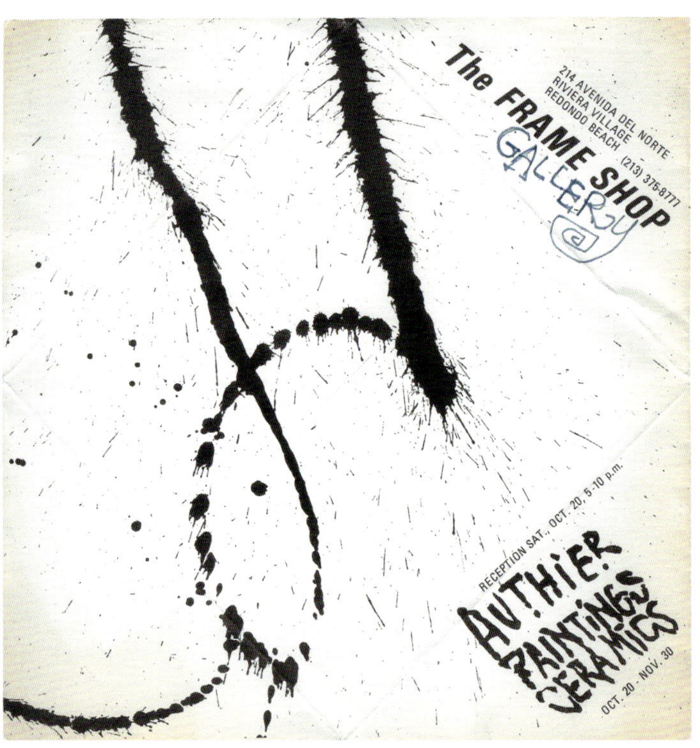
214 AVENIDA DEL NORTE
RIVIERA VILLAGE
REDONDO BEACH
The FRAME SHOP
GALLERY
(213) 375-8777
RECEPTION SAT., OCT. 20, 5-10 p.m.
AUTHIER
PAINTINGS
CERAMICS
OCT. 20 - NOV. 30

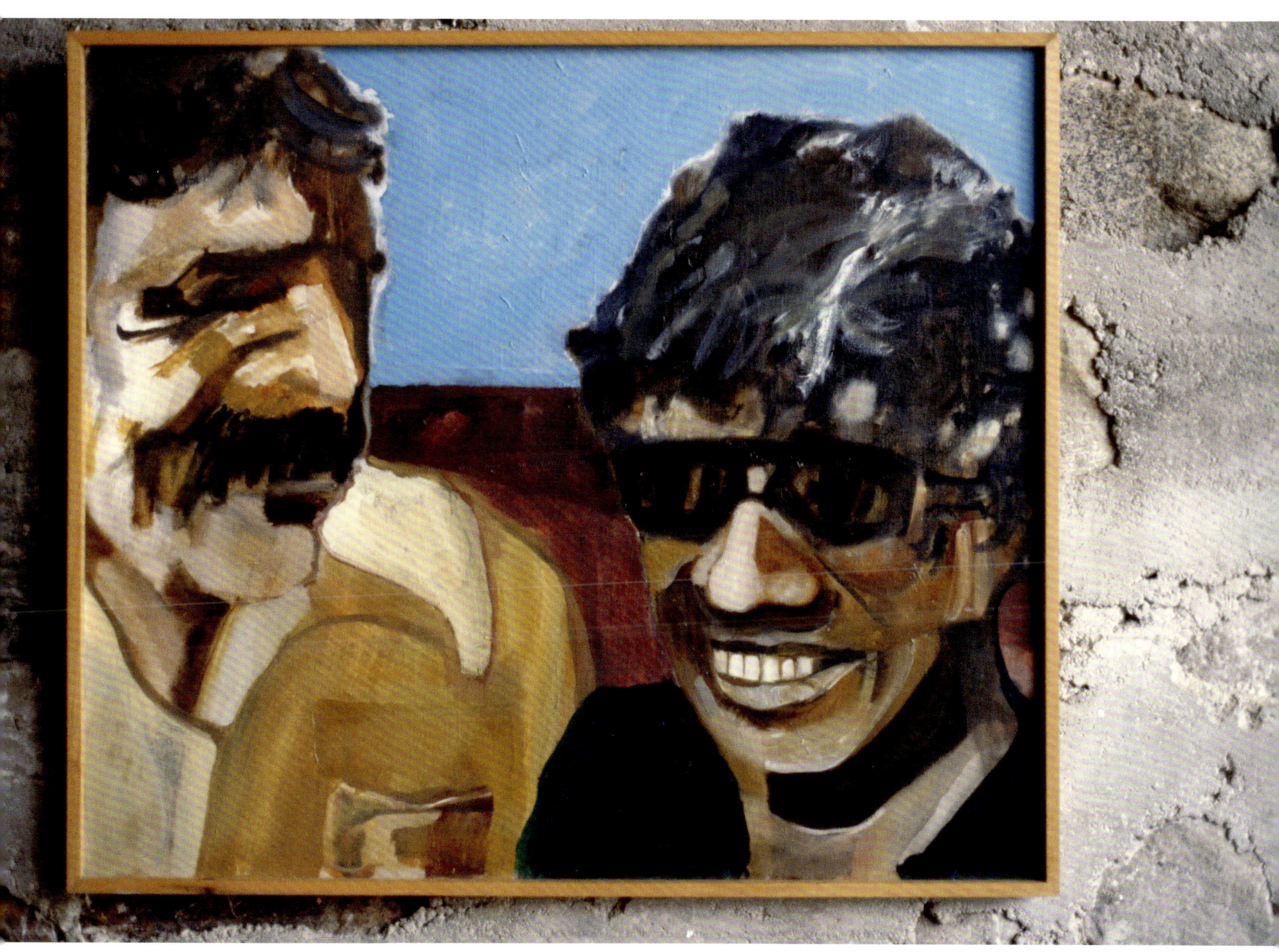

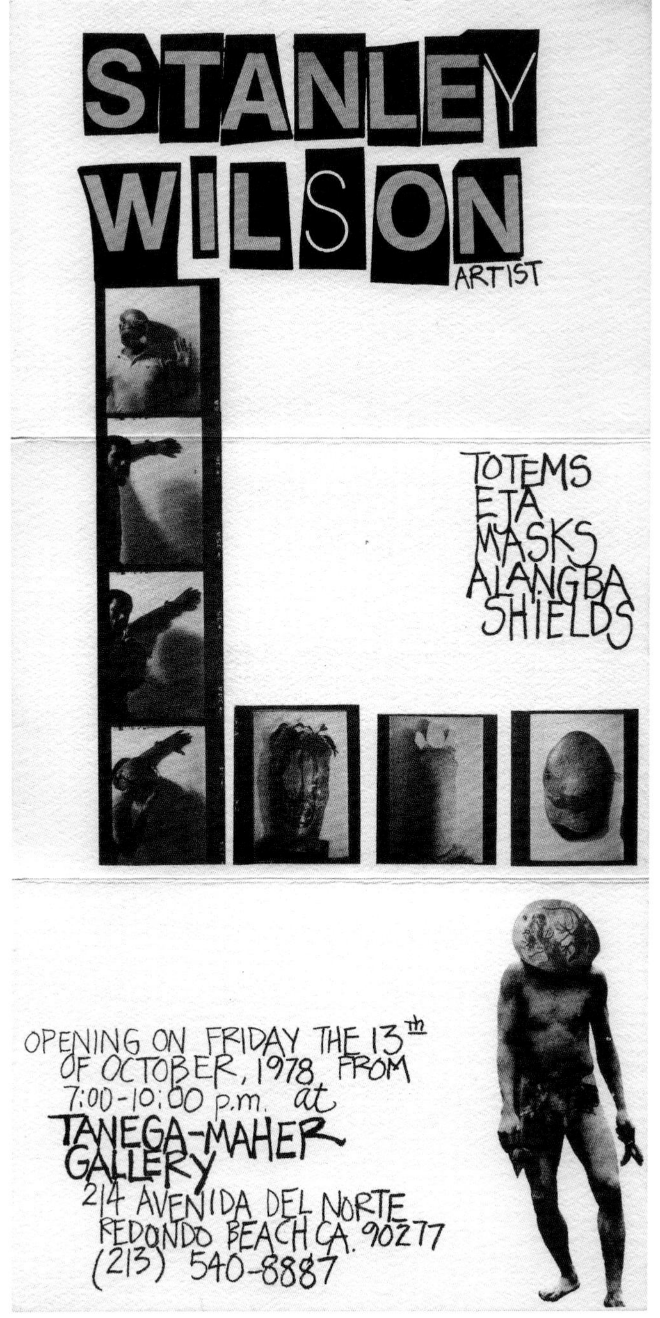

YOU ARE
INVITED TO
A SPECIAL
SALE AND
EXHIBITION
OF PRIMITIVE
ART FROM
NEW GUINEA

JUNE 1 TO 7

CELEBRATION:
SATURDAY,
JUNE 1

5:00-10:00 P.M.

Frame Shop Gallery 214 Avenida del Norte

Frame Shop Gallery 214 Avenida del Norte

REDONDO BEACH

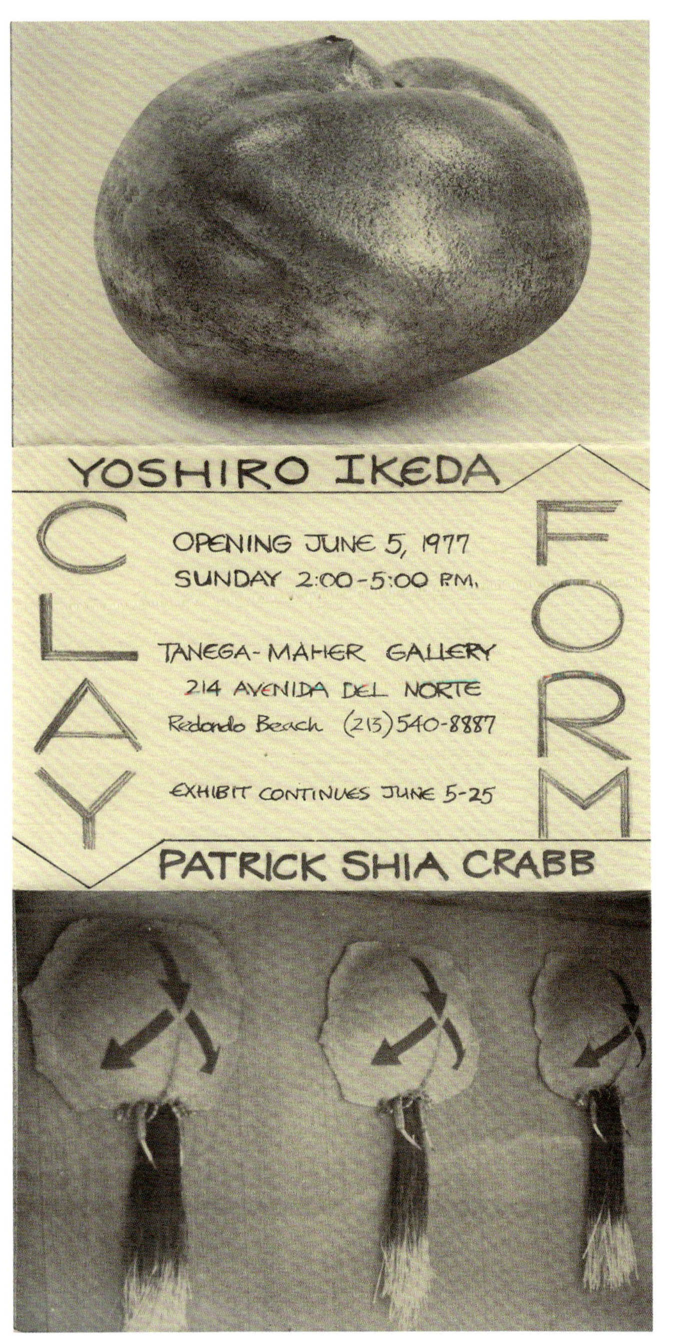

YOSHIRO IKEDA
CLAY FORM
OPENING JUNE 5, 1977
SUNDAY 2:00-5:00 P.M.
TANEGA-MAHER GALLERY
214 AVENIDA DEL NORTE
Redondo Beach (213) 540-8887
EXHIBIT CONTINUES JUNE 5-25
PATRICK SHIA CRABB

THE FRAME SHOP
NORMA and DAVIS GALLERY
CRAFTSMANSHIP USA YES
PAINTINGS
PRINTS
214 AVENIDA DEL NORTE, REDONDO BEACH,
CALIFORNIA 90277   (213) 375-8777

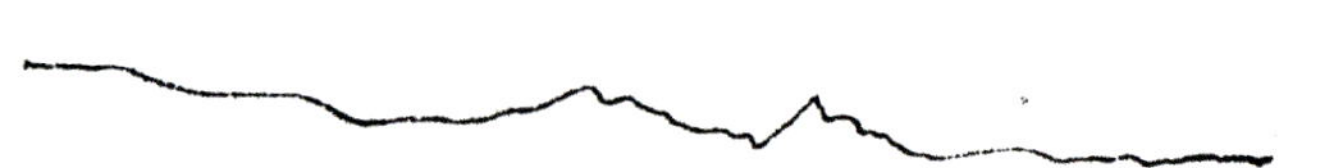

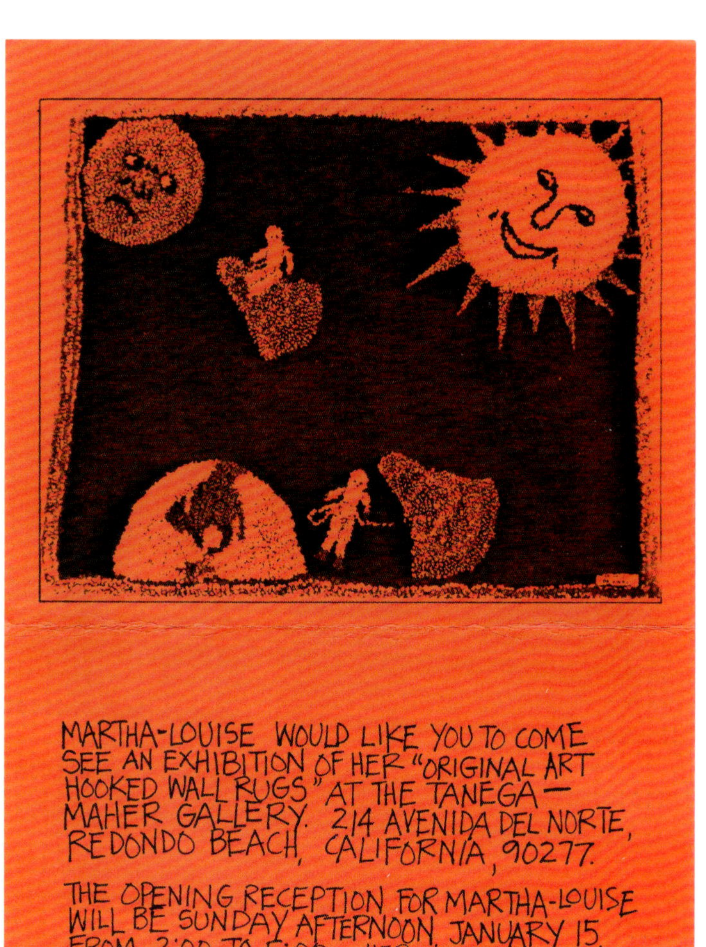

MARTHA-LOUISE WOULD LIKE YOU TO COME
SEE AN EXHIBITION OF HER "ORIGINAL ART
HOOKED WALL RUGS" AT THE TANEGA—
MAHER GALLERY. 214 AVENIDA DEL NORTE,
REDONDO BEACH, CALIFORNIA, 90277.

THE OPENING RECEPTION FOR MARTHA-LOUISE
WILL BE SUNDAY AFTERNOON, JANUARY 15,
FROM 2:00 TO 5:00. HER EXHIBIT WILL
CONTINUE THROUGH FEBRUARY 12.

GALLERY HOURS FOR 1978 ARE:
10:00 TO 6:00 – TUESDAY THROUGH FRIDAY
10:00 TO 4:00 – SATURDAY.
(213) 540-8887.

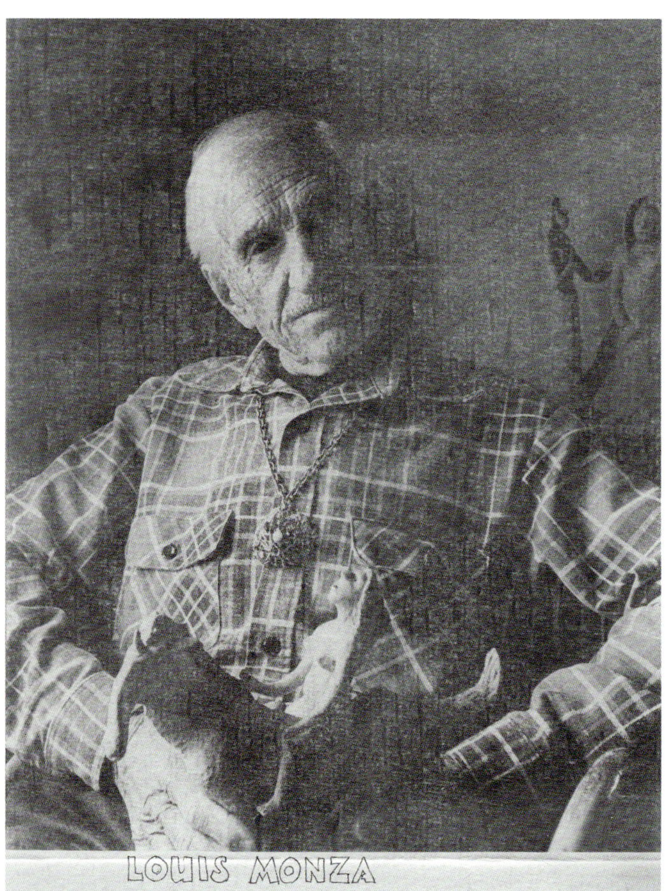

LOUIS MONZA
PAINTING AND SCULPTURE
FEBRUARY 4 TO 26
OPENING RECEPTION
FRIDAY, FEBRUARY 4, 1977
8 TO 10 PM
TANEGA MAHER GALLERY
214 AVENIDA DEL NORTE
REDONDO BEACH, CAL. 90277
(213) 540-8887

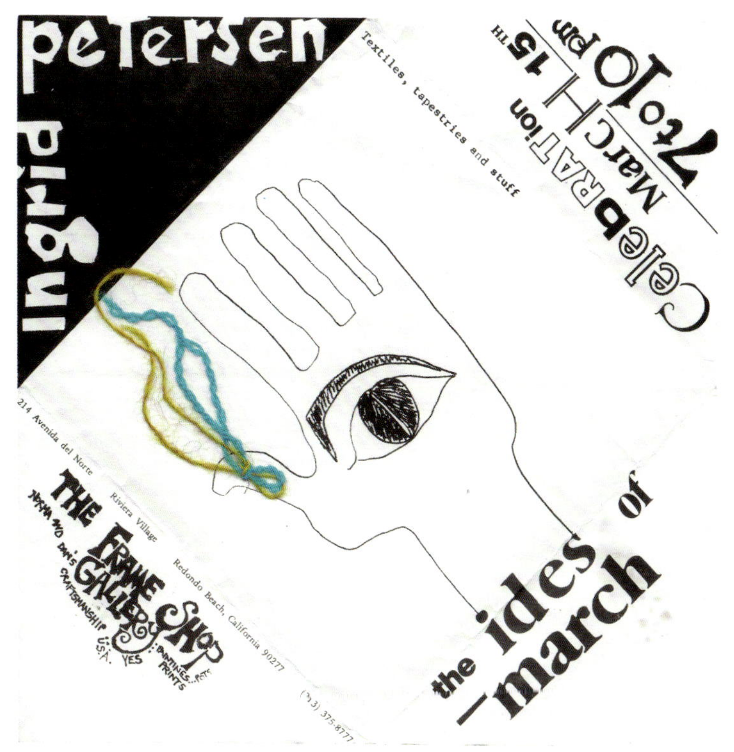

petersen
ingrid
Textiles, tapestries and stuff
CelebRATion MarcH 15th 2 to 10 pm
the ides of march
THE FRAME SHOP GALLERY
214 Avenida del Norte
Riviera Village
Redondo Beach, California 90277
(213) 375-8777

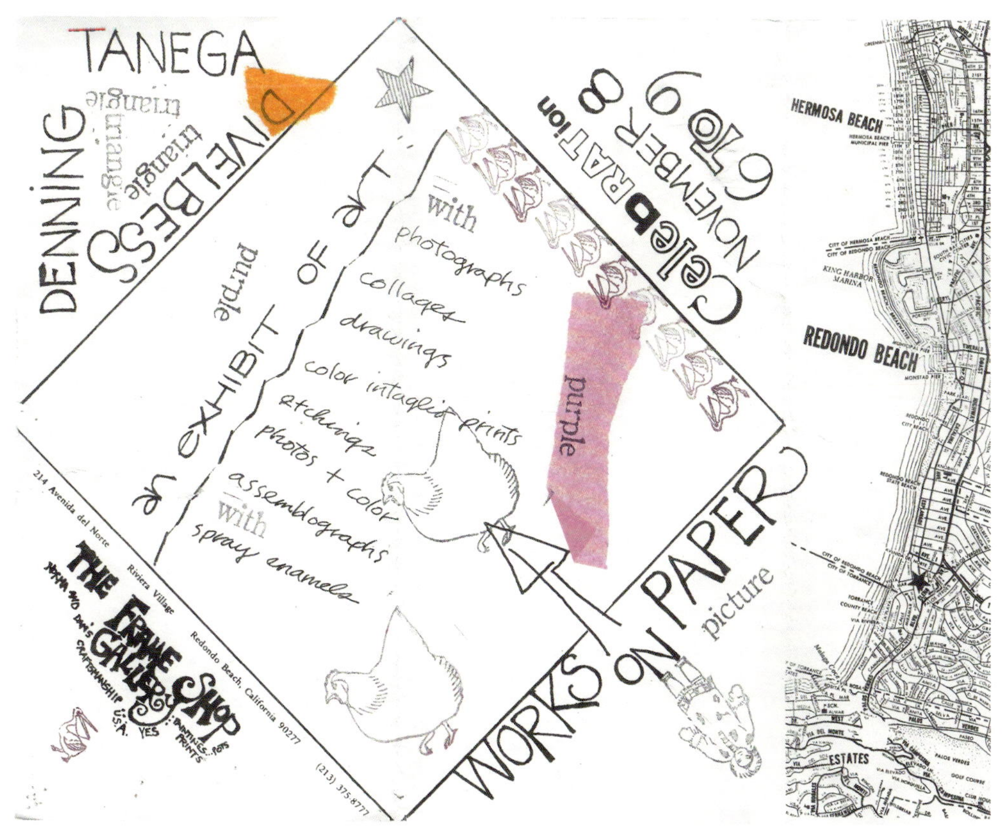

TANEGA
DENNING
DIVELBESS
triangle triangle triangle
purple
purple
EXHIBIT of art
with
photographs
collages
drawings
color intaglio prints
etchings
photos + color
assemblographs
with
spray enamels
CelebRATion NOVEMBER 6 to 9
WORKS ON PAPER
picture
THE FRAME SHOP GALLERY
214 Avenida del Norte
Riviera Village
Redondo Beach, California 90277
(213) 375-8777
HERMOSA BEACH
REDONDO BEACH
KING HARBOR MARINA

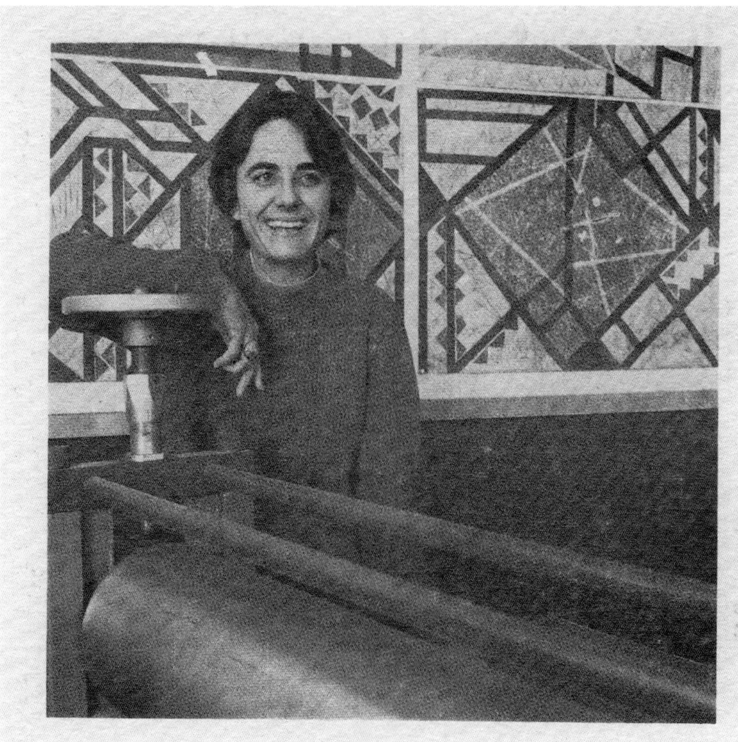

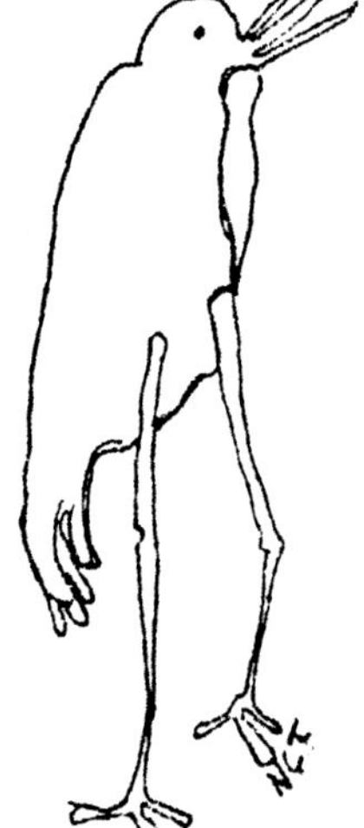

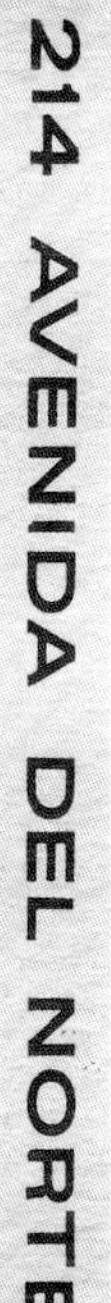

TANEGA—MAHER GALLERY

214 AVENIDA DEL NORTE

January 8-28, 1977
An exhibit of recent works
by Diane Divelbess.

You are invited to attend
the opening reception
Saturday, January 8, in
the evening from 6 to 9.

REDONDO BEACH, CAL

213 — 540 — 8887

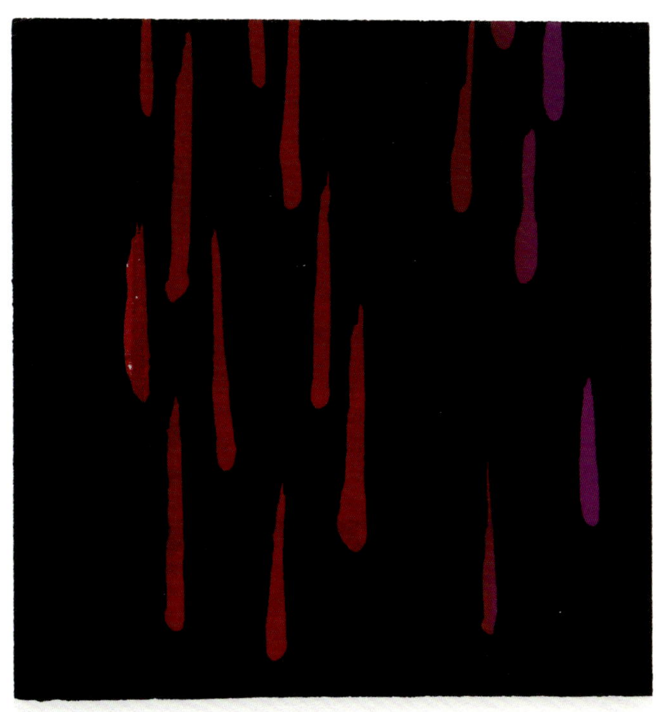

DIANE DIVELBESS
NEW WORKS WITH COLOR
NOVEMBER 10 – DECEMBER 9, 1984
RECEPTION: SUNDAY, NOVEMBER 11, 2-5 PM

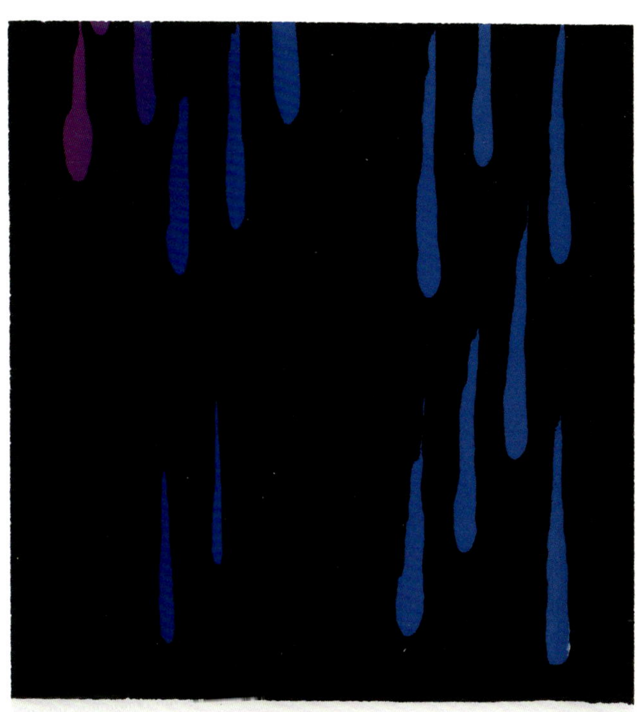

DIANE DIVELBESS
NEW WORKS WITH COLOR
NOVEMBER 10 – DECEMBER 9, 1984
RECEPTION: SUNDAY, NOVEMBER 11, 2-5 PM

DIANE DIVELBESS
Recent Works

Opening Sunday, November 5
Reception from 3:00 - 6:00 p.m.

Tanega-Maher Gallery
214 Avenida del Norte
Redondo Beach, CA 90277
213/540-8887

Exhibit through
November 30, 1978

Closed Sunday - Monday

"SOFT LANDING" 29¾" x 41⅛" DIANE DIVELBESS

MORNING + LINDA
DEW DROP INN

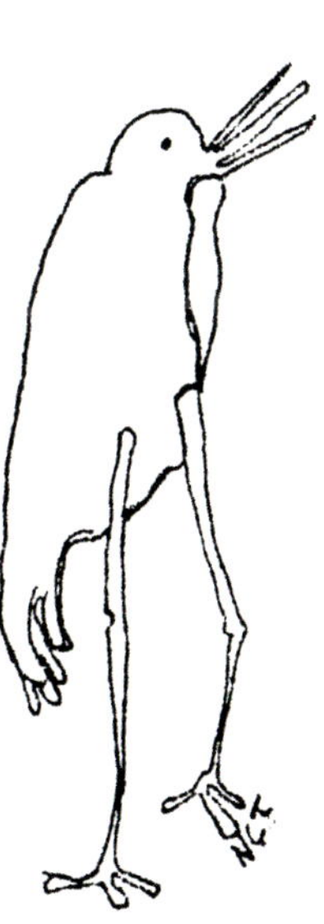

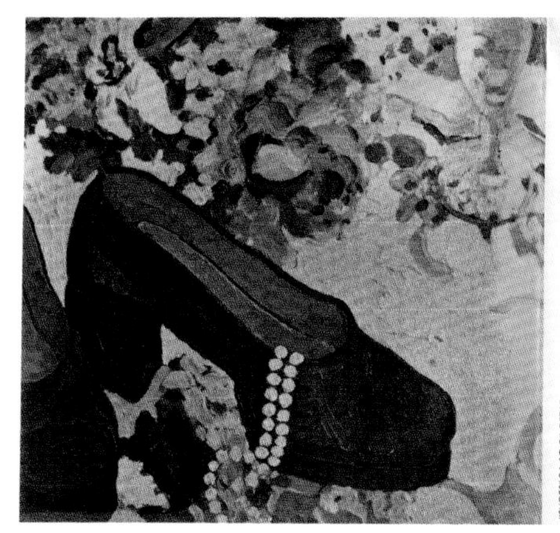

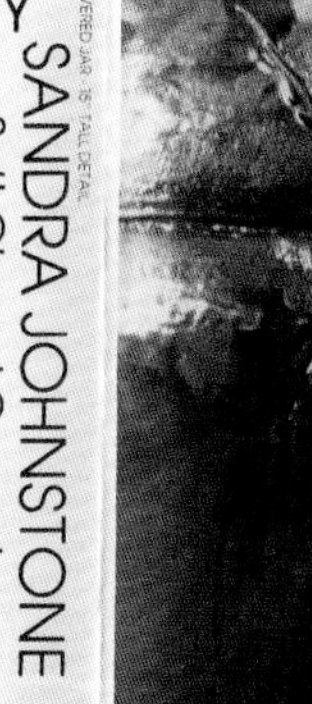

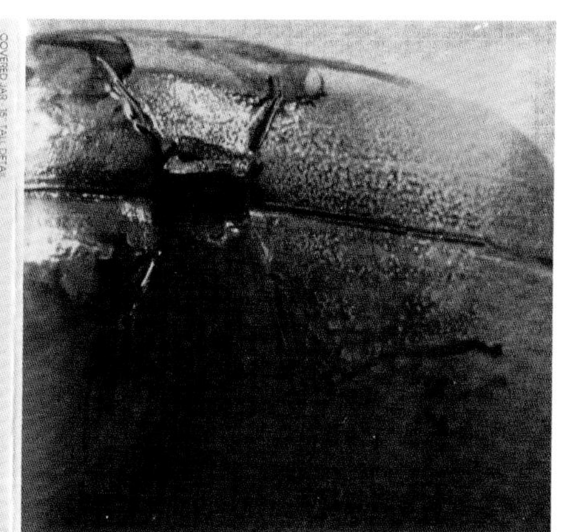

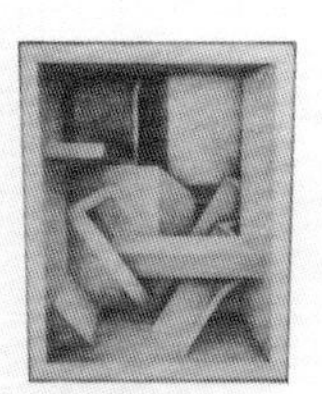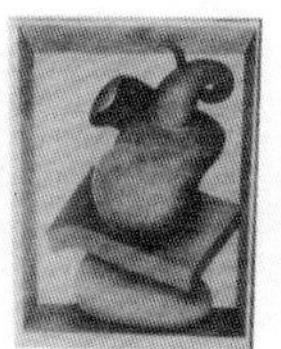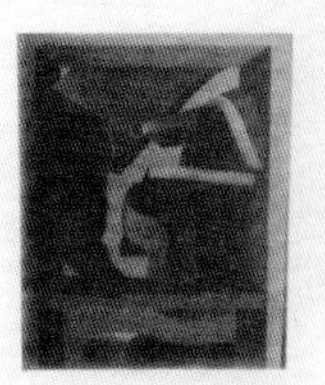

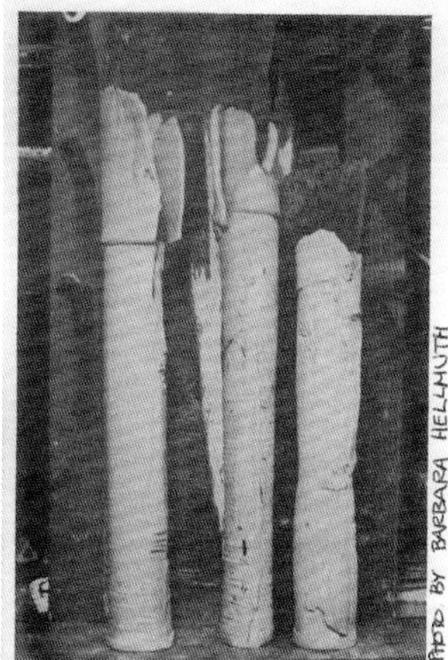

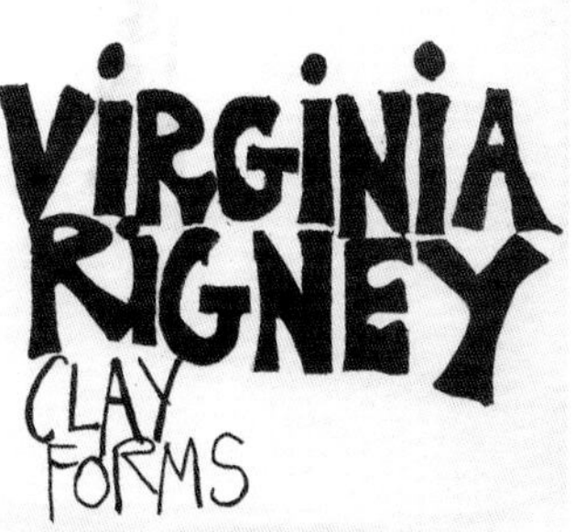

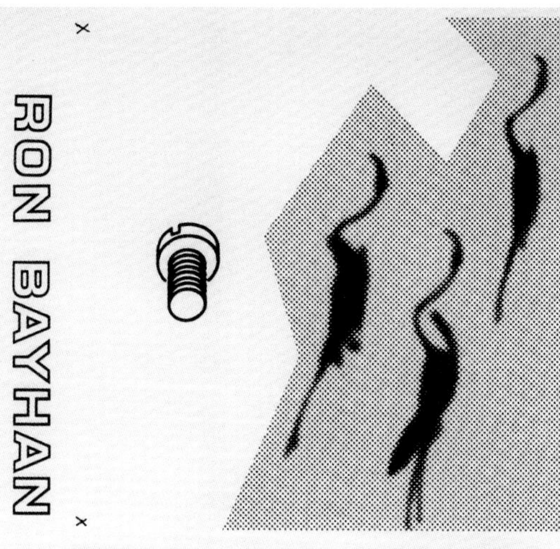

FRAME SHOP GALLERY
214 Avenida del Norte, Redondo Beach, Ca.   375-8777

April 18 through May 16, 1975   Opening April 18, 6-9 p.m.
Gallery hours: Monday through Saturday, 10 - 6

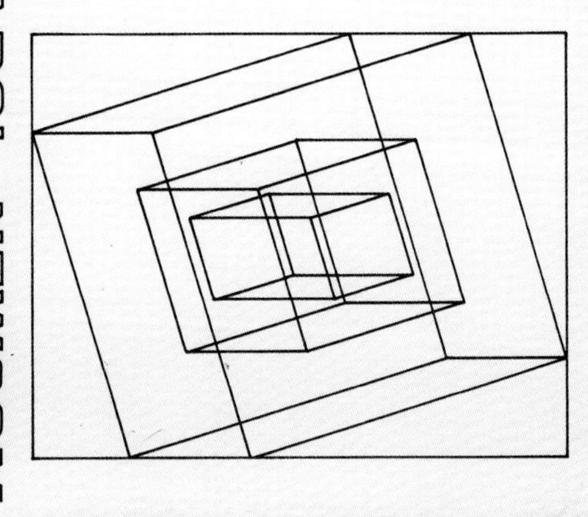

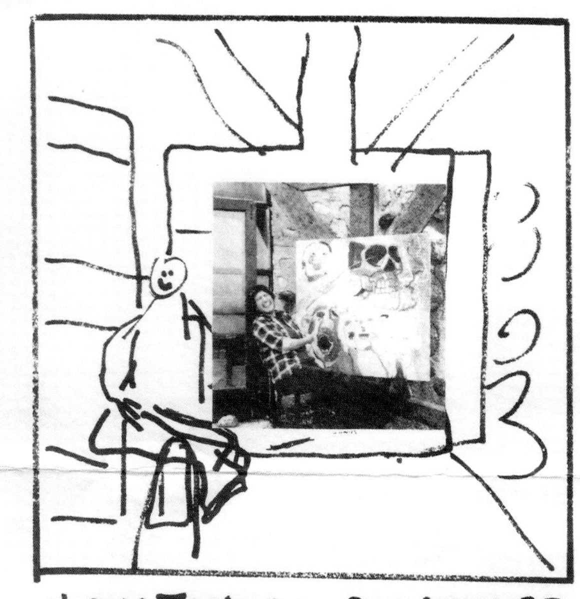

NORMA TANEGA PAINTINGS

MAY 20 - JUNE 20, 1978
OPENING: SAT. MAY 20TH 6-9 P.M.

TANEGA/MAHER
GALLERY
214 AVENIDA DEL NORTE
REDONDO BEACH, CA. 90277
(213) 540-8887

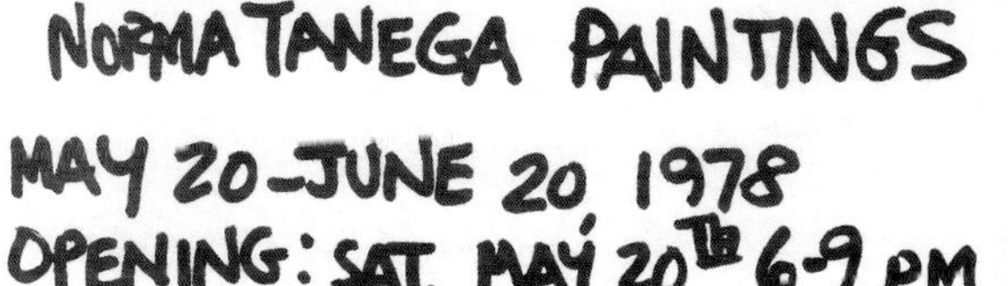

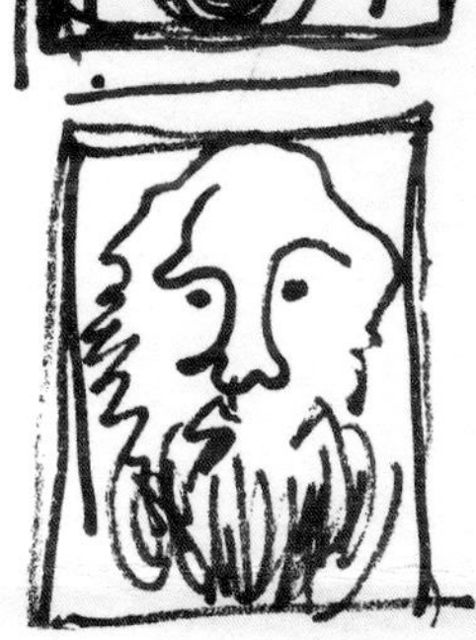

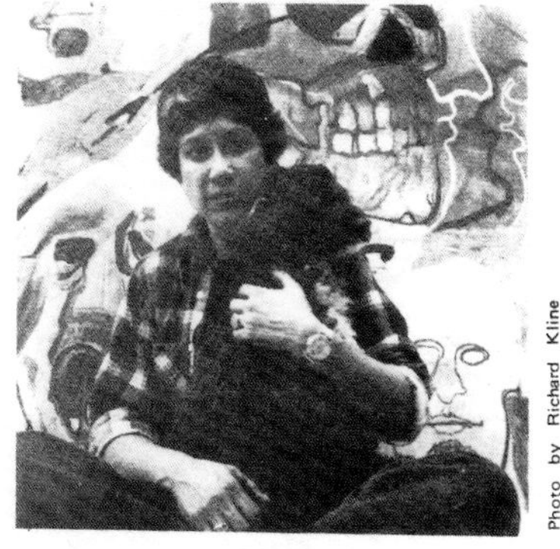

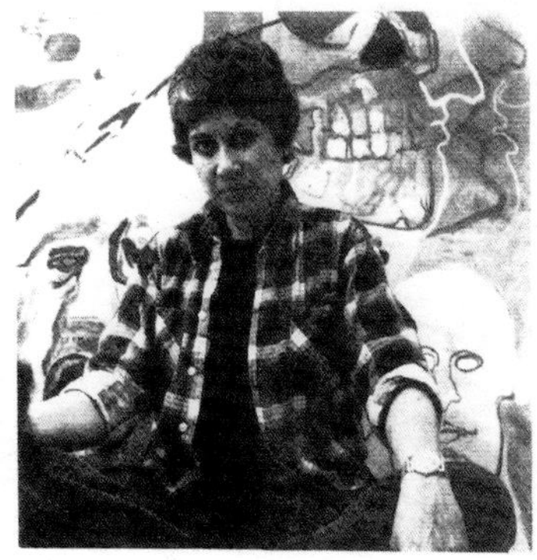

Photo by Richard Kline

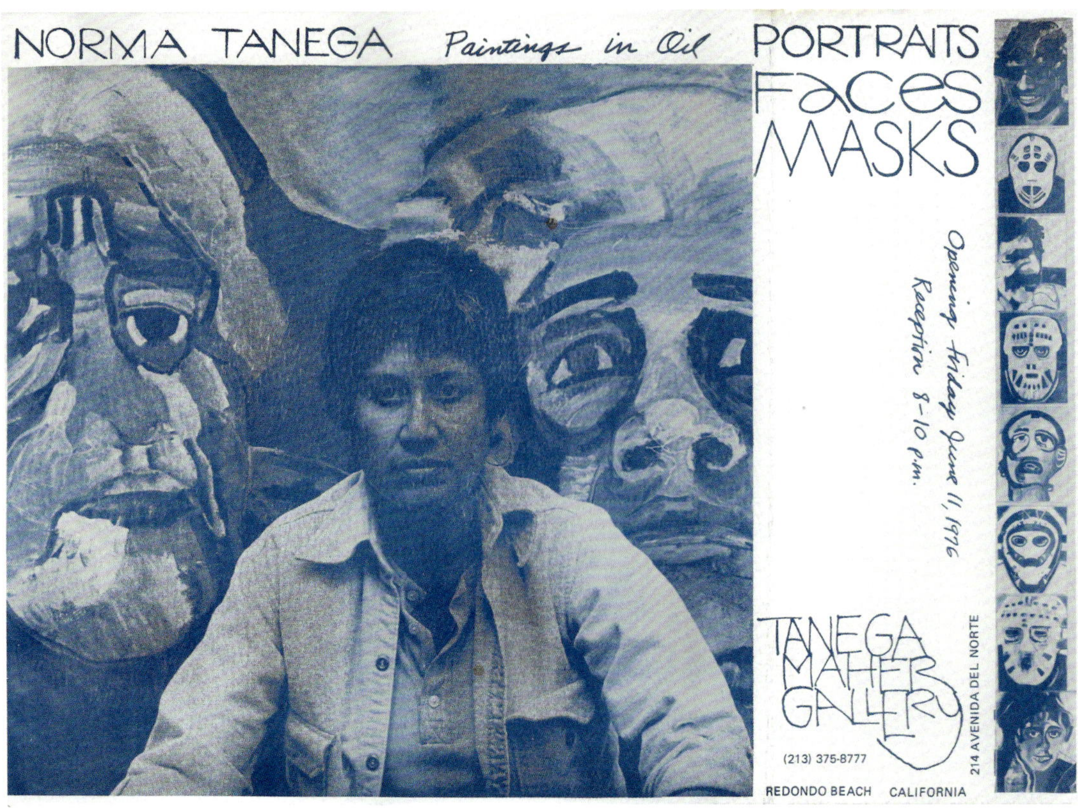

NORMA TANEGA
Paintings in Oil
PORTRAITS
FACES &
MASKS
Opening Friday June 11, 1976
Reception 8-10 p.m.
TANEGA MATHER GALLERY
(213) 375-8777
214 AVENIDA DEL NORTE
REDONDO BEACH   CALIFORNIA

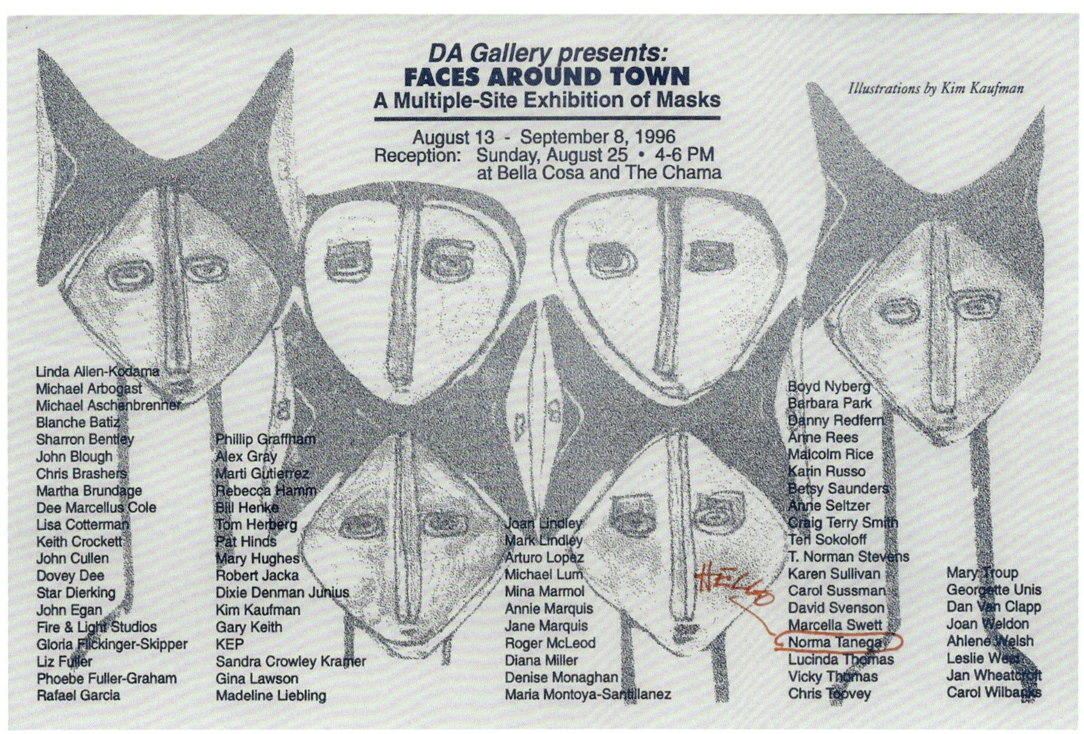

DA Gallery presents:
FACES AROUND TOWN
A Multiple-Site Exhibition of Masks
Illustrations by Kim Kaufman
August 13 - September 8, 1996
Reception: Sunday, August 25 • 4-6 PM
at Bella Cosa and The Chama

Linda Allen-Kodama
Michael Arbogast
Michael Aschenbrenner
Blanche Batiz
Sharron Bentley
John Blough
Chris Brashers
Martha Brundage
Dee Marcellus Cole
Lisa Cotterman
Keith Crockett
John Cullen
Dovey Dee
Star Dierking
John Egan
Fire & Light Studios
Gloria Flickinger-Skipper
Liz Fuller
Phoebe Fuller-Graham
Rafael Garcia

Phillip Graffham
Alex Gray
Marti Gutierrez
Rebecca Hamm
Bill Henke
Tom Herberg
Pat Hinds
Mary Hughes
Robert Jacka
Dixie Denman Junius
Kim Kaufman
Gary Keith
KEP
Sandra Crowley Kramer
Gina Lawson
Madeline Liebling

Joan Lindley
Mark Lindley
Arturo Lopez
Michael Lum
Mina Marmol
Annie Marquis
Jane Marquis
Roger McLeod
Diana Miller
Denise Monaghan
Maria Montoya-Santillanez

HELLO
Boyd Nyberg
Barbara Park
Danny Redfern
Anne Rees
Malcolm Rice
Karin Russo
Betsy Saunders
Anne Seltzer
Craig Terry Smith
Teri Sokoloff
T. Norman Stevens
Karen Sullivan
Carol Sussman
David Svenson
Marcella Swett
Norma Tanega
Lucinda Thomas
Vicky Thomas
Chris Toovey

Mary Troup
Georgette Unis
Dan Van Clapp
Joan Weldon
Ahlene Welsh
Leslie West
Jan Wheatcroft
Carol Wilbanks

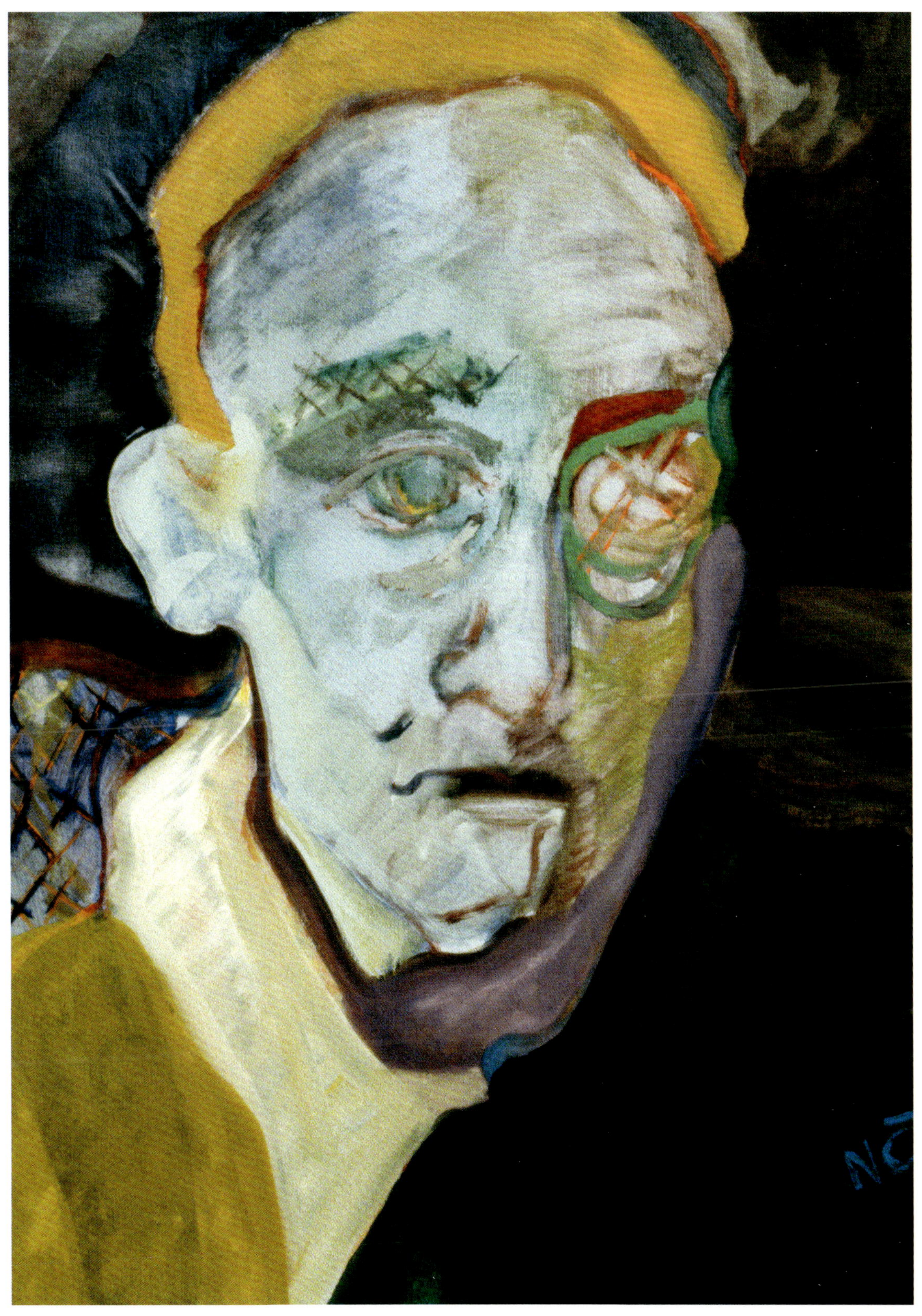

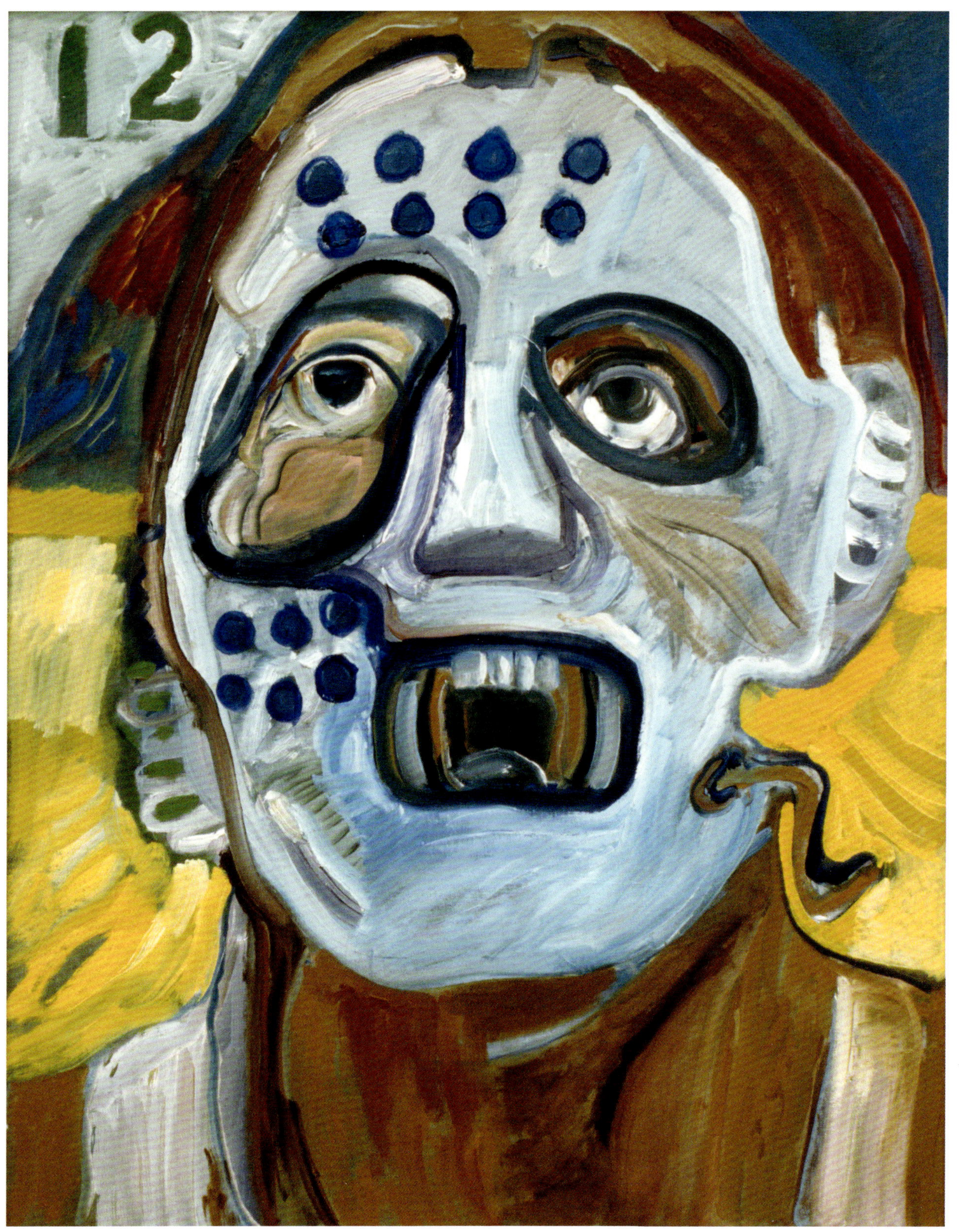

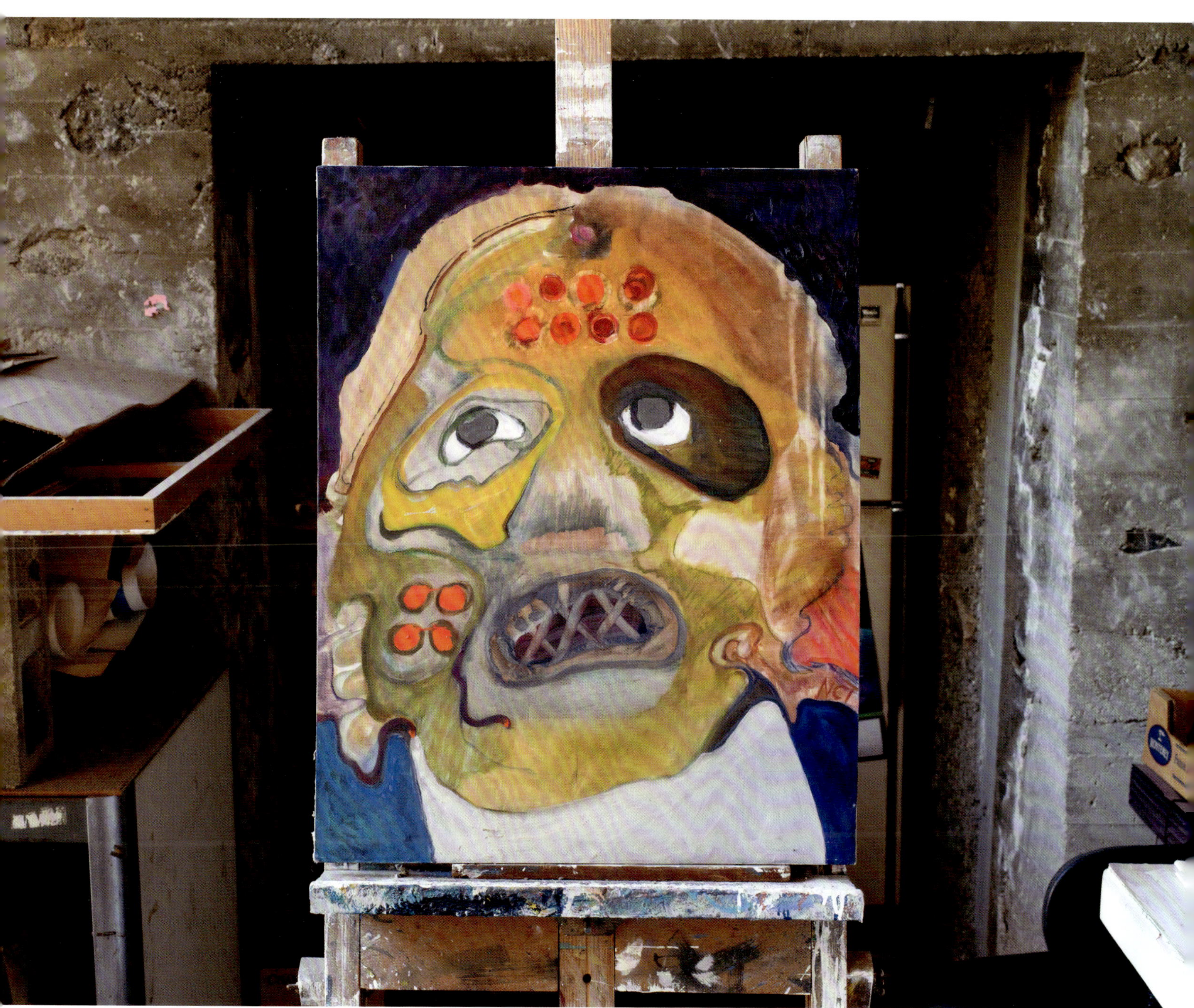

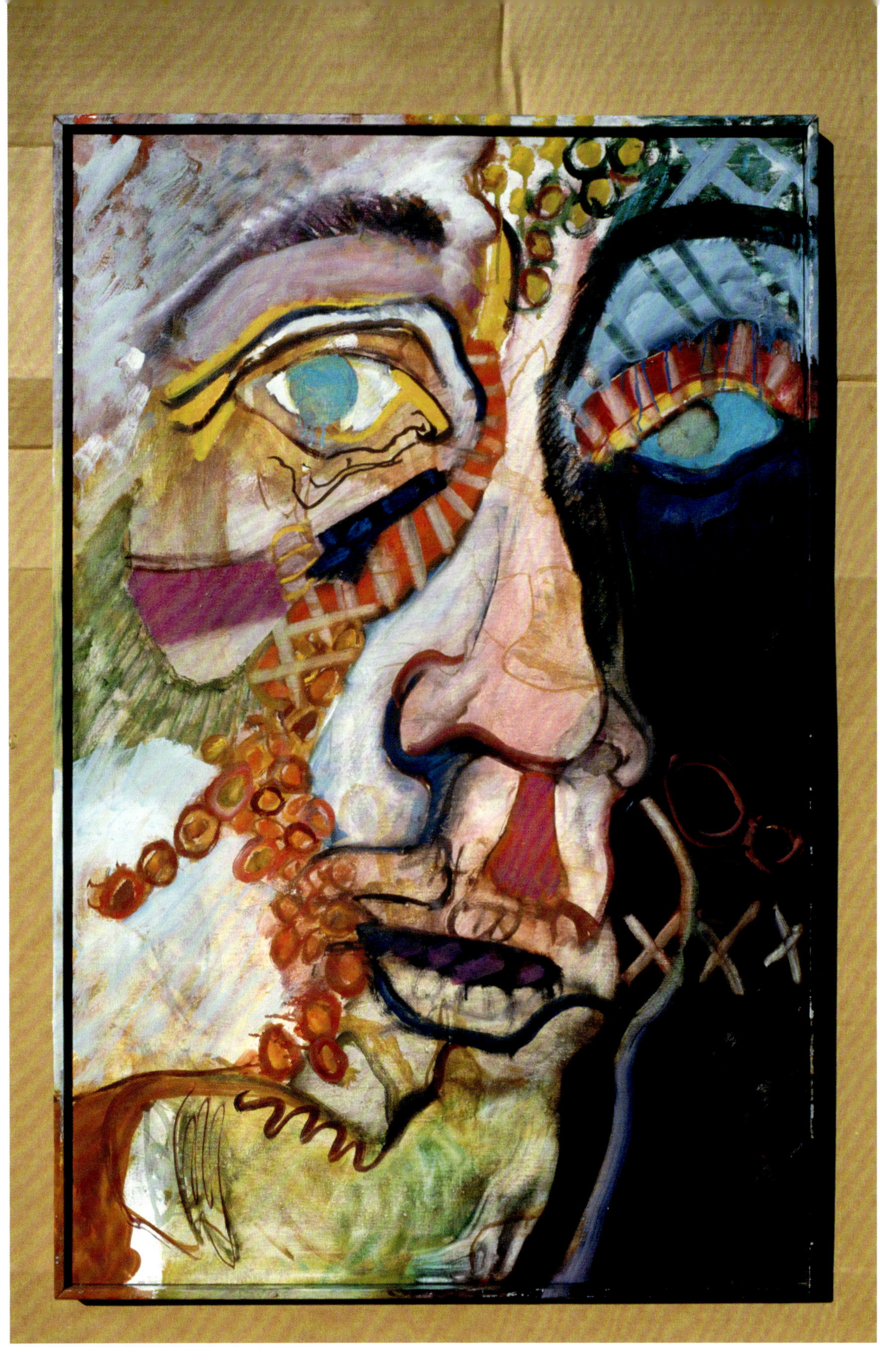

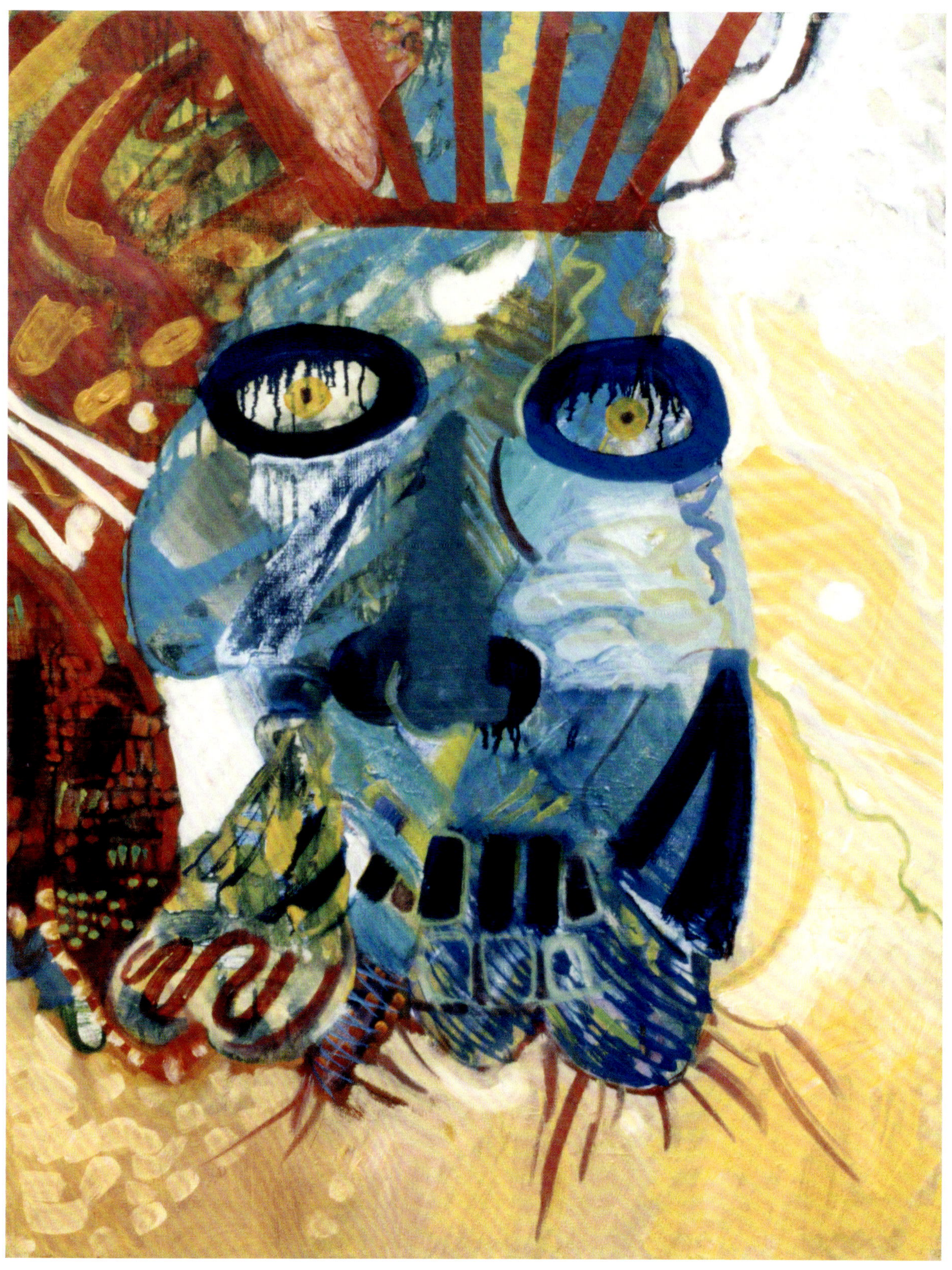

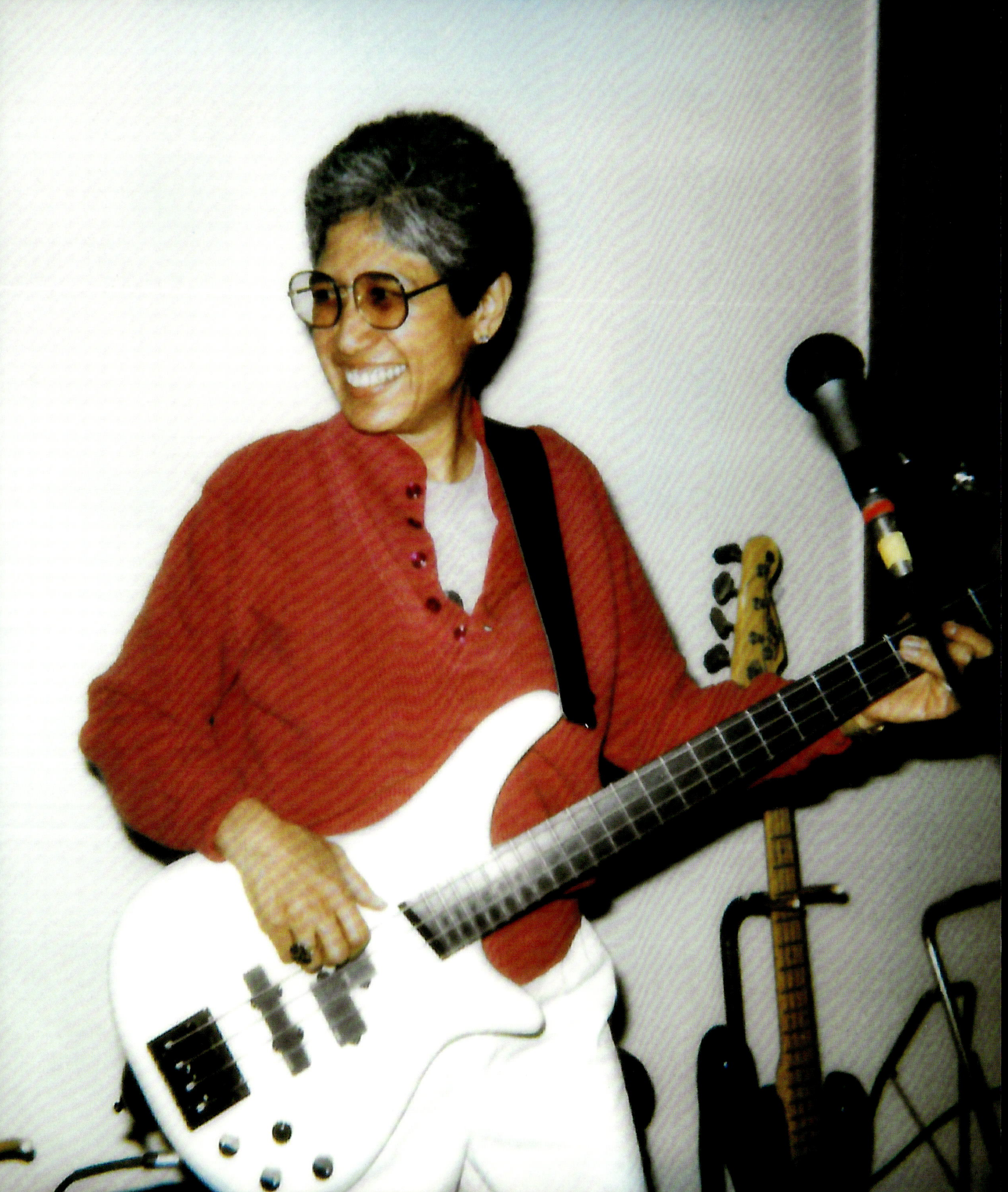

Collaborations

MOANA VERCOE: When I met Norma, she was teaching at Claremont Adult School and she continued teaching until the year before she passed away. There were restaurants throughout Claremont where Norma would walk in to be greeted by calls of "Teacher!" Norma loved her students and they loved her. Her hairdresser was a former student. Her handyman was a former student. She took pride in her teaching, and was extremely proud of her students.

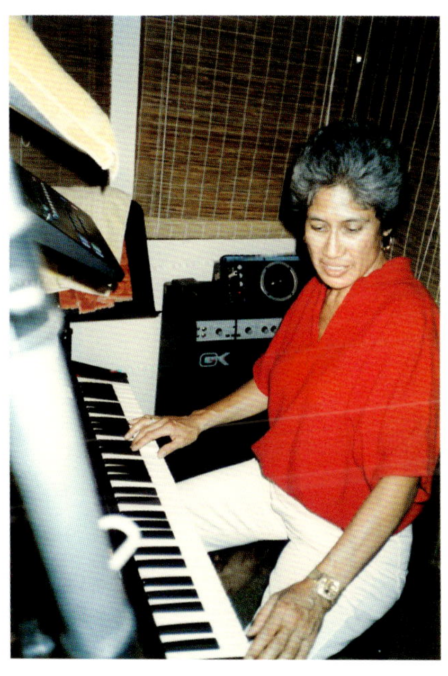 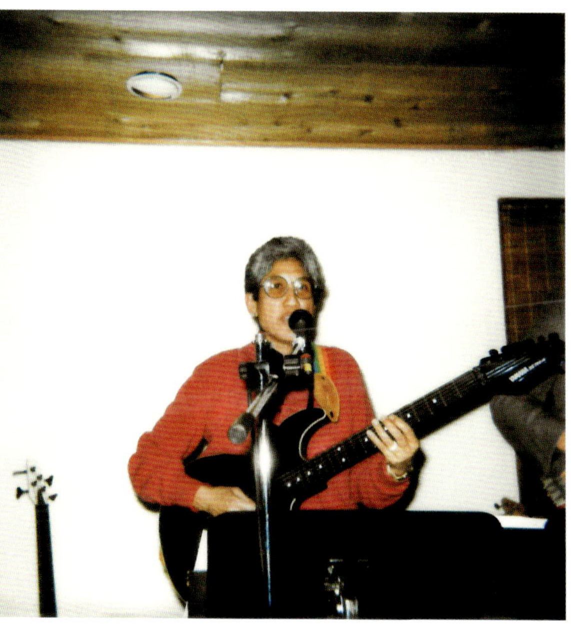

MARIO VERLANGIERI: I was a teenager when I met Norma. I think I was fifteen or sixteen. My mom, my younger sister, and me, we went to the Folk Music Center and said, "Hey, we're looking for a drum teacher." And someone, I'm not sure who it was, recommended Norma. And so we showed up one day to her studio to have a drum lesson, and that's how it started. We were known to her as "the Tribe"—that was the nickname she gave us. None of us knew who Norma was at that point; she was just this awesome music teacher. And as we got to know her better, we learned more about her: she told us about her life as a folk singer, and her life as a painter. Little by little, we started to get her story and really connect with her. And she really connected with us, I think, because she saw our love for music and loved that we were doing it as a family, you know? At some point I started taking piano lessons with her—and not just piano, but music theory lessons. Norma loved really exploring that and teaching me all sorts of musical things, exposing me to different styles. She taught me how to play the blues in her studio, which was important to me, and then she started teaching me bass guitar.

STANLEY C. WILSON: As one of her money makers, Norma also taught English as a second language for the Claremont Unified School District. She would always talk about how that was such an inspirational class for her to teach, because it was all newly immigrated people, many of whom spoke very little English, and she really had to get into their minds and hearts. And she had no problem with that at all; I mean, her students loved her. And I can see why. I mean, she was that type of person. And she did that for a number of years for Claremont Unified School District while she kept her art career going and kept her music career going.

MAXINE BOROWSKY JUNGE: I know that music was really, really important to her. She gave me all her albums, and talked to me more about her musical adventures in that second half of her life than we ever talked about art. Music was her "other" passion and was in the forefront in her later years.

NORMA TANEGA FAN CLUB

This certifies that

is a member in good standing

from   to   president

NORMA TANEGA FAN CLUB

THIS CERTIFIES THAT

IS A MEMBER IN GOOD STANDING

FROM ________ TO ________   PRESIDENT

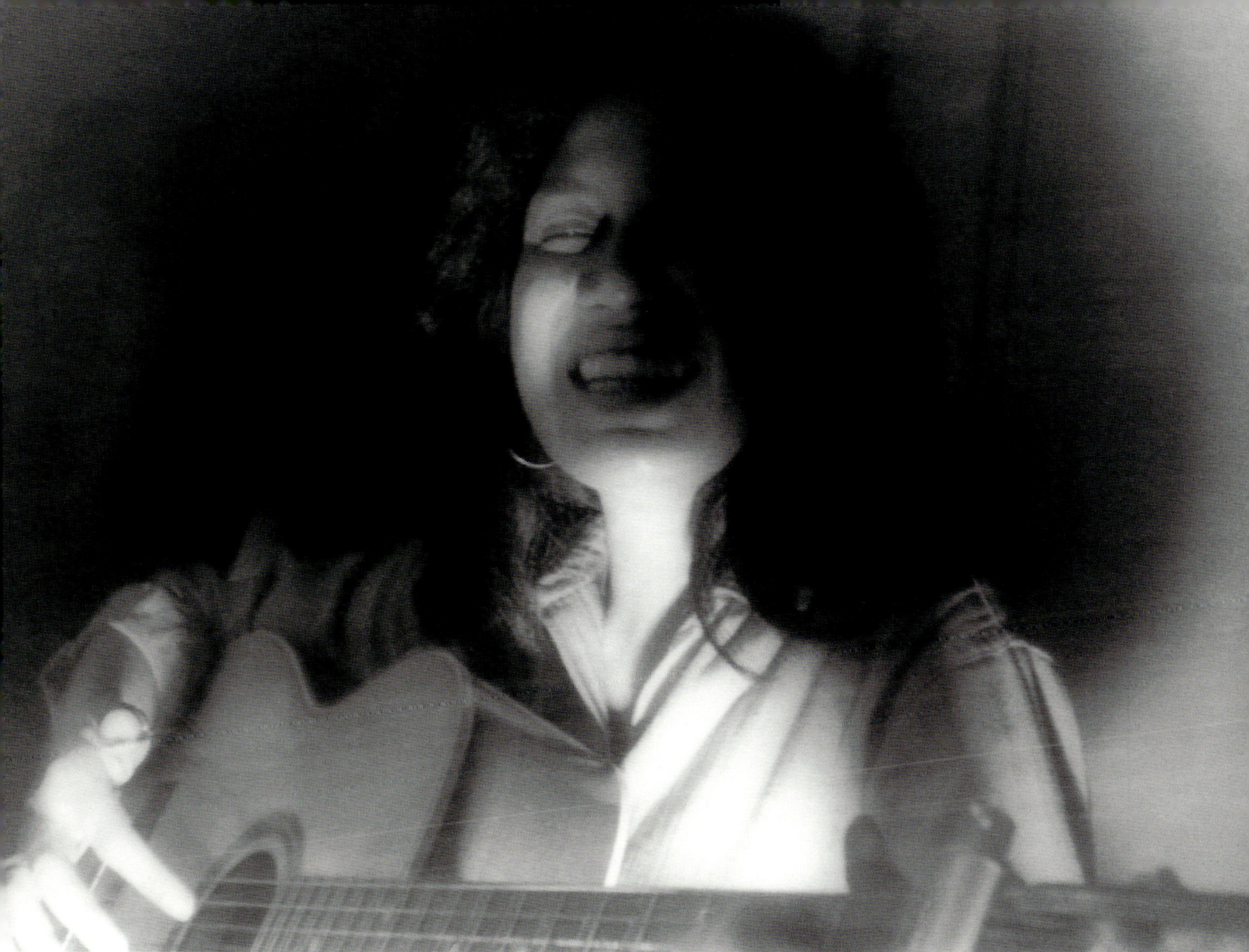

NORMA TANEGA FAN CLUB
THIS CERTIFIES THAT
Norma Tanega
IS A MEMBER IN GOOD STANDING
FROM '67 TO '80
PRESIDENT
TANEGA MUSIC
PRIVATE LESSONS:
GUITAR • BASS • PIANO • DRUMS
RECORDING TECHNIQUES • SYNTHESIZER • BANDS
NORMA TANEGA
4111 MT. BALDY ROAD
CLAREMONT, CA 91711
(714) 624-2034

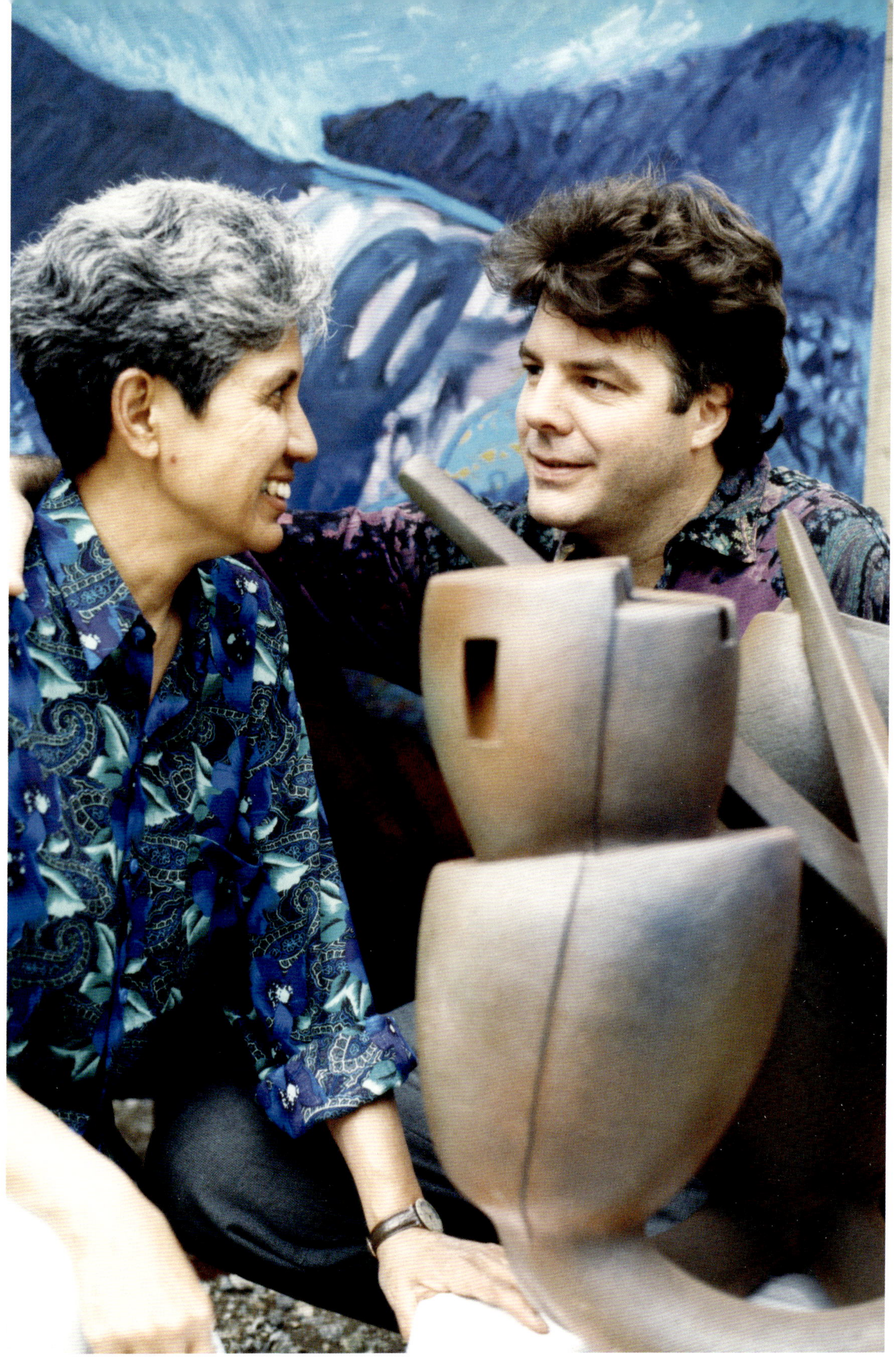

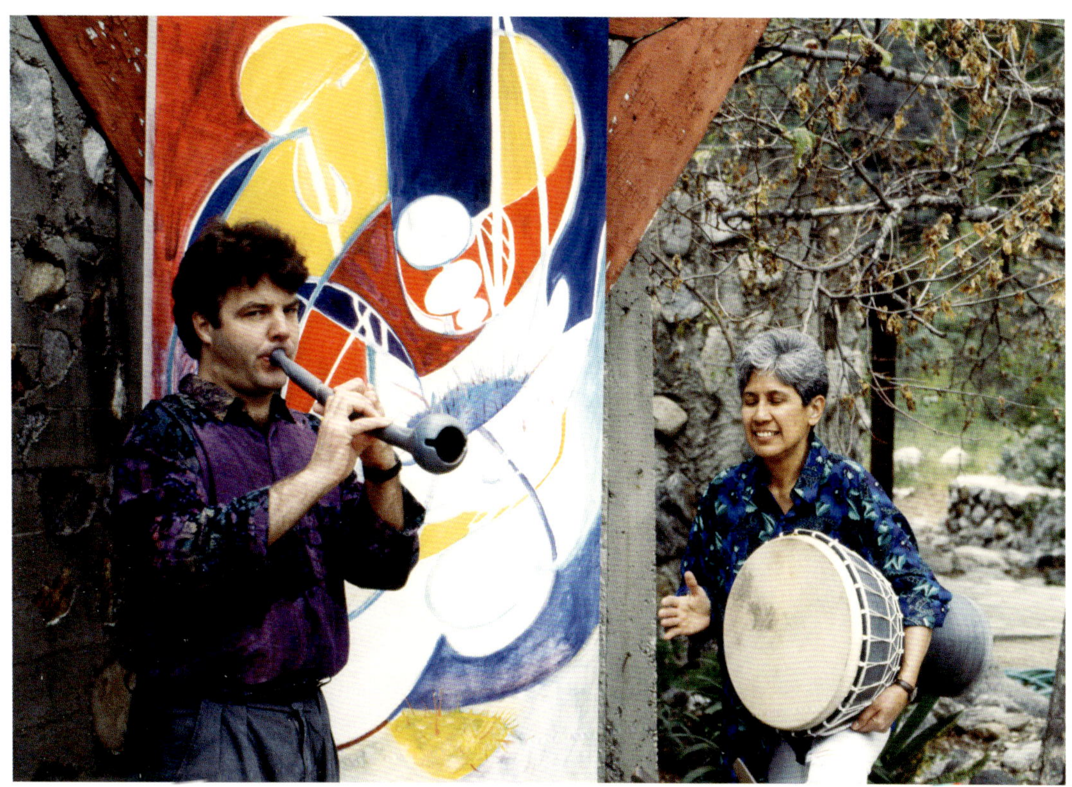

NCT with Brian Ransom

ROBERT GRAJEDA: I was around Norma when she was participating in quite a few musical endeavors; I believe there was the Brian Ransom Ceramic Ensemble, where she played bells created by the ceramicist Brian Ransom.

BRIAN RANSOM: I had my MFA show at Claremont around 1987 and I had compiled my first serious attempt at tuned ceramic instruments. I had bells tuned in quarter tones and a tuned set of congas and lots of experimental stuff, and I think in that era, I made my first clay trumpet, too, which had brass valves that I pirated off the trumpet my parents gave me. So, I was looking for musicians, and after Norma answered my ad, I went up to her house. It was just the most amazing place, and Norma was obviously just exactly who I was looking for, and she helped me find a couple more people. We'd play a lot; we'd work on her stuff and she worked on my stuff and then eventually, she said, "You know, I must have drums." So, I made her—sort of one by one—a lot of the drums that were up there.

AIDA PAVLETICH: Brian Ransom brought his clay instruments to Norma's studio, where she kept her grand piano, percussion, sound equipment, and Yamaha keyboard. When they performed, Brian played a clay sax he made, and an ocarina the size and shape of a young boy. He made a set of tuned clay bells for Norma, set up on a steel rack that she kept in the studio, playing them carefully with tympani mallets, as the instruments were fragile.

BRIAN RANSOM: Then, one day I get a phone call from the LA *Times*, saying that somebody had read an article that had been written about me in *Ceramics Monthly*, a really obscure ceramics magazine. They ended up coming out to Norma's with a photographer, and they took all these pictures of Norma and me and all the instruments. That Sunday, the article came out, and then that Monday, everything changes. I had gallery representation, a sold-out show in West Hollywood . . . we became the house band at the Pacific Asia Museum in Pasadena, and then we played a couple of afternoon shows at SFMOMA. We went on a couple different tours, and so many hilarious, cool things happened. One of the funniest things was when we were playing an opening for the Arts Council in San Jose at Rosicrucian Park. Rosicrucians are Egyptologists, and they actually have mummies and a tomb and they had a planetarium. And we got to the planetarium and we were all piled into our bandmate Hartt Stearns's kind of mini–motor home thing with all the instruments. It was like a traveling circus. We get there, and we're setting up inside this planetarium, and this guy—this kind of tall, thin, graying man with sort of yellowing cuffs—says, "My name is Mark. I'll be doing your lights tonight for your show." And we all look at him and, "Mark, what have you got? What can you do?" He goes, "Anything from meteors at sunset to the Big Bang." I said, "Let's start with meteors at sunset, and just see where it goes."

MARIO VERLANGIERI: At some point, she started a new band, which was with Tom Skelly, who was a Claremont artist and guitar player.

TOM SKELLY: My first involvement with Norma was to record, mix, and participate as a musician on several of her music group recordings, including the Ceramics Ensemble, with Brian Ransom and guests, and Hybrid Vigor.

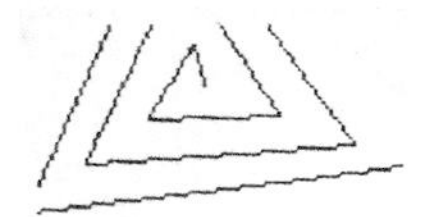

CERAMIC ENSEMBLE
CONCERT

Brian Ransom & Norma Tanega
with Ben Harper

October 22, 1992
Music Room 102
12 noon
FREE

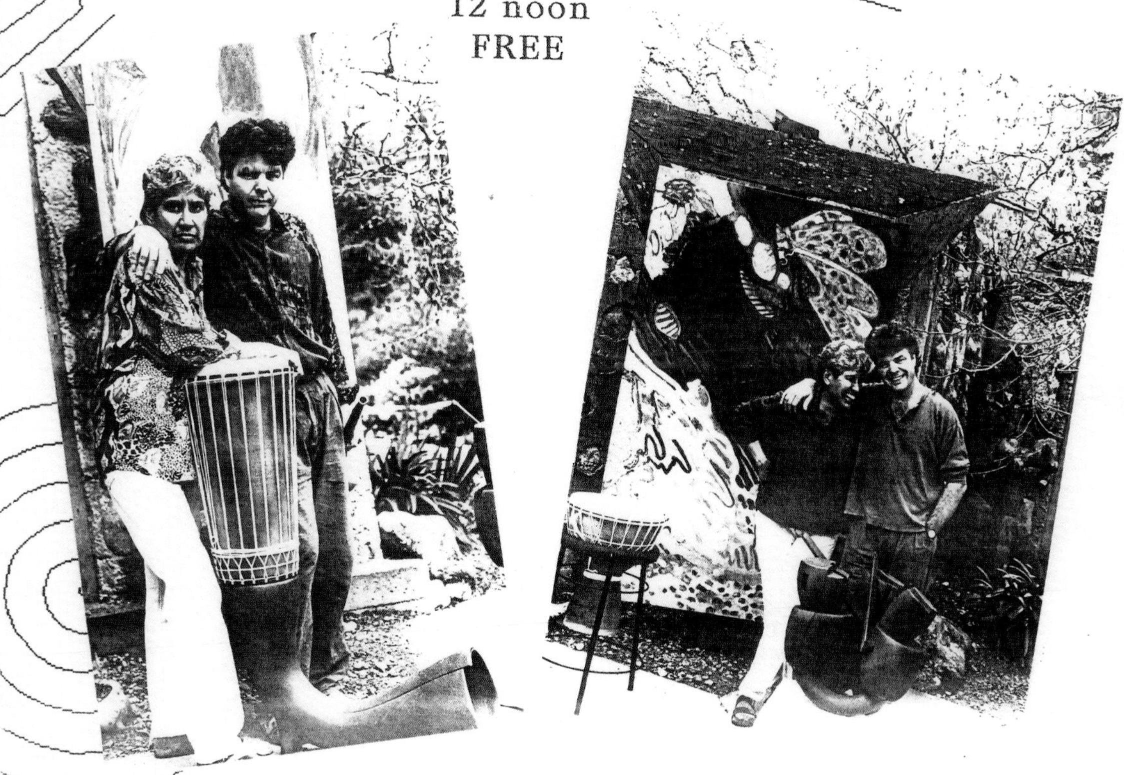

Riverside Community College presents Brian Ransom and Norma Tanega with Ben Harper perfoming on Ransom's ceramic sculpture instruments. Norma's paintings and Brian's sculptures can be seen at the RCC Gallery at City campus through NOV. 20 th.

TRY TO TELL A FISH ABOUT WATER

Artist/composer/musician, Brian Ransom has combined his visual and musical talents to create a unique set of finely tuned musical instruments which primarily use ceramics as their resonators. Many of the highly sculptural forms he creates are the result of musical ideas in a pure sense. He uses his musical ideas as impetus for performances which incorporate spacial movement, sound, and visual imagery.

The music, which at times has ancient nuances and at other times has a cutting contemporary feel, is influenced by folk musical traditions from around the globe (African, Indian, South American) as well as jazz and modern music. A performance by the Ceramic Ensemble is unlike any other.

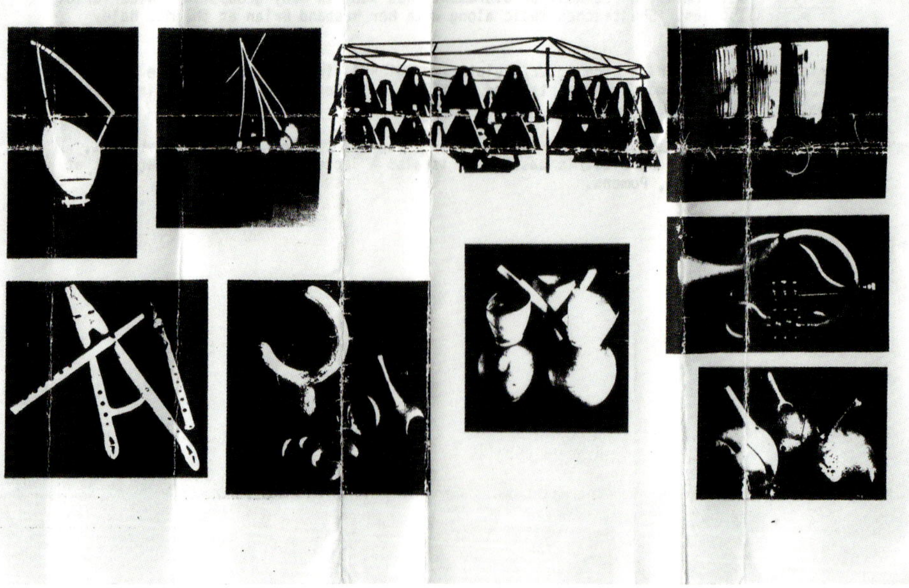

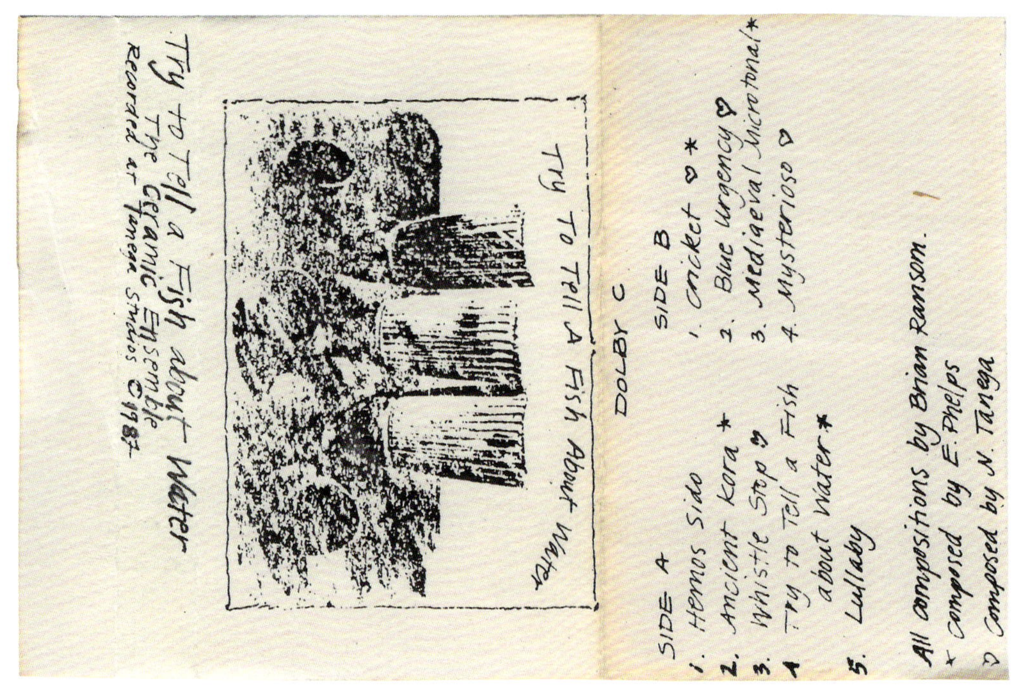

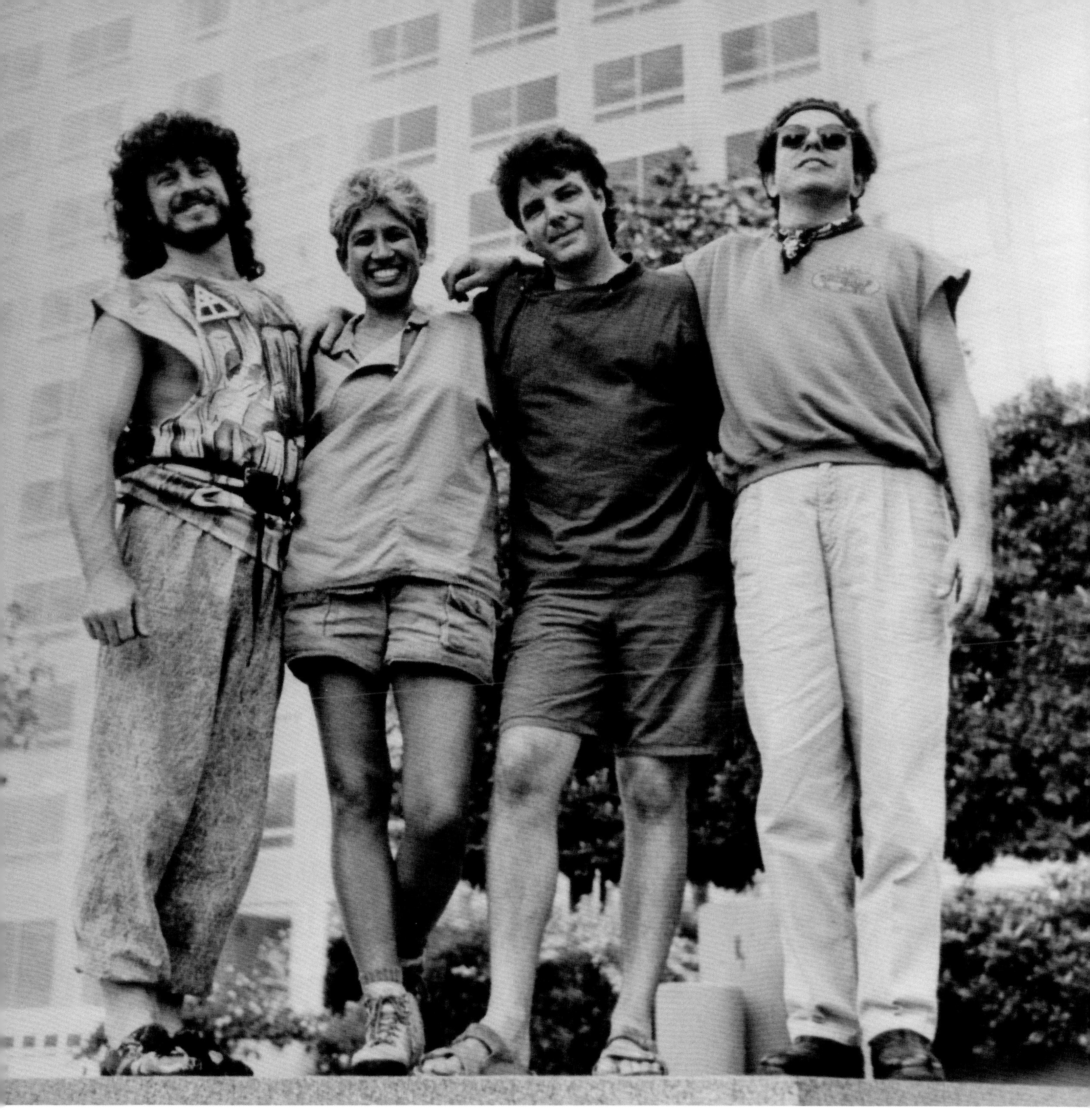

The Ceramic Ensemble: Hartt Stearns, NCT, Brian Ransom, and Ernesto Salcedo

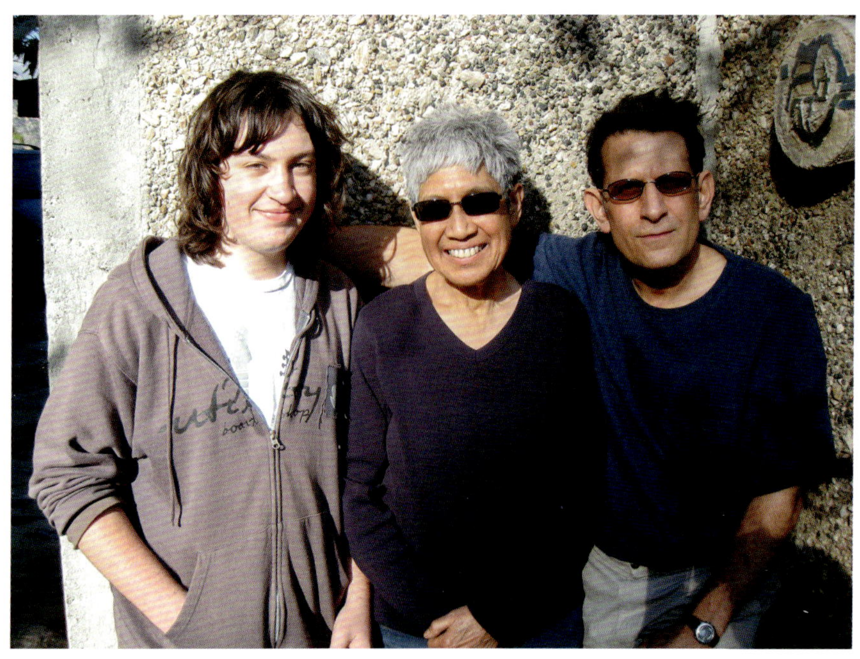

Baboonz: Mario Verlangieri, NCT, and Tom Skelly

REBECCA HAMM: In 1997 to 1998 I was in my sixteenth year of working with Desperation Squad, a highly original and satirical punk band. That's when I began working with Norma and Mike Henderson on the Hybrid Vigor project. Together we wrote and composed the material: our collaborative works were mostly instrumental, driven by Norma's amazing drumming and sound experiments. Mike created emotive and expressive sound landscapes with his guitar, and I would come in with lyrics and an occasional song melody, and we'd improvise them into something we could perform and record. The local venues at that time were plentiful and lots of fun. I truly enjoyed shaping experimental vocals, percussion, and sound performances into a professional event, and along with Norma and Mike, we presented a highly entertaining and involving show.

TOM SKELLY: When those projects ended, Norma and I continued our friendship through visits and attending art and music venues. Because of her unused knowledge and interest in past pop music, I suggested we form a guitar, bass, and percussion trio to play pop music arrangements of evergreens and movie songs.

MARIO VERLANGIERI: Norma and Tom had been talking about doing a project for a while, and they were looking for a bass player. I guess they had someone in mind originally, but he couldn't do it for some reason, and Norma was like, "Well, I know this kid that is good enough and would love to bring him on." And so that's how Baboonz started.

TOM SKELLY: The trio was unique in that it represented three generations of musicians. Norma became very excited to venture into an area she knew well and talked about but left behind in the early seventies, and her big grill-like smile and contagious laugh allowed me to feel our friendship with the comfort that we shared the same vocation.

MARIO VERLANGIERI: I was the young one with the least experience; I'd been playing guitar for a while and I had my own bands, but I had no business playing with Norma. I think I'm one of the great examples of her really reaching out and wanting to bring other people along with her, and connect. She really liked me, and she gave me the chance, and I was able to hang in there with Norma and Tom. And that was such a great opportunity. It was just an honor to be able to sit there, and play with them, and learn from them.

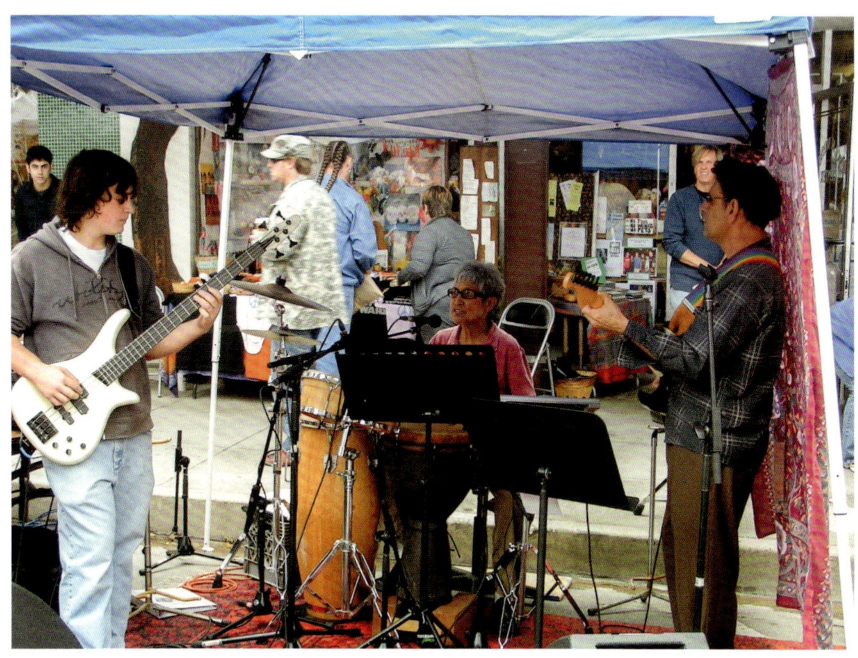

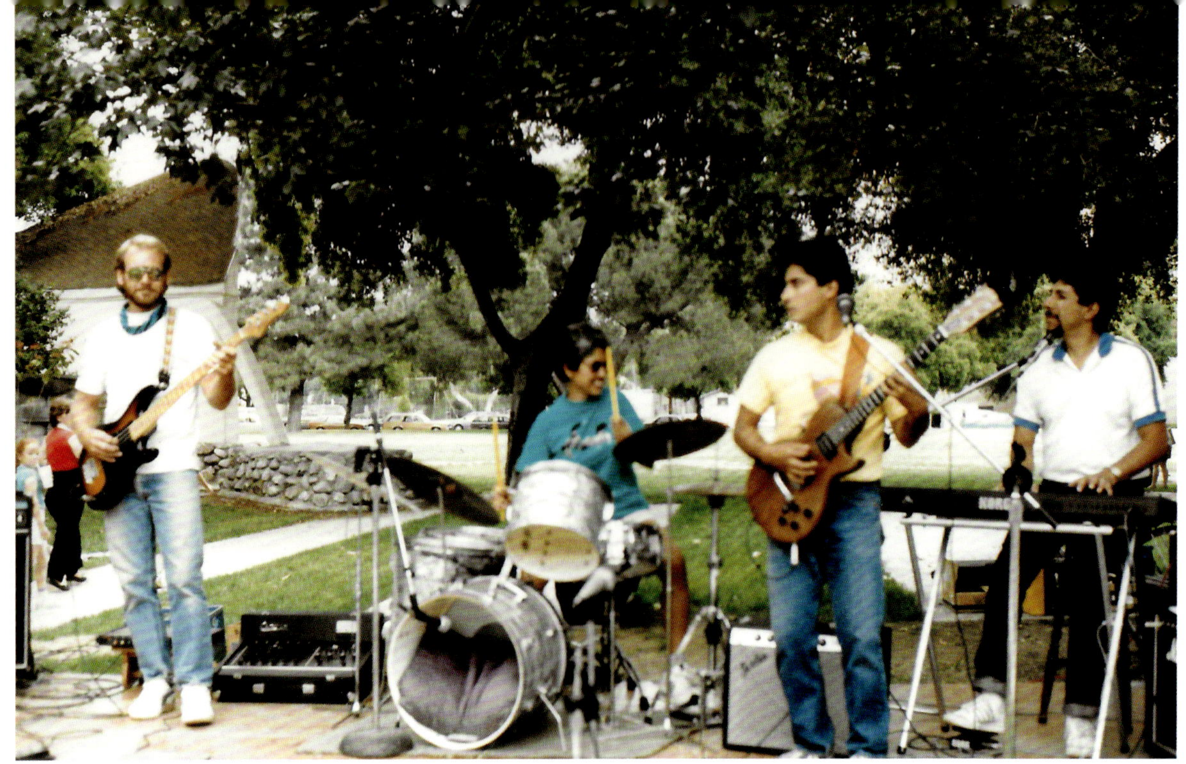

Playing with friends, circa 1985: Russ, NCT, Gilbert, and Robert Grajeda

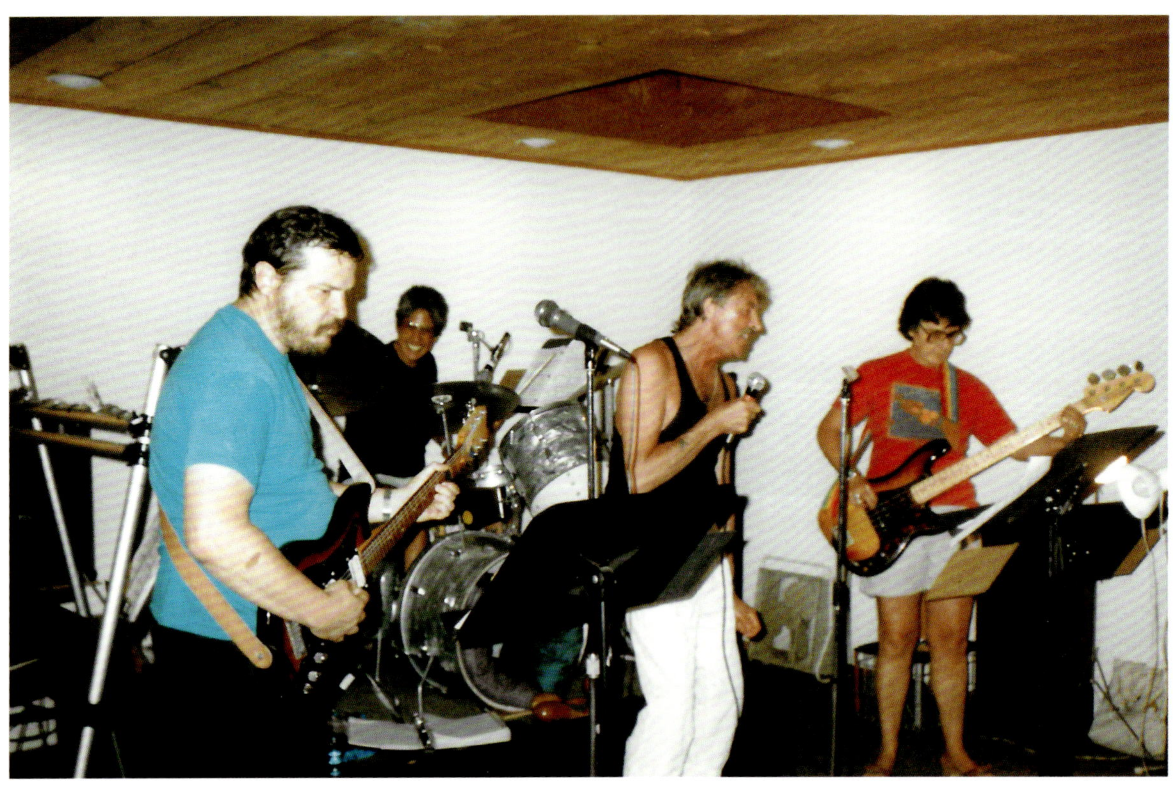

Paul Frindt, NCT, Don Paul, and DD in the music room

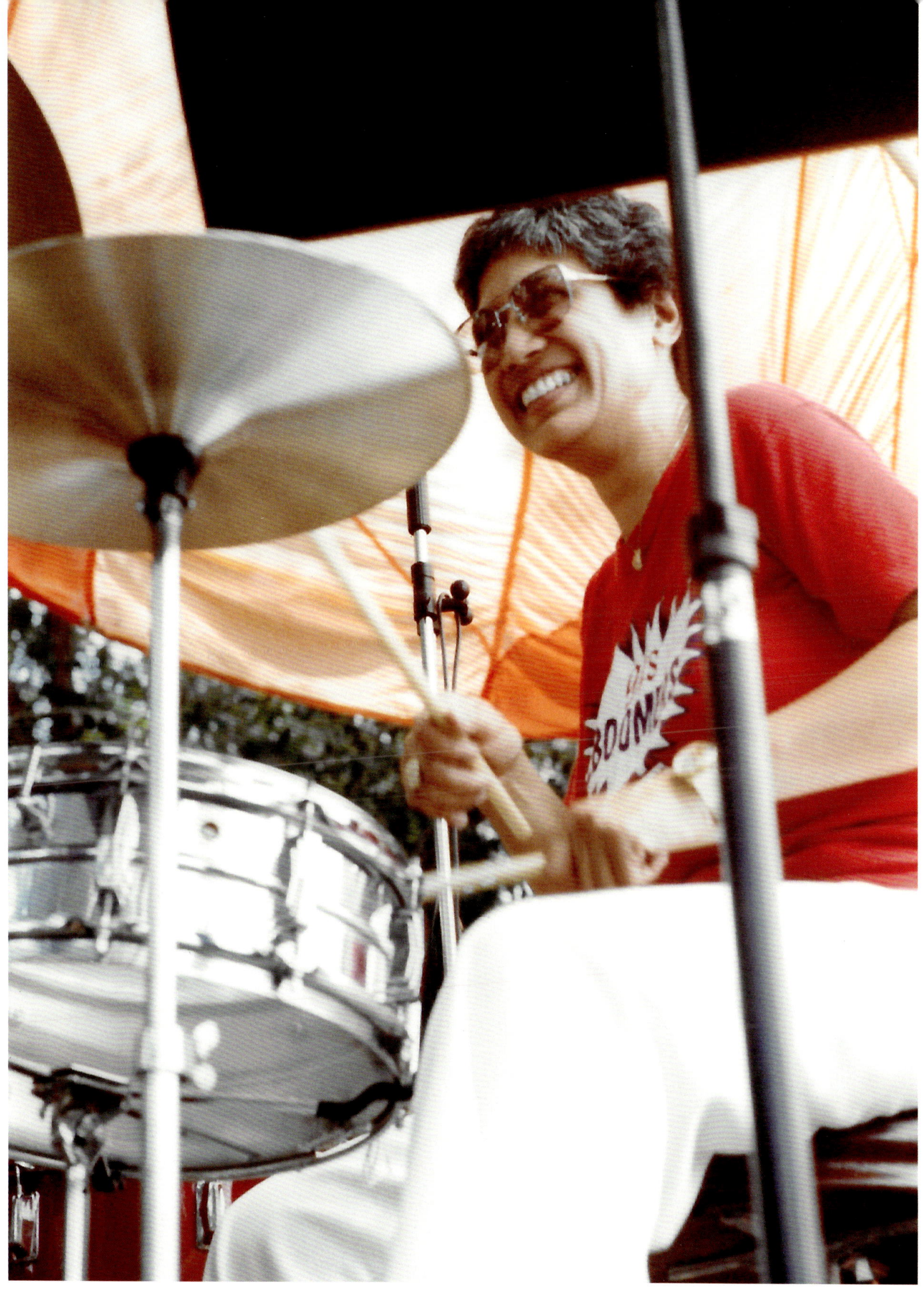

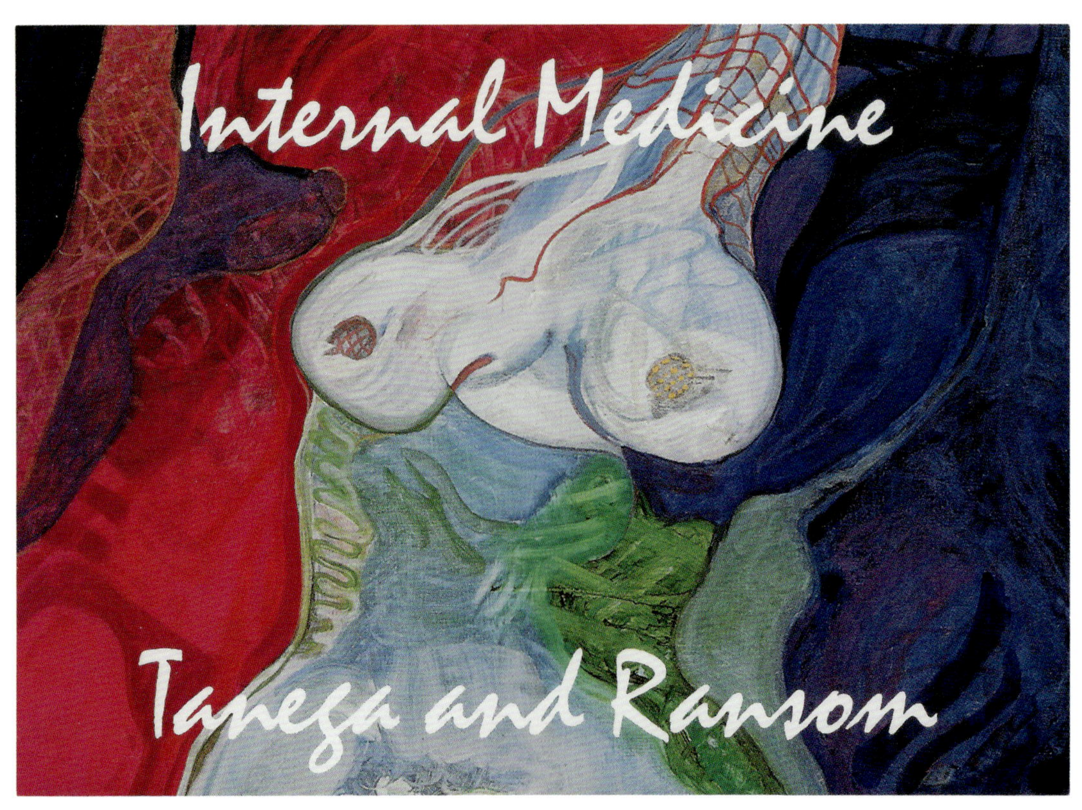
Internal Medicine
Tanega and Ransom

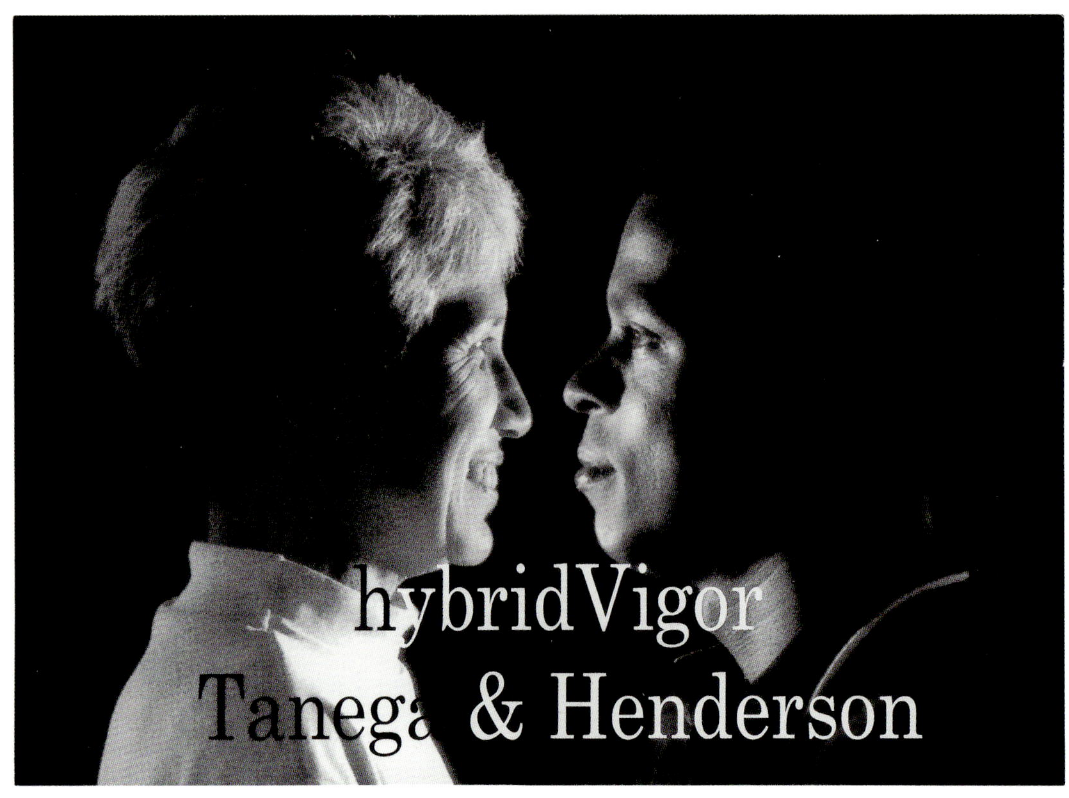
hybridVigor
Tanega & Henderson

Run Runner

Words written and performed by Aida Pavletich
Music composed and performed by Norma Tanega

Produced by Norma Tanega

©1993 by Aida Pavletich and Norma Tanega

Listen.....rrrrrakatakatakatakatakrakataaa...
Listen.....you ain't nuthin' butta...
Listen.....water from your dripping hair.
Listen.....love, like war rarely takes prisoners without some irrevocable change to the human condition. We all need to connect, to be warmed by a smile, a touch, a word of love. The moods and worlds that Aida and Norma create with words and sounds are images of now, of feelings we can recognize as our own, of feelings we can observe and understand better. Listen to these slices of experience and look around. You will laugh, you will remember, maybe you will be saddened. Aida takes the language through some hip turns, gives fresh slants to the puzzle of living. Norma is her wingman in sound, creating instantly recognizable yet perfectly new sounds and rhythms that soar and rock and snort along with Aida. The words and sounds interlock seamlessly. The matching of these two artists seems inevitable. Their vision is one of hope and compassion and it compels you to listen....perhaps you will be changed.

Aida Pavletich is a Los Angeles writer, photographer and editor whose publications include "Rock-A-Bye, Baby: The Popular Female Vocalist in America" (Doubleday, 1980) and "Sirens of Song" (paperback edition, Da Capo, 1982)

Norma Tanega is a California performer, composer and artist whose most well-known pop song is "Walkin' My Cat Named Dog."

Also on Addictive Audio by Aida Pavletich and Norma Tanega: "Saturday Dancer" and "Ways Away."

Recorded at Tanega Studios, 4111 Mt. Baldy Rd. Claremont, CA 91711 (213) 663-6993 (909) 624-2034

Addictive Audio 21593

Art Direction by Ellen Brouse
Photo by Diane Schnitzer • Notes by Robert Grajeda

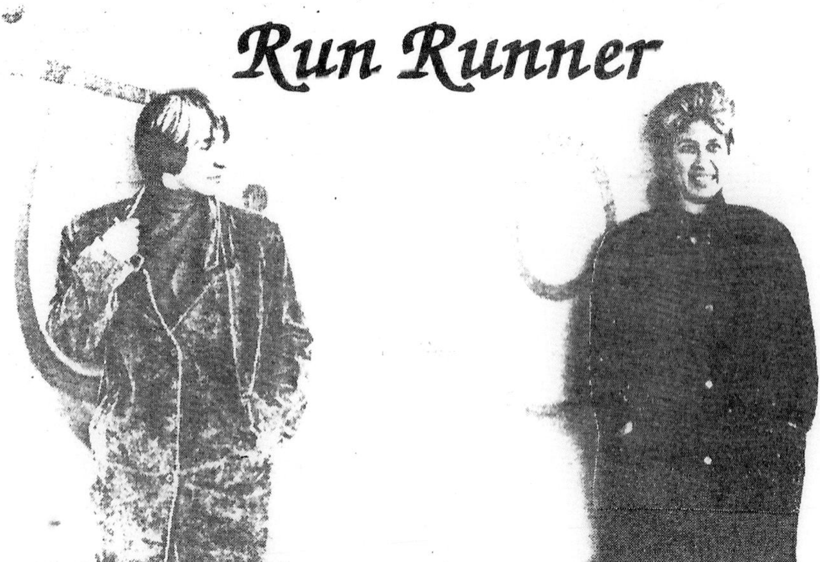

Run Runner

Words: Aida Pavletich   Music: Norma Tanega

Side A
Linguistics 2:44 • Women of World Wars 4:00
Love Is Never Cold 2:19 • I Saw Elvis 2:25 • Cold War 5:05
Baths of Caracalla 4:44 • The One Who Takes the Falls 3:03

Side B
Tattoo 1:02 • Phantom Mercedes 3:20 • Reputation 4:33
Don't Know About Love 1:42 • Rosary 1:52
Run Runner (Enola Gay) 7:47 • Home Free All 3:52

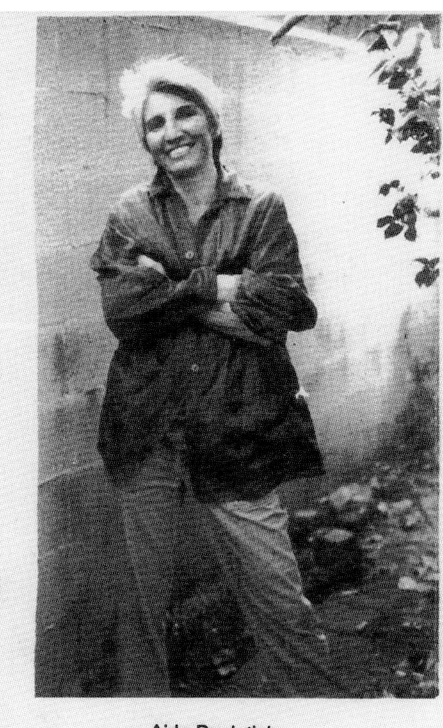

Aida Pavletich
Photo by Kathleen Reinoehl

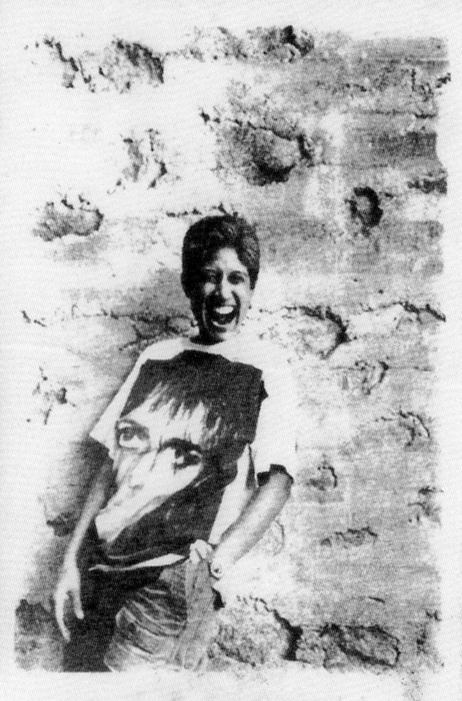

Norma Tanega
Photo by Aida Pavletich

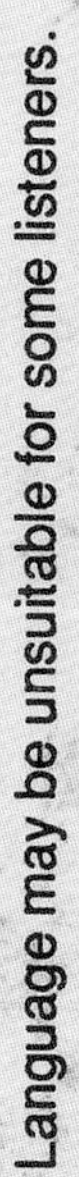

Saturday Dancer

Words: Aida Pavletich
Music: Norma Tanega

Side A

Saturday Dancer 3:49 • Ice Curtains 1:12 • Bar 2:24 • First Lover 3:53 • Satin Latin 0:42
Expurgatoria 0:55 • Angel 0:59 • Memorial Day 1:24 • Eryngo 1:07 • Danse Macabre 1:50

Side B

Why I Don't Sleep with 20 Cats 2:47 • Insect 1:22 • Homogenous Erogenous 3:09
Rendez-vous 2:11 • Oh Marilyn 3:45 • White People's Music 3:08
To Meet A Friend 1:21 • Night 0:52 • Sunday Morning 3:20

Saturday Dancer

Words: *Aida Pavletich*
Music: *Norma Tanega*

Saturday Dancer

Words written and performed by Aida Pavletich
Music composed and performed by Norma Tanega

Produced by Norma Tanega

© 1988 by Aida Pavletich and Norma Tanega

Aida Pavletich is a Los Angeles writer, photographer and editor whose publications include "Rock-A-Bye, Baby: The Popular Female Vocalist in America" (Doubleday, 1980) and "Sirens of Song" (paperback edition, Da Capo, 1982). She has written for radio station KRLA's "Big 11 Countdown" and for The Hollywood Reporter, the L.A. Free Press and the Pasadena Star-News.

Norma Tanega is a California performer, composer and artist whose most well-known pop song is "Walkin' My Cat Named Dog." Her albums include "Walkin' My Cat Named Dog" (New Voice) and "I Don't Think It Will Hurt If you Smile" (RCA Ltd.).

Saturday Dancer is a rap opera. The words paint a picture of an evening in the life of a Saturday Dancer, who goes out on a Saturday night, filled with hope and illusion, to look for true love at the dance hall. Throughout this quest Saturday Dancer meets old loves, new loves, future loves and loves that can never be. Saturday Dancer encounters the taxi dancer in "First Lover," the soldier in "Memorial Day," and Death in "Danse Macabre." The night is filled with myriad characters from memory and imagination. Like life, the quest and seduction of Saturday Dancer moves on from failure to conquest. "Pay for the ticket but the dance is free..."

Recorded at Tanega Studios, 4111 Mt. Baldy Rd.
Claremont, CA 91711 (213) 663-6993 (714) 624-2034

Addictive Audio 11288

Art Direction by Mehdi Sahrai

AIDA PAVLETICH: In the eighties, Norma had gotten a Yamaha keyboard with programmed voices: the machine held an orchestra of woodwinds, horns, strings, and could repeat licks as Norma hit the "remember this" button. As she had mics and a cassette recorder, we began to lay down tracks for an enterprise I told Norma to name. She came up with Addictive Audio. On weekends, we were loud and raucous as we played in the studio. We laughed incessantly. We made a series of three audiotapes—Norma's music, my text—that became *Saturday Dancer*, *Ways Away*, and *Run Runner*. I set up duplication and we each took half of the short-run, neatly shrinkwrapped audiotapes . . . Then, through the nineties, I worked as a production supervisor at the Century Cable Public Access studio, where I had a heaven's worth of video equipment, trained interns, taught the weekly production classes, and made shows to air on their channel 3. "Come," I told Norma, "bring your instruments and another musician."

ROBERT GRAJEDA: When I first got into the band that Norma was leading as a teacher, she named us the Mobius Band. Then afterwards, we finished doing the student thing and we had a band called the Channel Three.

AIDA PAVLETICH: I made several episodes of a program called *Duo*, with Norma accompanied by guitarist Mike Henderson, and on other occasions Robert Grajeda. She brought her percussion instruments, including a Chinese gong, bells, congas . . .

ROBERT GRAJEDA: We started to collaborate. I kind of was still a student at that time, and I was trying to get into the avant-garde style of music that that particular band was playing. Our influences were more than folk, pop, even classical . . . There were a lot of things that we collaborated on. We did a duo as the Latin Lizards, where Norma played hand drums and electronic drums and sang, and then I played keyboards and sang, etc. I cherish the time that the Latin Lizards were her main focus. With Norma's help and support, I learned a lot about being a pro versus just doing it as a hobby: understanding what that really meant.

MARIO VERLANGIERI: I think Norma made her art—and her music, and her paintings, everything—because she wanted to do it. It was her vision. She did it for herself and for the people around her, and that was it.

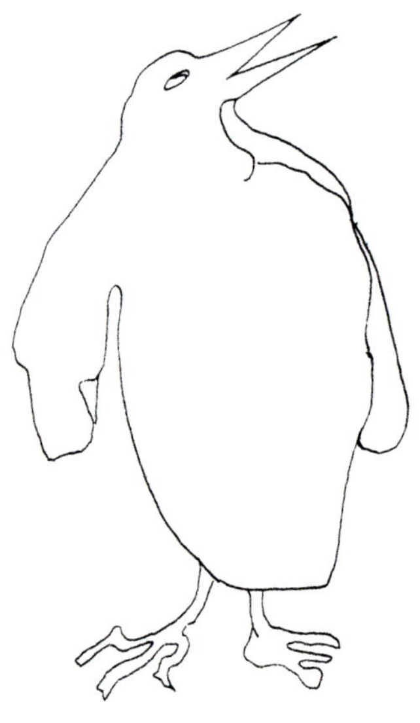

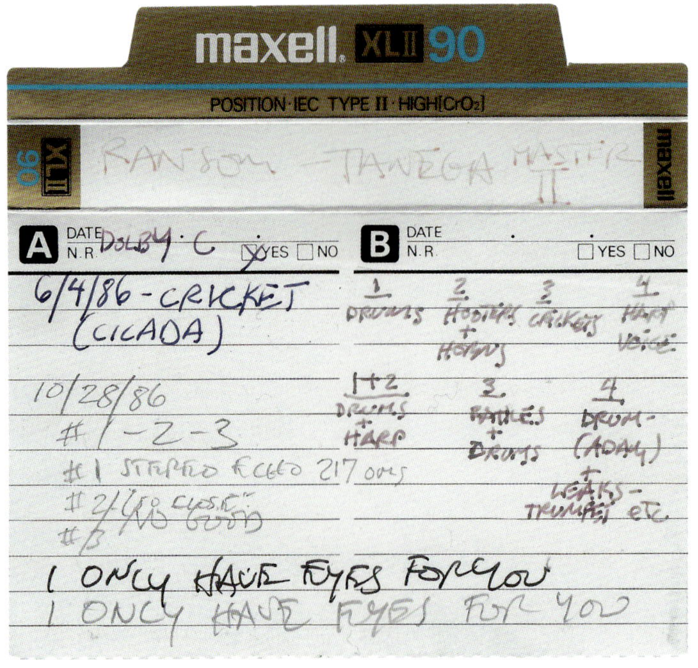

maxell XLII 90
POSITION · IEC TYPE II · HIGH [CrO₂]
RANSOM — TANEGA MASTER II
A DATE N.R. DOLBY · C   YES NO
B DATE N.R.   YES NO
6/4/86 - CRICKET (CICADA)
10/28/86
#1 - 2 - 3
#1 STEREO ECHO 217 ohs
#2 "TOO CLOSE"
#3 NO GOOD
I ONLY HAVE EYES FOR YOU
I ONLY HAVE EYES FOR YOU
1 DRUMS
2 HOODAS + HOANS
3 CRICKETS
4 HART VOICE
1+2 DRUMS + HARP
3 RATTLES + DRUMS
4 DRUM (ADAM)
LEAKS - TRUMPET etc

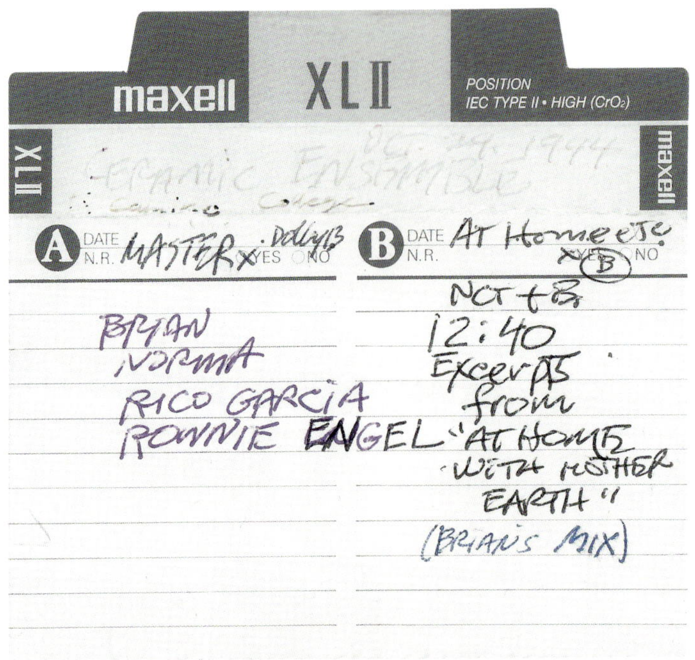

maxell XLII
POSITION IEC TYPE II · HIGH (CrO₂)
CERAMIC ENSEMBLE OCT 24 1944
Camino College
A DATE N.R. MASTER DOLBY B   YES NO
B DATE N.R. AT HOME etc   YES NO
BRYAN
NORMA
RICO GARCIA
RONNIE ENGEL
NOT+B
12:40
EXCERPTS from "AT HOME WITH MOTHER EARTH"
(BRYAN'S MIX)

maxell UDS-II 90

POSITION·IEC TYPE II·HIGH[CrO₂]

BRIAN RANSOM 4/9/87
CERAMIC ENSEMBLE — LIVE — CAL POLY

A DATE APRIL 9, 1987 N.R. LIVE-   ☐ YES ☒ NO

B DATE CAL POLY. N.R.   ☐ YES ☒ NO

A	B
HEMOS SIDO	BLUE URGENCY
TRY TO TELL FISH	LULLABY
ABOUT WATER	
WHISTLE SONG	PERFORMANCE
CRICKET	LIVE AT
MYSTERIOSO	CAL POLY
ANCIENT SONG	APRIL 9, 1987

maxell XLII-S 60

POSITION · IEC TYPE II · HIGH (CrO₂)

SATURDAY DANCER — 1988
PAULETICH / TANEGA / MASTER

A DATE OCT. 13, 1988 N.R. DOLBY C ☐ YES ☐ NO

B DATE . N.R.   ☐ YES ☐ NO

A	B
Saturday Dancer	Why I Don't Sleep
ICE CURTAIN	With Cats
Bar	Insect
First Lover	Homogenous
Sextim Latim	Elogenous
Expurgatoria	Rendez-vous
Angel	Oh Marilyn
Memorial Day	White People's
Eryngo	Music
Danse Macabre	To Meet A Friend
	Night
	Sunday
	Morning

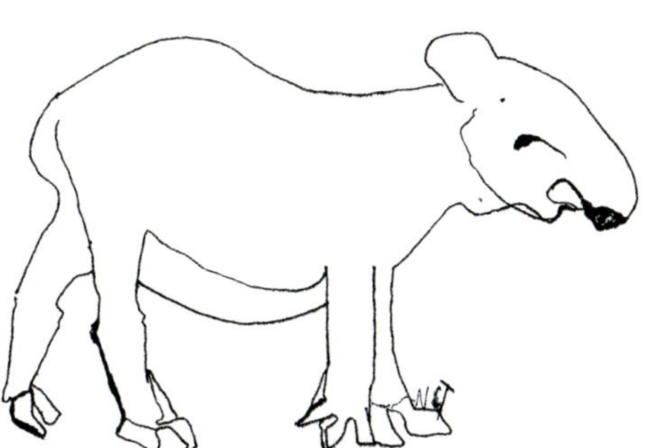

MAXINE BOROWSKY JUNGE: Many people who call themselves "artists" are not artists in the more profound sense, needless to say. A real artist, you might exhibit, you might perform, but essentially you do it for yourself. That was Norma.

ROBERT GRAJEDA: We had this relationship tension of taking the project into an artful place rather than just simply saying, "Let's see how slick we can get, so we can make music that'll chart." It was sometimes a challenge. I remember drinking and dialing one night, calling Norma up and saying, "Look, where are we going to go? What are we going to do in the future? I don't want to continue to be a wannabe and I don't think you want to be a has-been either." In spite of my remark, her response was kind and reflected her experience with artist anxiety. She said, "Look, Robert, we play what we know and our songs speak for themselves." I always appreciated her and loved her for that. I remember that she then went on to mention that we had a Latin Lizards gig coming up. Typical diehard Norma!

MARIO VERLANGIERI: She taught me a lot about gigging, and taking every gig seriously, even if it was for a few people in a backyard. We did small gigs like that, and we brought the same game as if we were playing a much bigger show, you know?

ROBERT GRAJEDA: Norma had been there, done that, at the top of the heap—and what she saw was that you can make it as elaborate as you want or as simple as you want. These were just human beings, singing their hearts out.

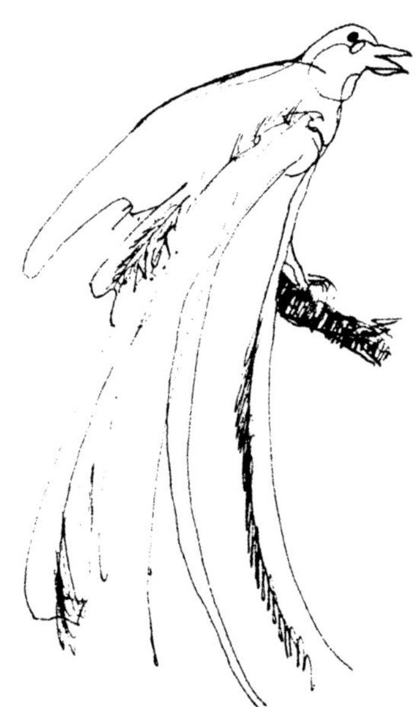

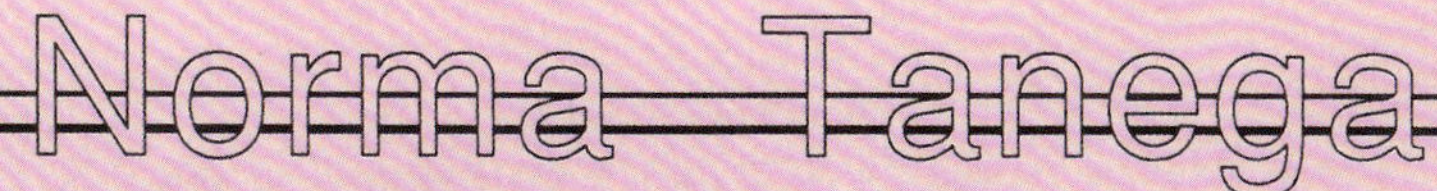

MASTER ARTIST/EDUCATOR IN VISUAL ARTS FOR THE CALIFORNIA ARTS PROJECT

FUSION

PAINTER...MUSICIAN...TEACHER

at
California State University
1000 East Victoria Street
Carson, CA 90747

University Art Gallery

(Park in lot 3. The Art Gallery is located on the first floor,
next to the main entrance of the Humanities and Fine Arts building).

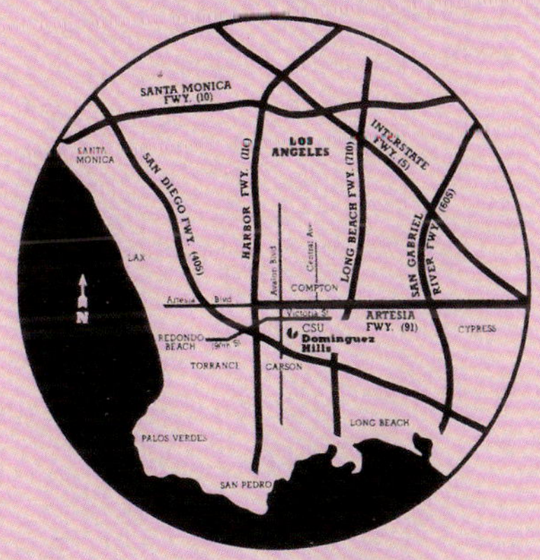

**There will be a performance of original music by
Norma Tanega and Brian Ransom at 3:30**

Thursday, July 19, 1990
3:00 - 4:45

Free parking in lot #3 only, for more information call
Toni Marich   (213) 516-3960 or 516-3761 (Messages)

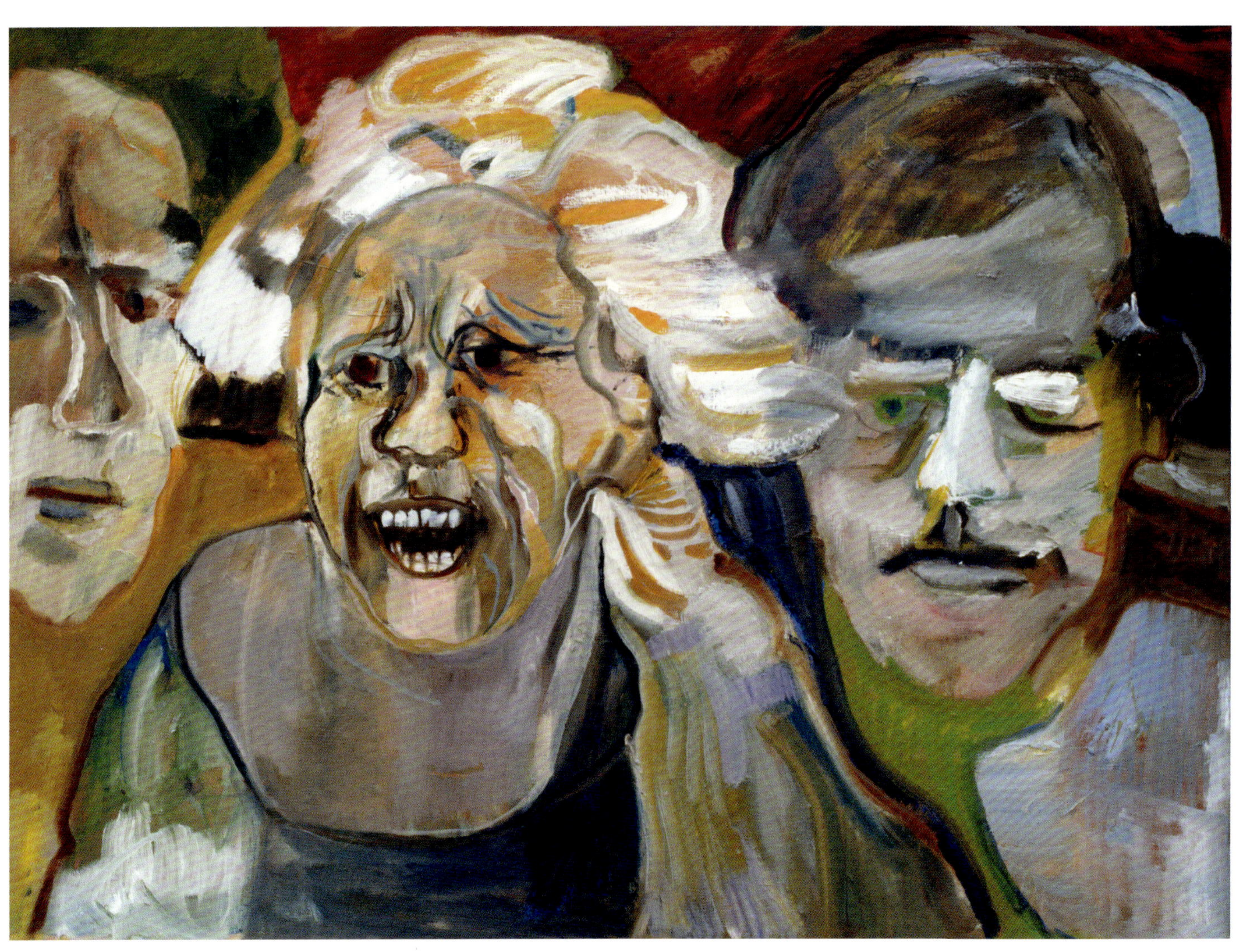

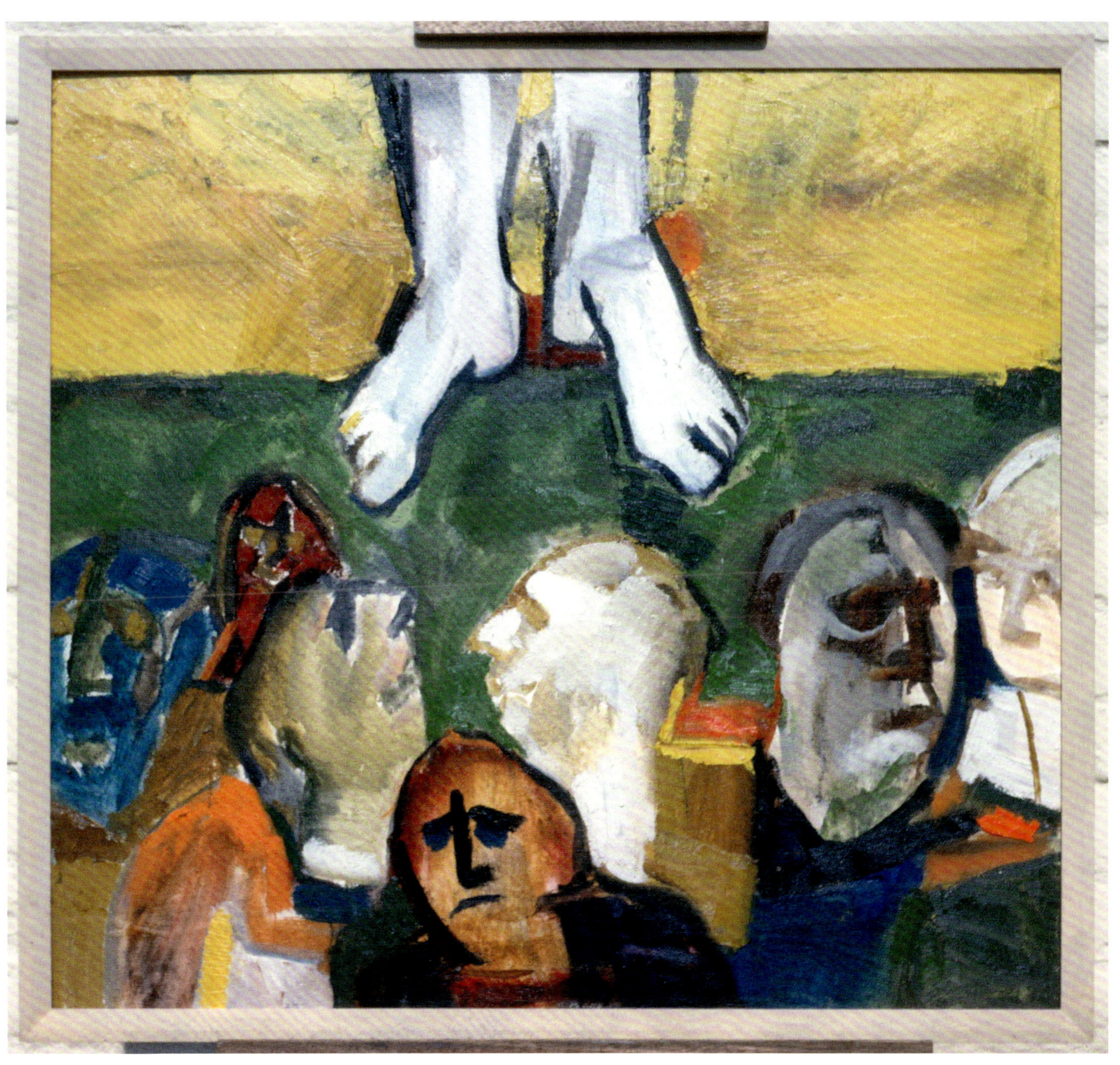

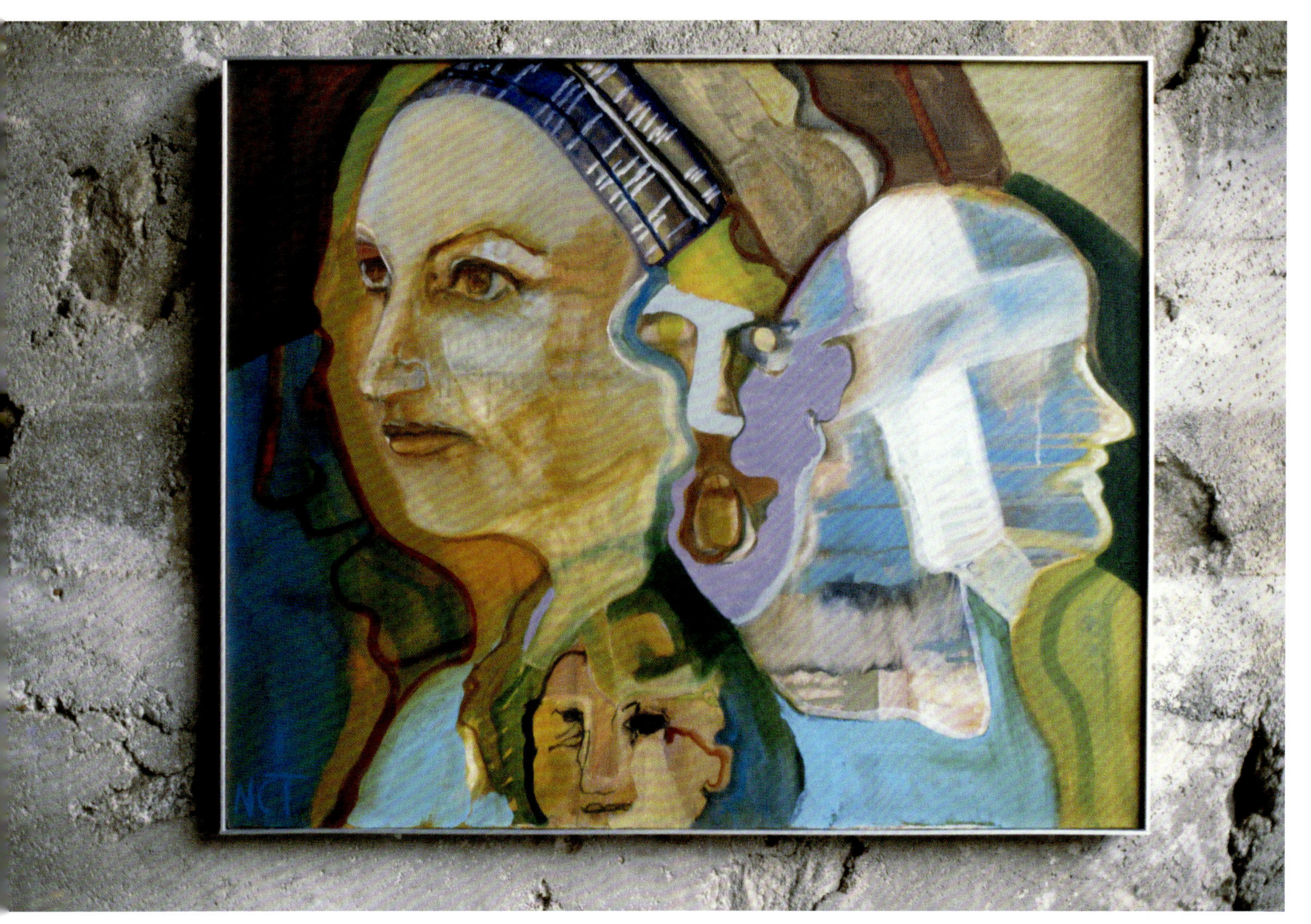

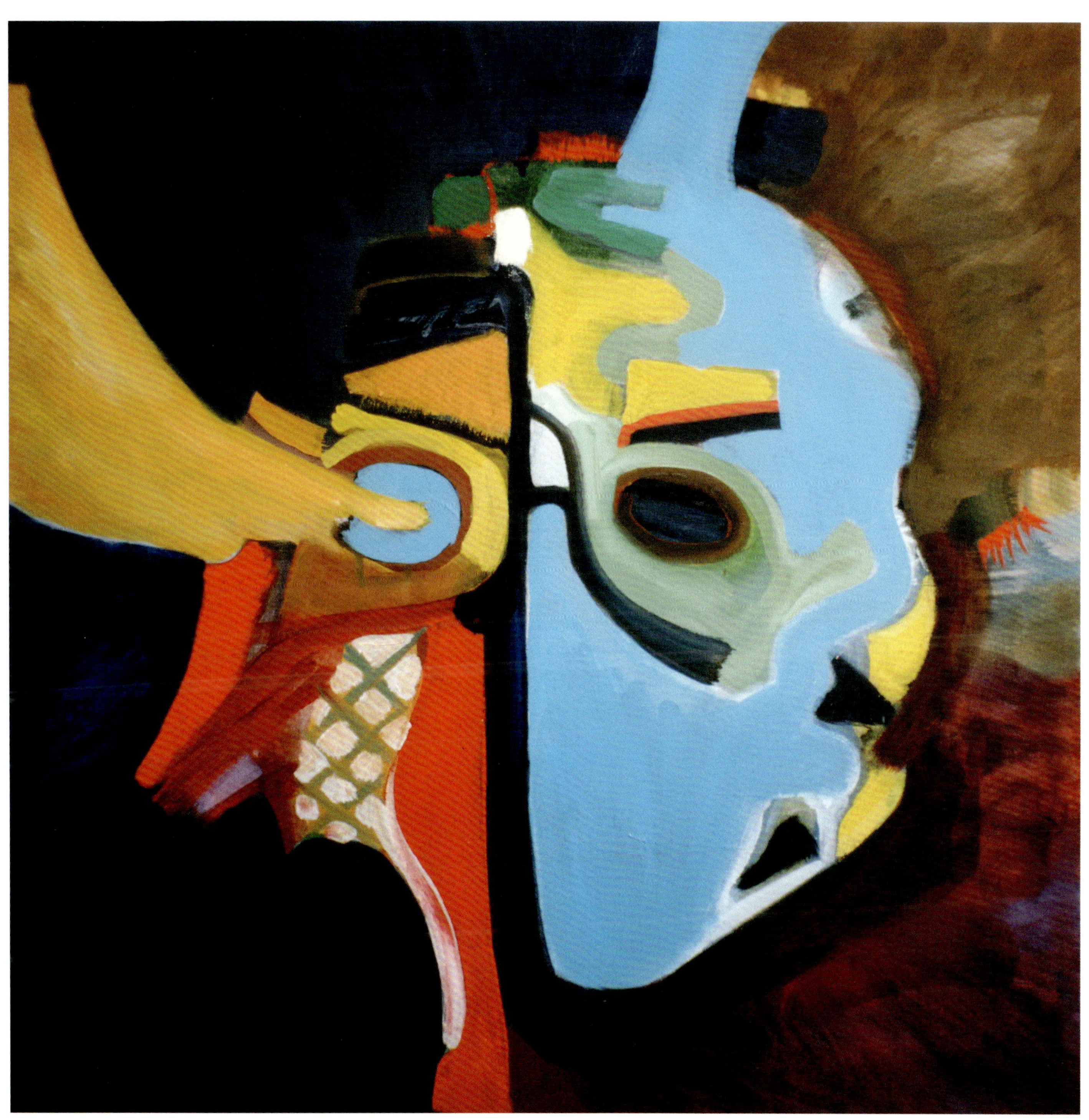

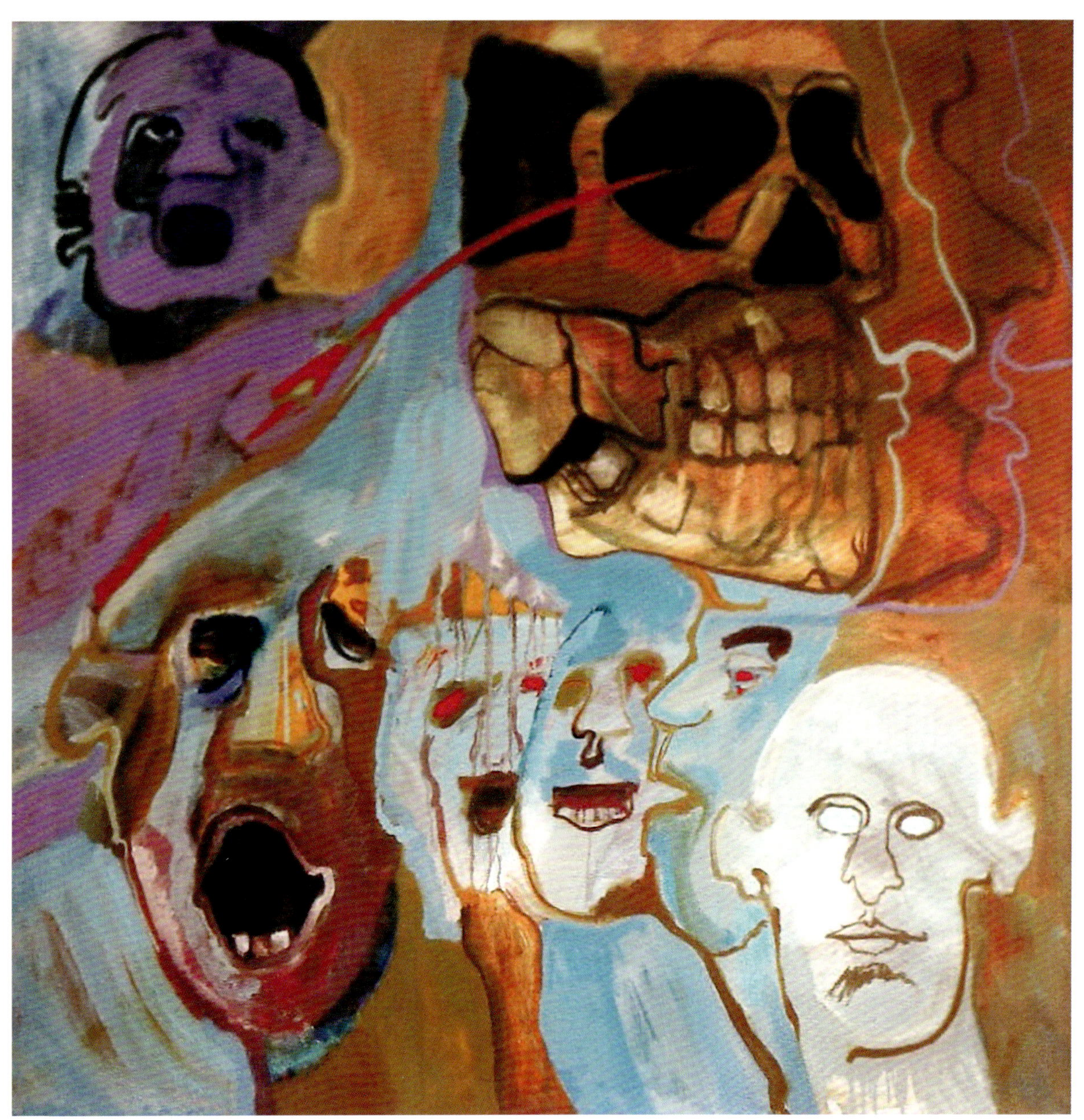

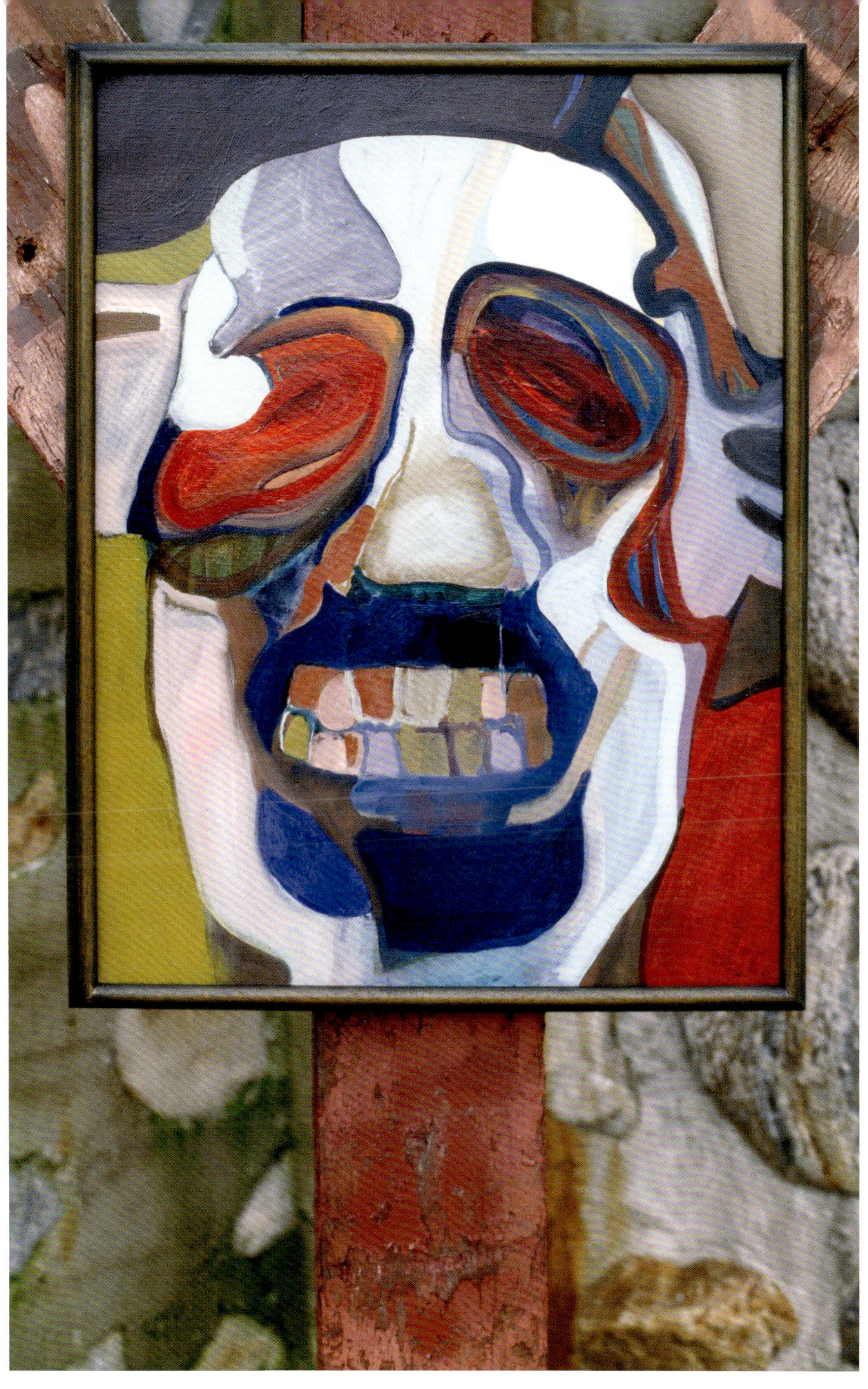

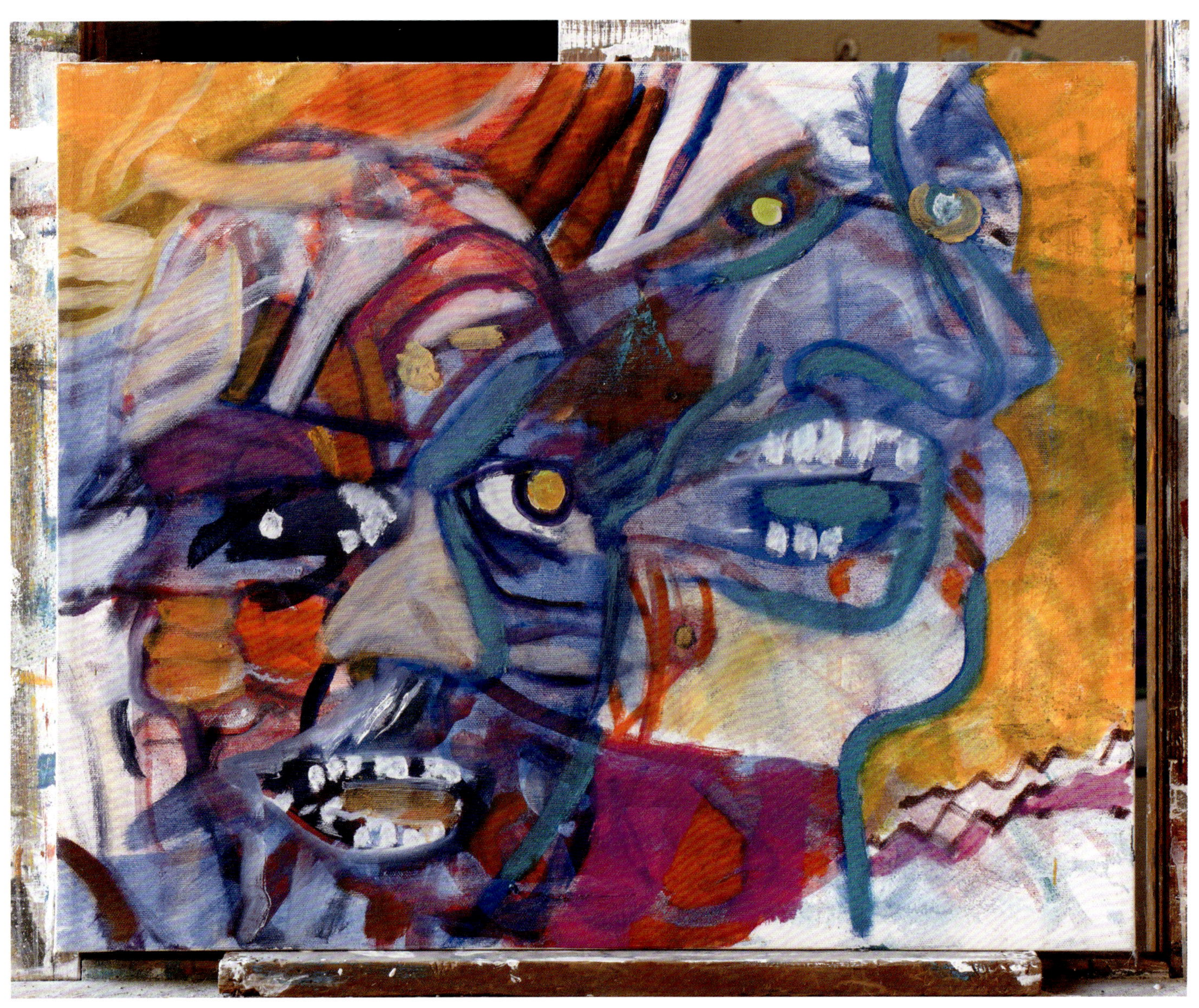

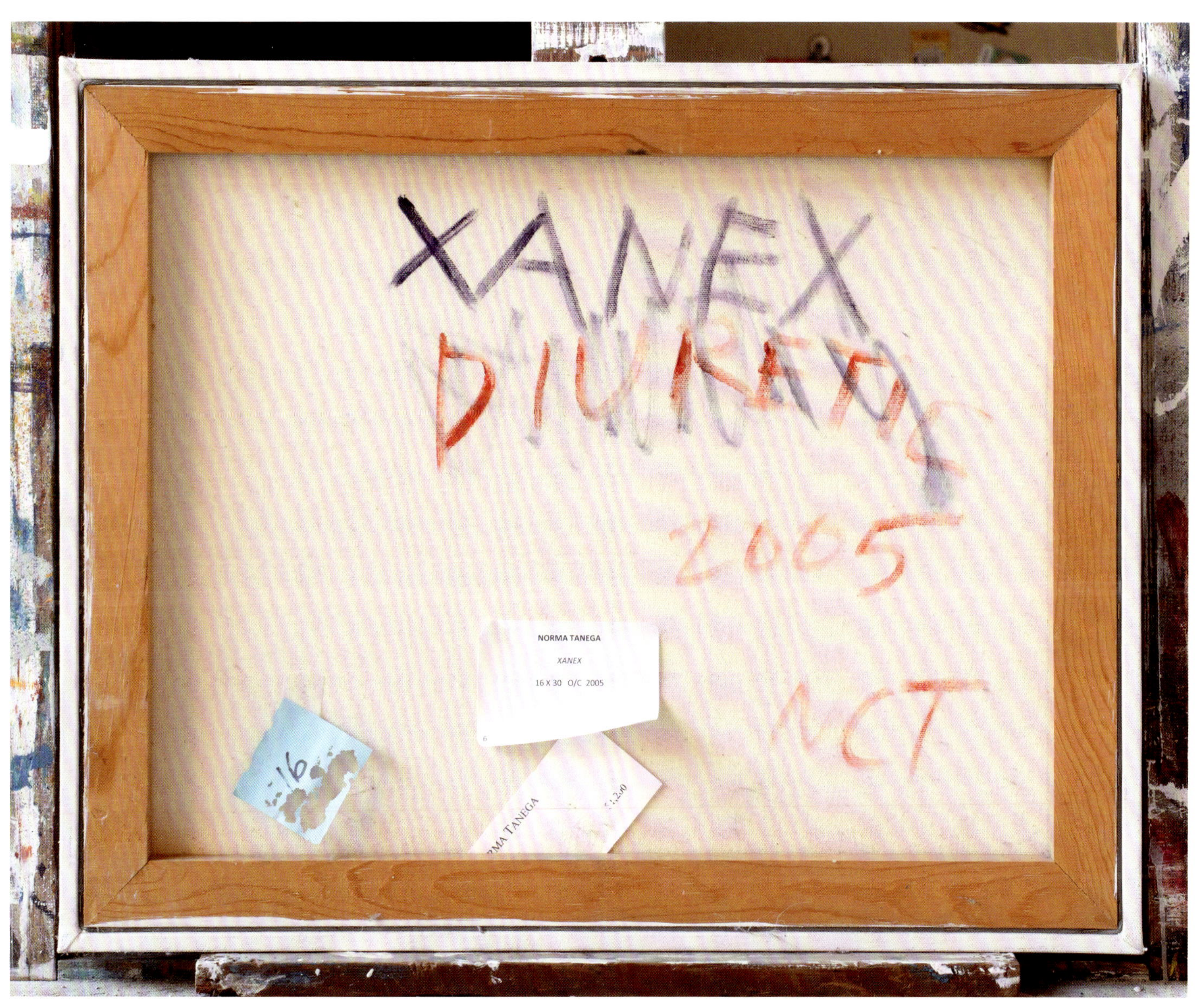
XANEX
DIURETIC
2005
NCT
NORMA TANEGA
XANEX
16 X 30 O/C 2005

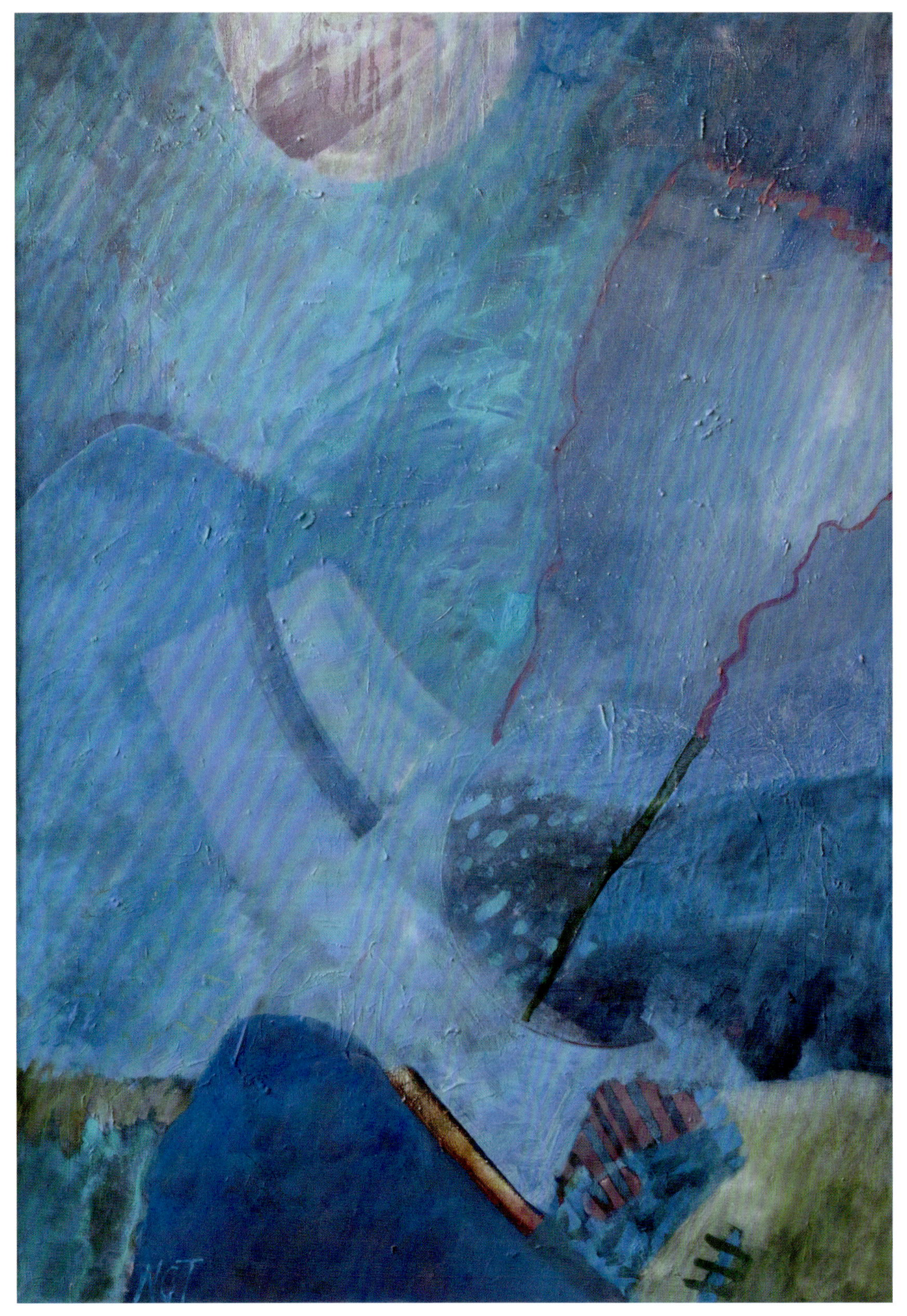

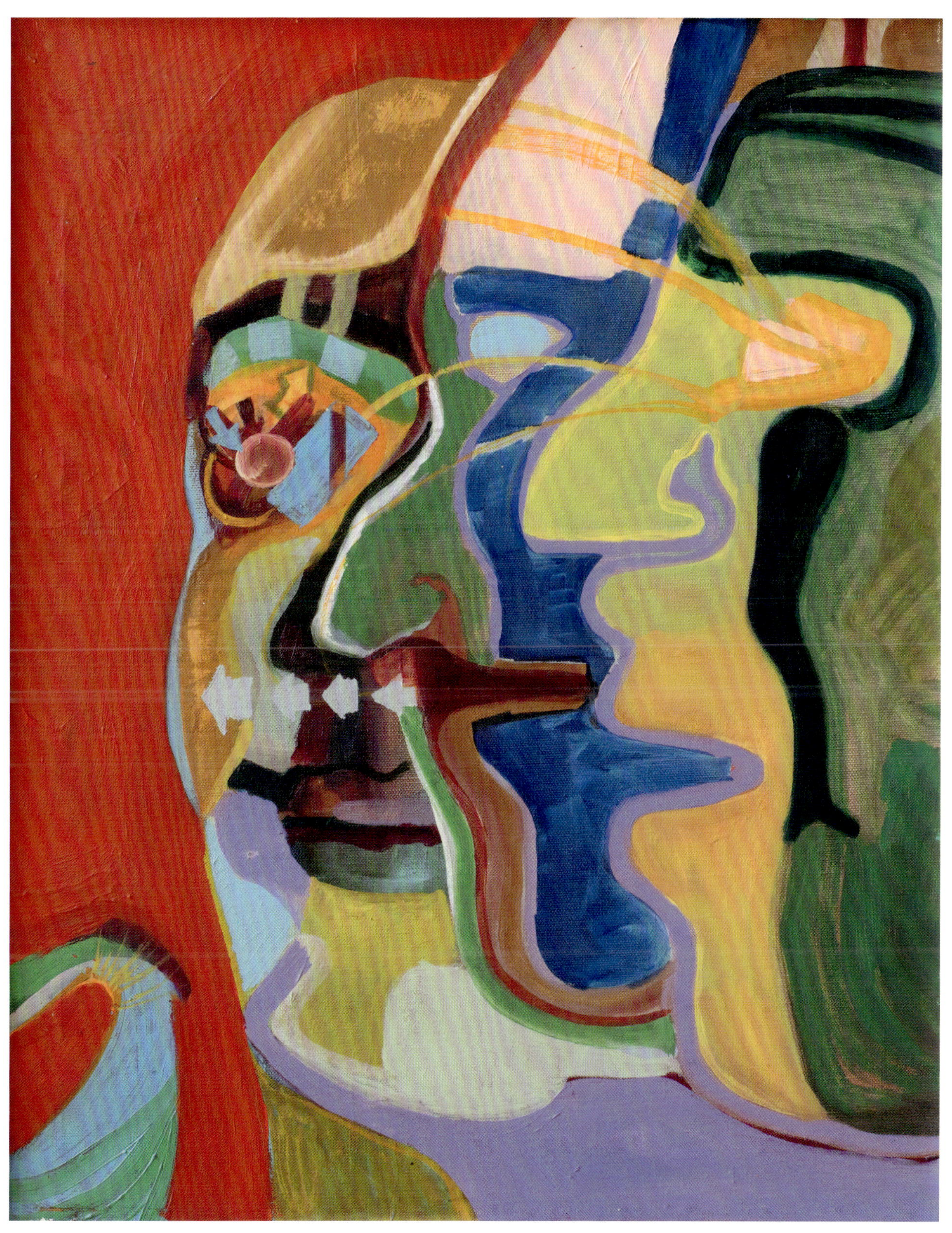

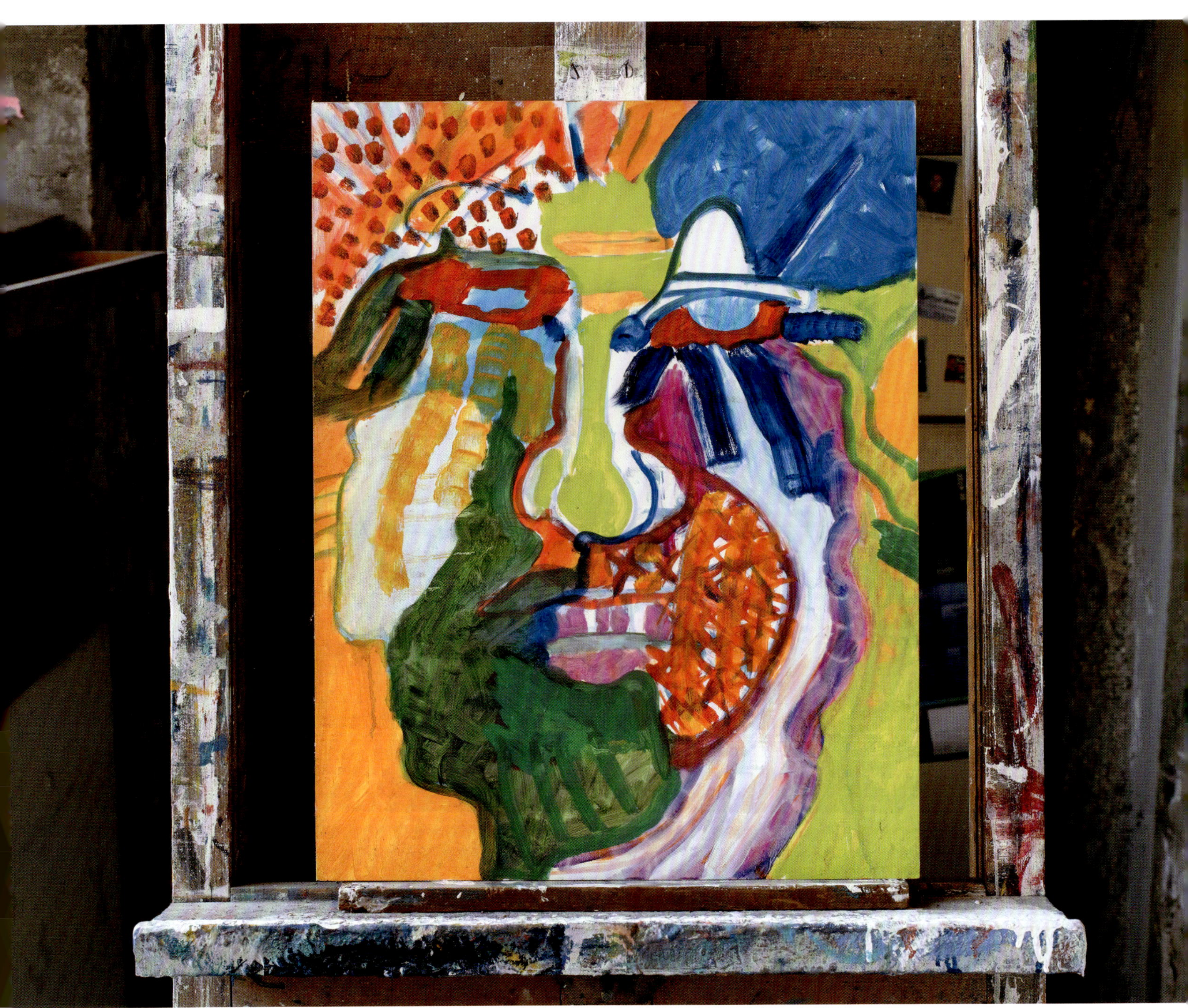

I often find making a "statement about (my)work"
rather difficult because I always feel that the
work is the statement and words are superfluous.
Nevertheless, the focus of my painting for the
past ten years has been in two categories:
faces/masks and landscapes. The latest landscapes have become more abstract in shape and form.
The early landscapes were more recognizable as roads and mountains. The color has
always been abstract. As the recognizable
images become less important, the paintings have
become more emotionally intense.

AUGUST 27, 1982
NCT.

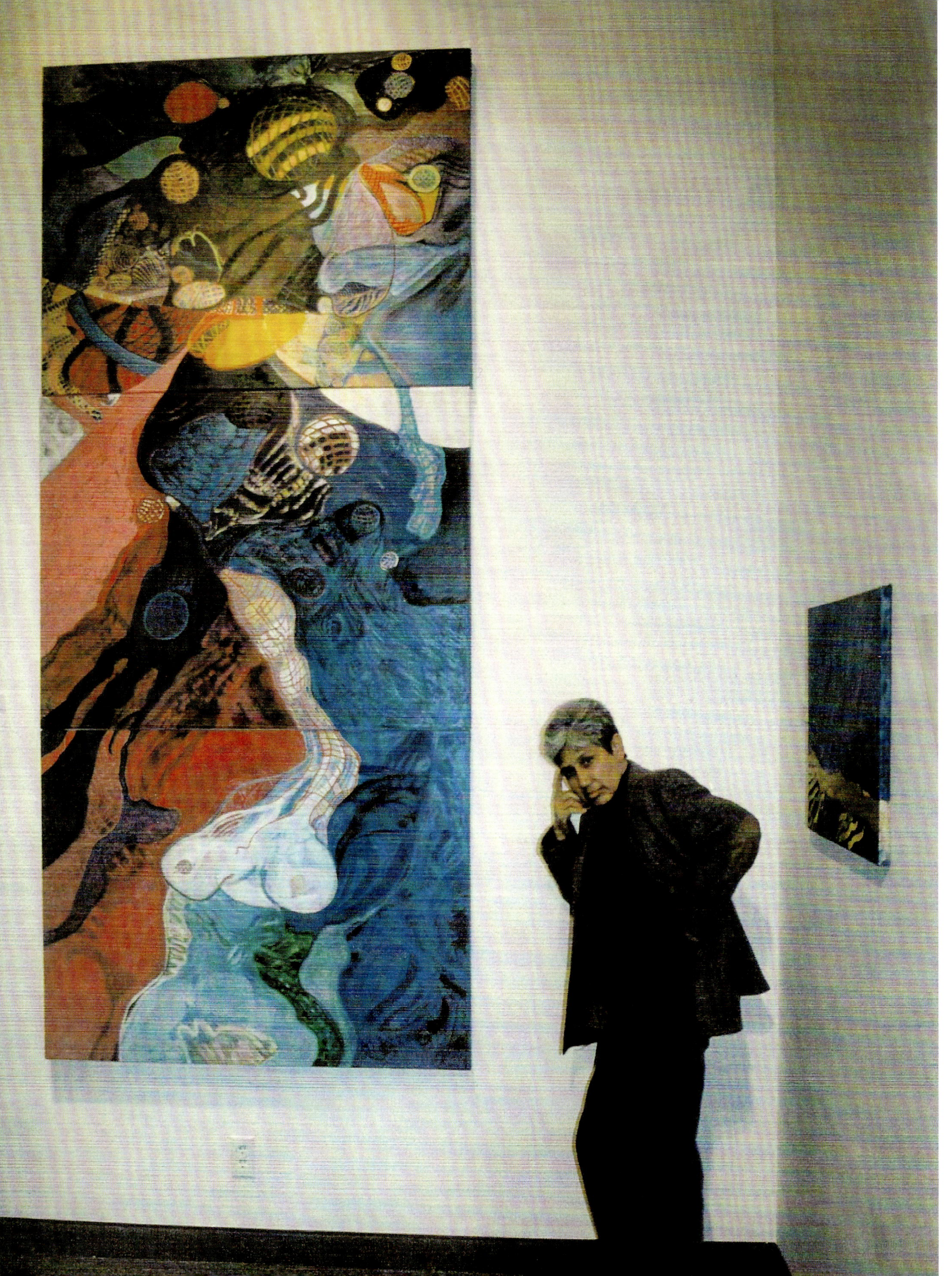

Visions

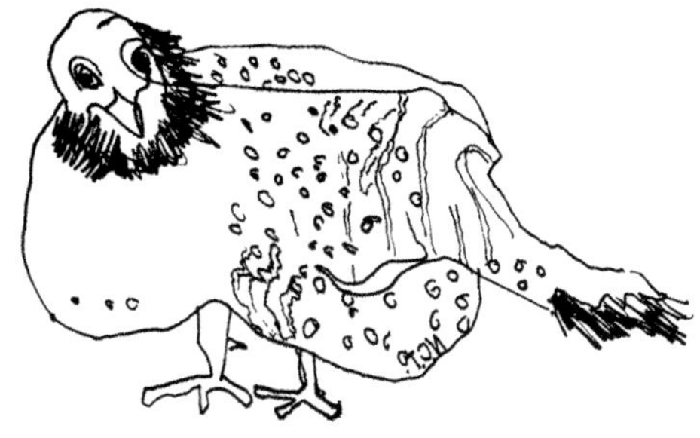

STANLEY C. WILSON: We think about the term "renaissance man" or "renaissance woman." Norma was really typical of that, in the sense that she wasn't only one thing. She was not only a visual artist; she was not only a painter; she was not only a draftswoman. She also was a musician. And she thought in those ways, with her many skills. She thought about her many applications. She was also a teacher and she taught music. She taught art and she was totally involved with the people who were in her life and around her. I mean, you expect an individual to excel maybe in one area, but Norma excelled in many areas. She was eclectic, in the sense that she was able to manifest all of those abilities and do it well.

MOANA VERCOE: Norma mastered the point of synthesis between creative energy and the discipline of formalism. She was technically brilliant, maybe even a savant. Although Norma was in her third life, there was a childlike quality to her immense energy that offset how proficient and precise she could be. Beneath her easygoing nature was a prodigious talent and immense intellect.

TOM SKELLY: Norma and I developed a deep interest in what she called "big ears," where we enjoyed paying attention to sound art and how music is composed and digested both socially and psychologically. My impression of Norma was that she was a person who had a deep interest in music and art and how these played out in one's personal and social lives.

MOANA VERCOE: She loved playing with sounds and meaning. For example, the Baboonz remix CD—which is musically brilliant, but not conventional listening—is titled *Eight Songs Ate Brains*. I wonder if she had some form of synesthesia, because Norma was just as comfortable using sounds as she was using colors and forms, or words.

DAVID SHEARER: The thing that struck me the most about Norma's paintings was just the, I guess, kind of raw energy that she had in her work. Very gestural, some of it even literal.

BRIAN RANSOM: I loved her paintings from the first time I saw them. And in those days, she wasn't very well represented. She gradually got a lot more known; in the beginning, she just painted because she loved to.

DAVID SHEARER: It reminded me of some of the early New York graffiti artists: Basquiat and Keith Haring and people like that, who were just really kind of expressing themselves in a way that was unique and had its own imprimatur, its own signature. And she had developed that. You could really tell that she was not parading the art for anyone other than herself. She was just expressing herself. It was just like the music was; it was an artistic expression, with this rawness, but yet, still, this very individual approach.

BRIAN RANSOM: Just as an artist, I'll say that I really responded to the scale of the paintings—this really large-scale stuff. I was just stupefied by them. We would talk about it and she'd say, "I'm flipping it today. I'm doing it over. I'm going to paint on the back." Norma was always just steaming off in another direction.

DAVID SHEARER: She had really kind of dropped off the radar. She kept up more with the music than the art, and still was performing later in life. I don't know if she got disillusioned with the art scene, or exactly what happened.

CATHERINE McINTOSH: I'm not sure why the galleries didn't carry her work, or if she ever did have a show. I mean, if you don't show up at the art openings, you don't get that well known among potential buyers. I think Norma almost resisted that, as part of her anti-establishment streak.

TOM SKELLY: Even though we were both painters, we were of the opinion that music offered a deeper connection to being the language of the soul because it was invisible and fluid. Painting locked on to a tangible and frozen object which functioned more as the architecture of emotion. She was not interested in going out unless it would be of great interest to her—such as seeing a concert of Harry Partch or Evelyn Glennie. Our "big ears" absorbed these concerts and offered great inspiration for playing music, or simply for fun conversations.

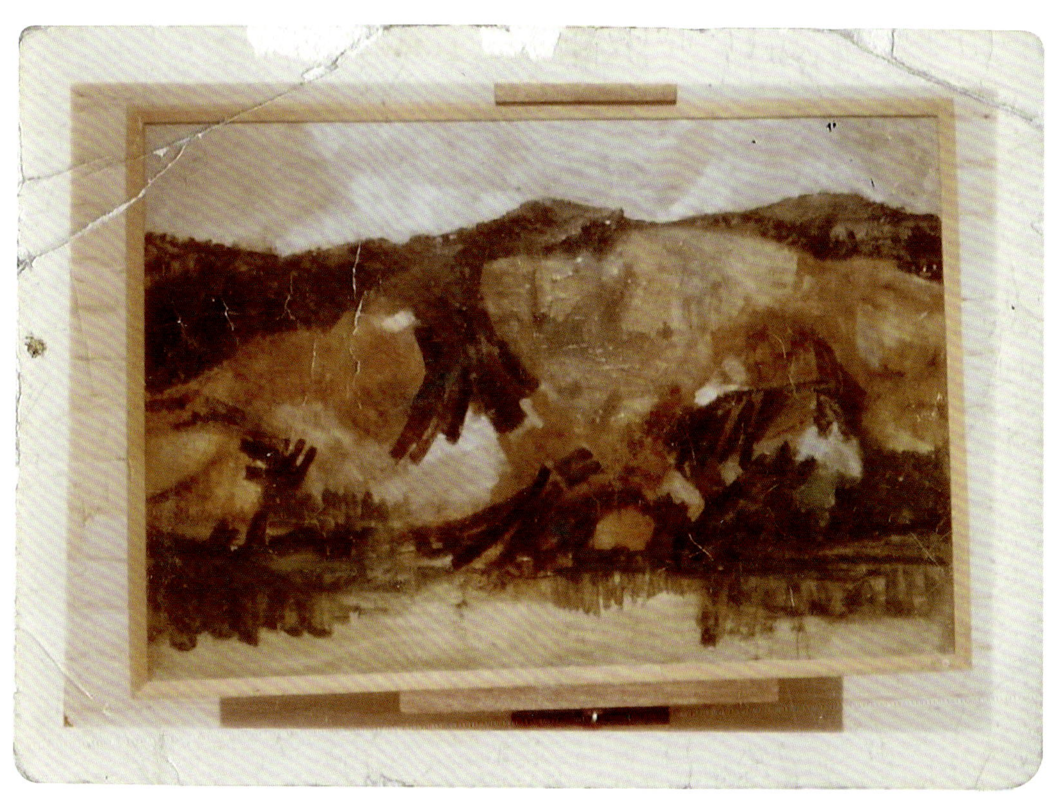

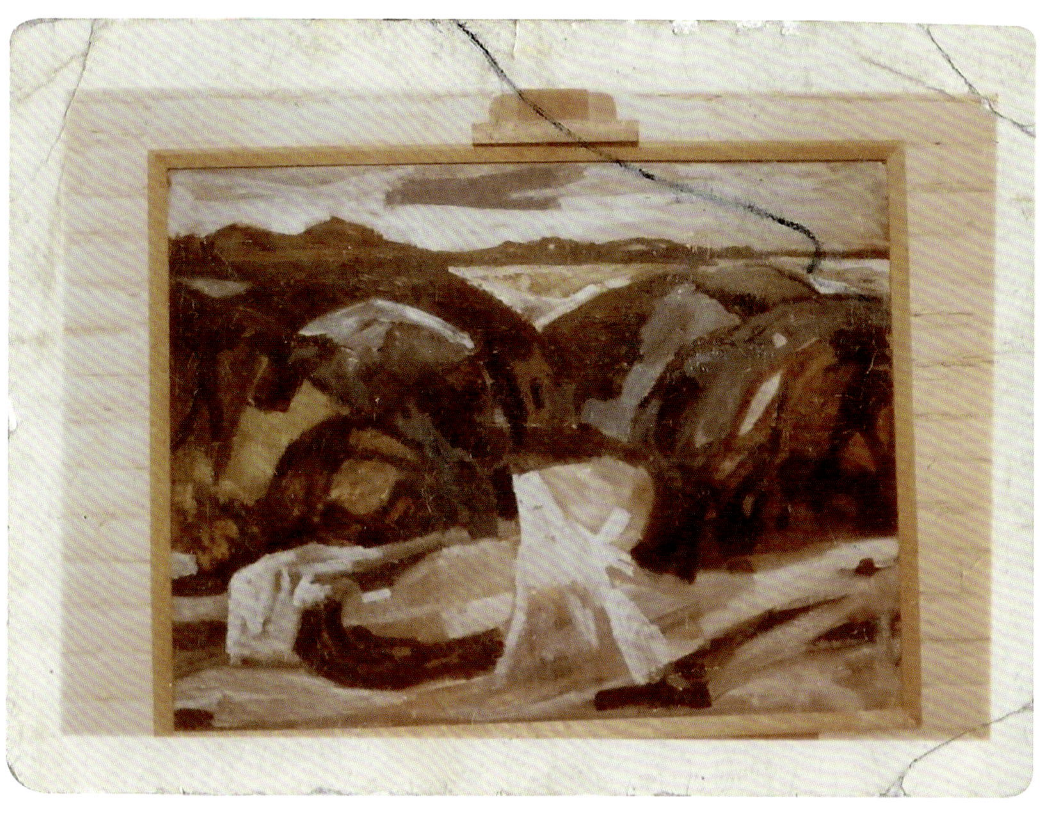

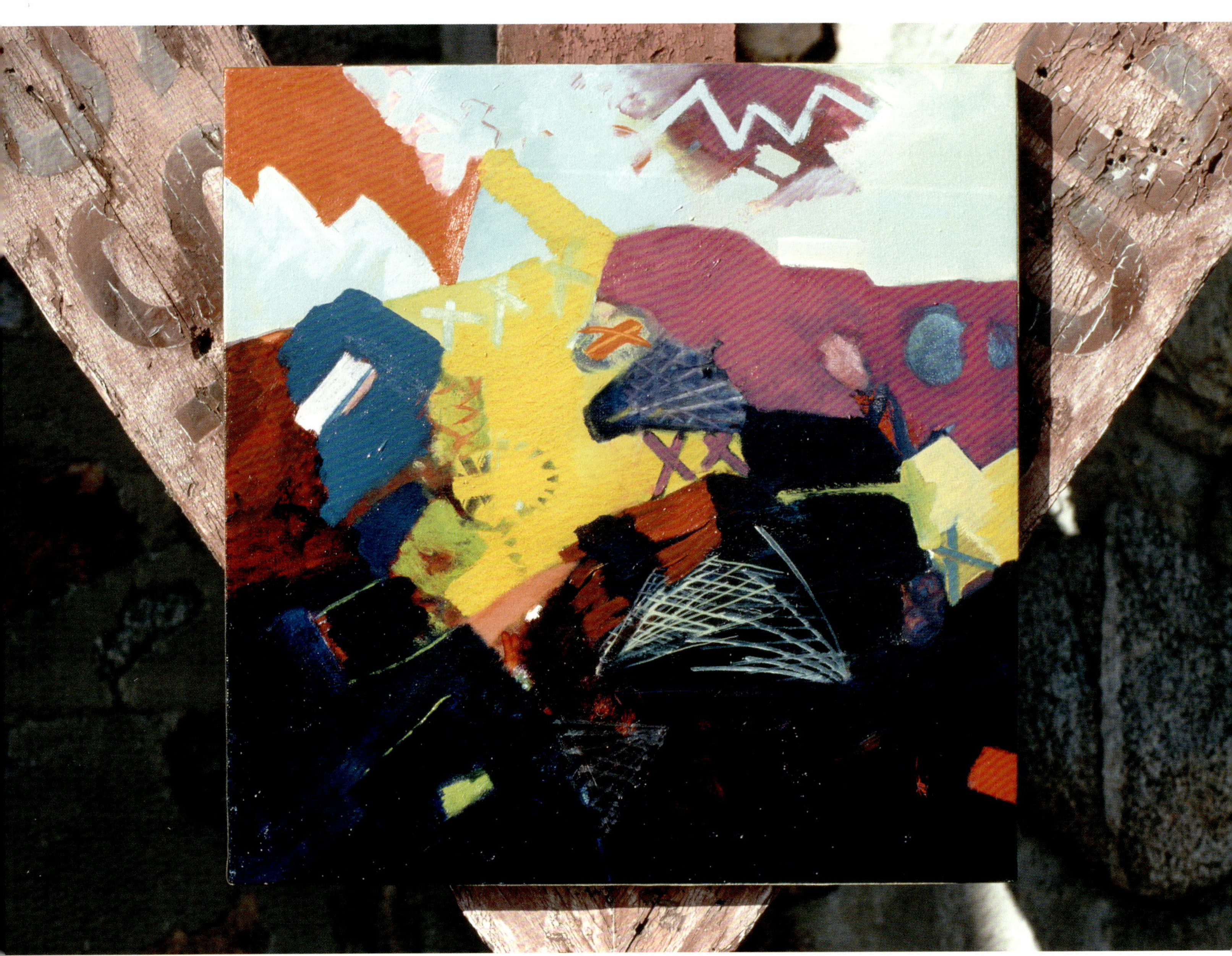

DAVID SHEARER: At the point we met, Norma was kind of a recluse. Actually, one of our interns from Scripps was an architecture major, and she was fascinated by Norma and her Foster Rhodes Jackson–designed studio and home. So, we were able to make arrangements for her to meet with Norma, and to basically do an interview. So, she went and interviewed her and came back just ecstatic, like, "Wow, this woman's incredible." And right here in Claremont, and really, nobody knew too much about her. So, that was when I said, "Well, let's talk to her about maybe doing an exhibition of her work."

BRIAN RANSOM: Norma would make really odd choices—often, like, really sort of obtuse. These really funny, wacky portrait things, and self-portraits, and you'd just be kind of looking on in amazement. I love that she always painted in oil. There was always that beautiful smell in the studio, of the oil and linseed and turpentine—old school. Not even flammable, but toxic. Can't buy that stuff anymore. I don't even know if they sell it in LA.

DAVID SHEARER: We put together a show, and we tried to put something together that represented the various periods, and the various themes that she was addressing, like activism, pharmaceutical drugs—she had these mental-health paintings, some very specific themes that she was inspired by. We kind of tried to put together something major, that would be a survey of her work, and an overview of what her artistic life had been.

CATHERINE McINTOSH: I came back to town and got involved with the Claremont Museum of Art, which my mother founded, in 2009. We started to focus on a number of local artists who were in their eighties. Norma was one of those artists—unfortunately, she passed away before we made it down the history line to get to her generation. I was really happy that Claremont Heritage put together a show of her work while she was still alive.

DAVID SHEARER: Maybe the impetus for her doing this show, the reason why she did the show was more financially driven. Because she was kind of in a tough spot at the point she was in, and she needed to raise some funds.

MARIO VERLANGIERI: Norma always told me—going back to the whole idea of the business of being an artist—"Well, you gotta eat."

DAVID SHEARER: We talked a lot about pricing, and Norma, of course, had a kind of following of people in the area. So we were able to sell some things.

CATHERINE McINTOSH: I think, in a lot of ways, her pieces were too personal to be very sellable. She wasn't painting to sell paintings; she was painting to express her own feelings.

DAVID SHEARER: I think Norma loved the exhibition. And on opening night—she didn't actually perform, but we put together a film, a short film of just her work and we had some musicians that were around, and they did a kind of tribute.

CATHERINE McINTOSH: Norma's work seemed very contemporary, from what I see. Most of the paintings in her studio were more psychological. Sometimes, Mount Baldy was referenced, too; it looked very abstract, but it was a reference to a landscape.

DAVID SHEARER: She was also really feeling like people had forgotten about her; I think that was another reason why she wanted to do the show, too. Not just to sell things, but to really put out a representation of her life's work and what she had done; what she had accomplished.

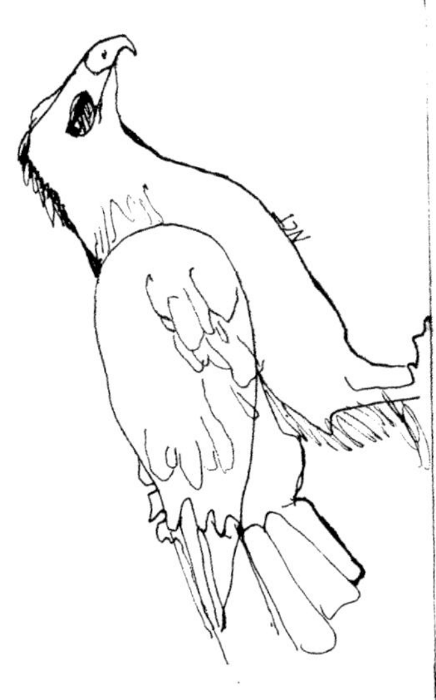

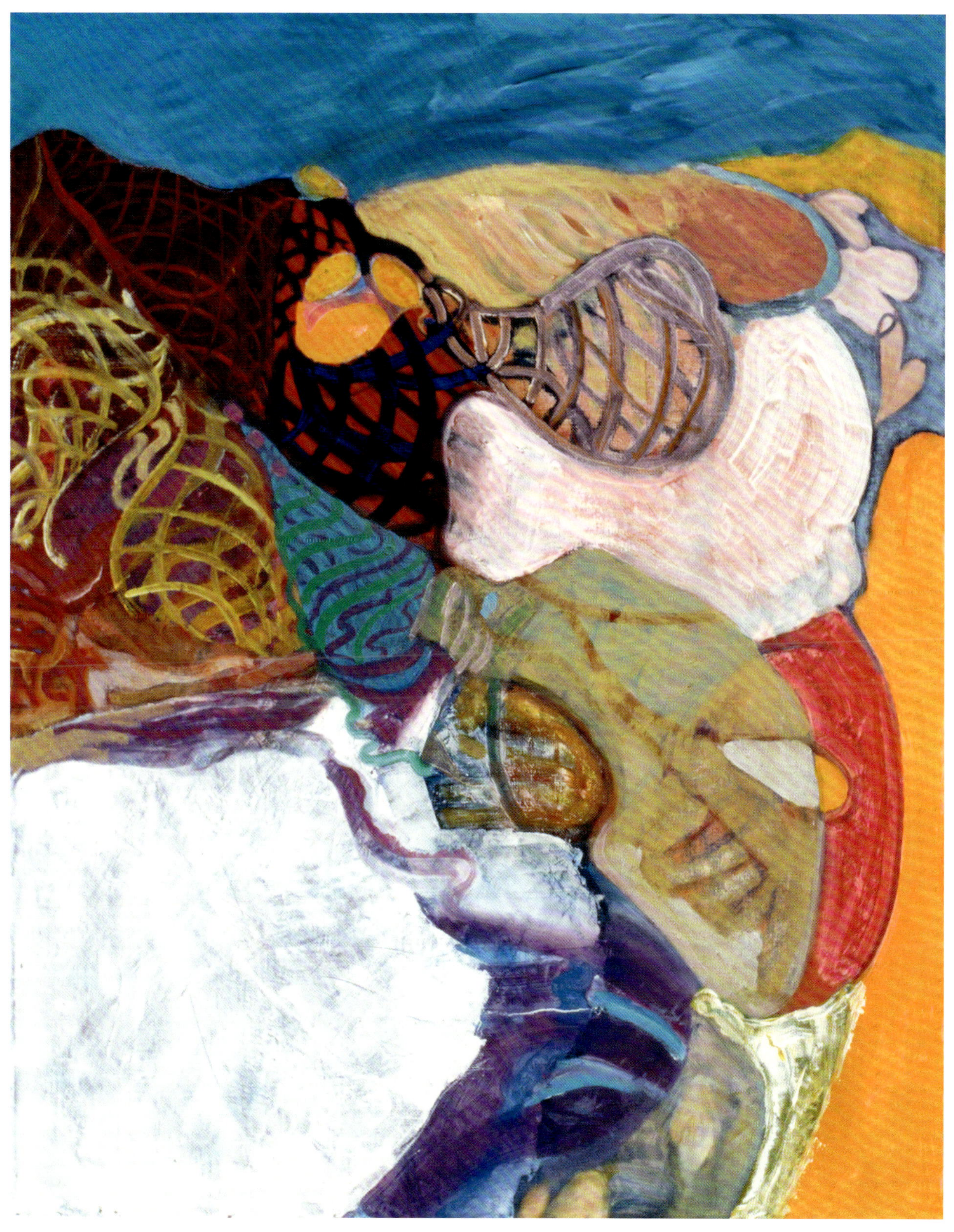

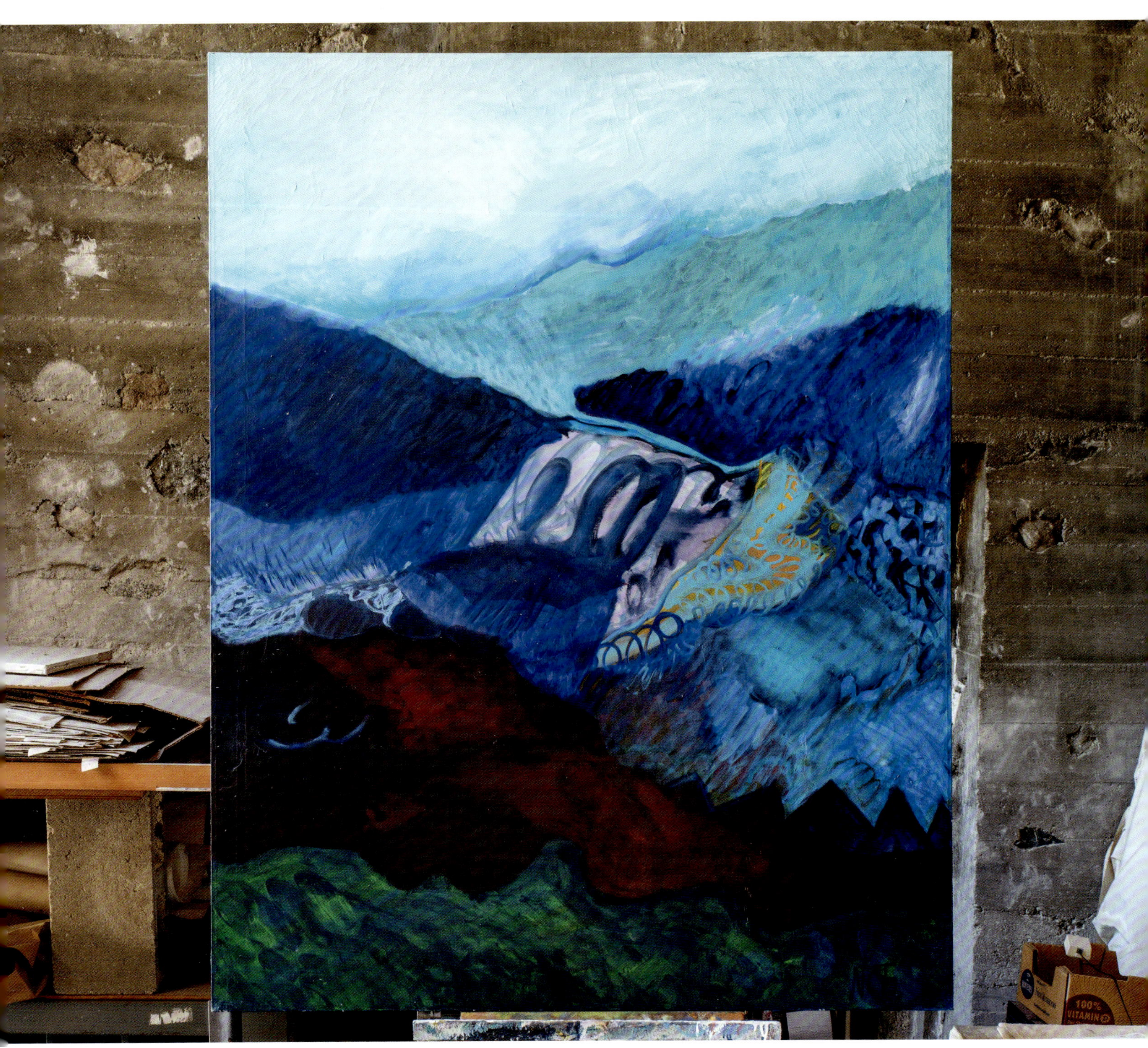

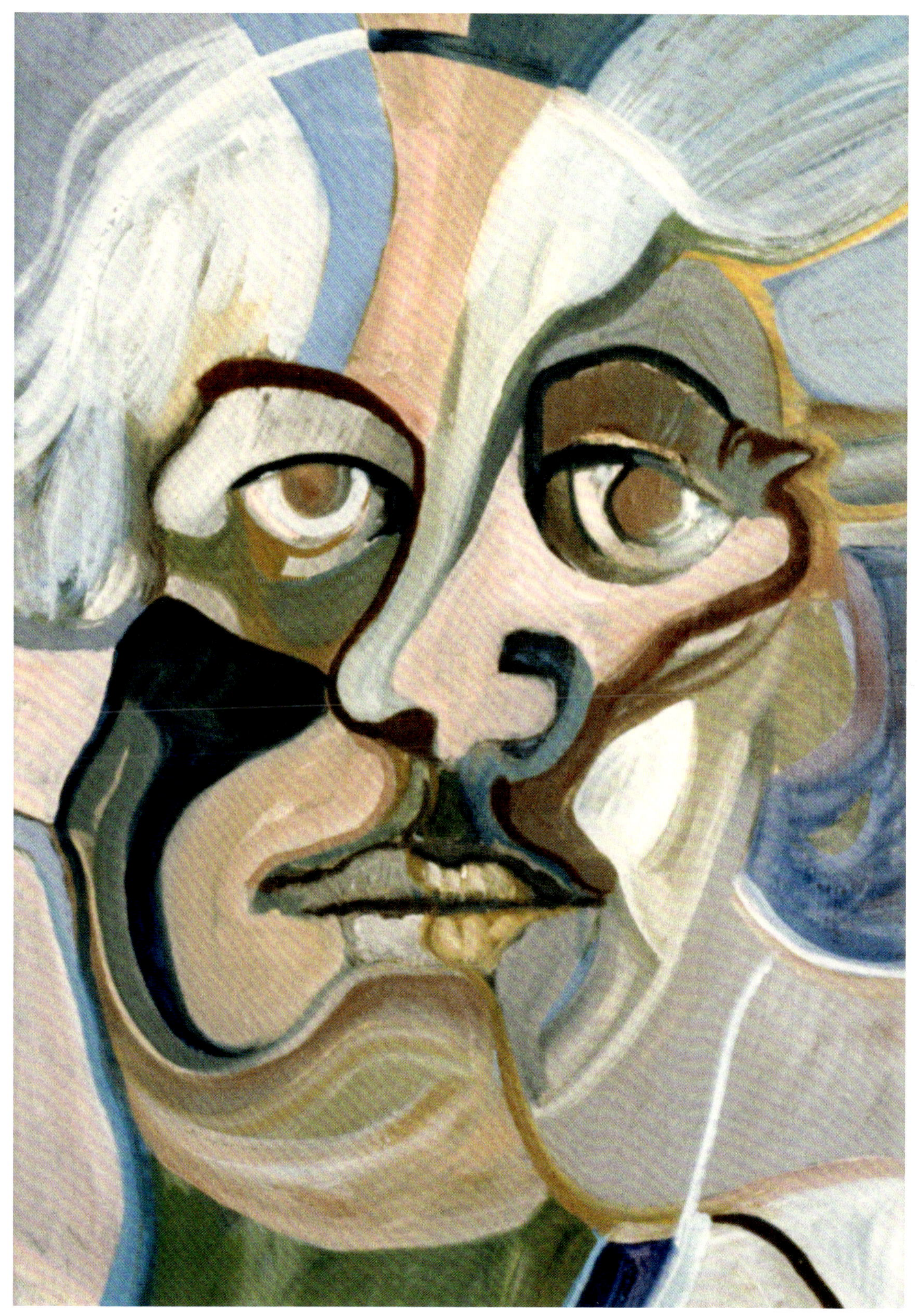

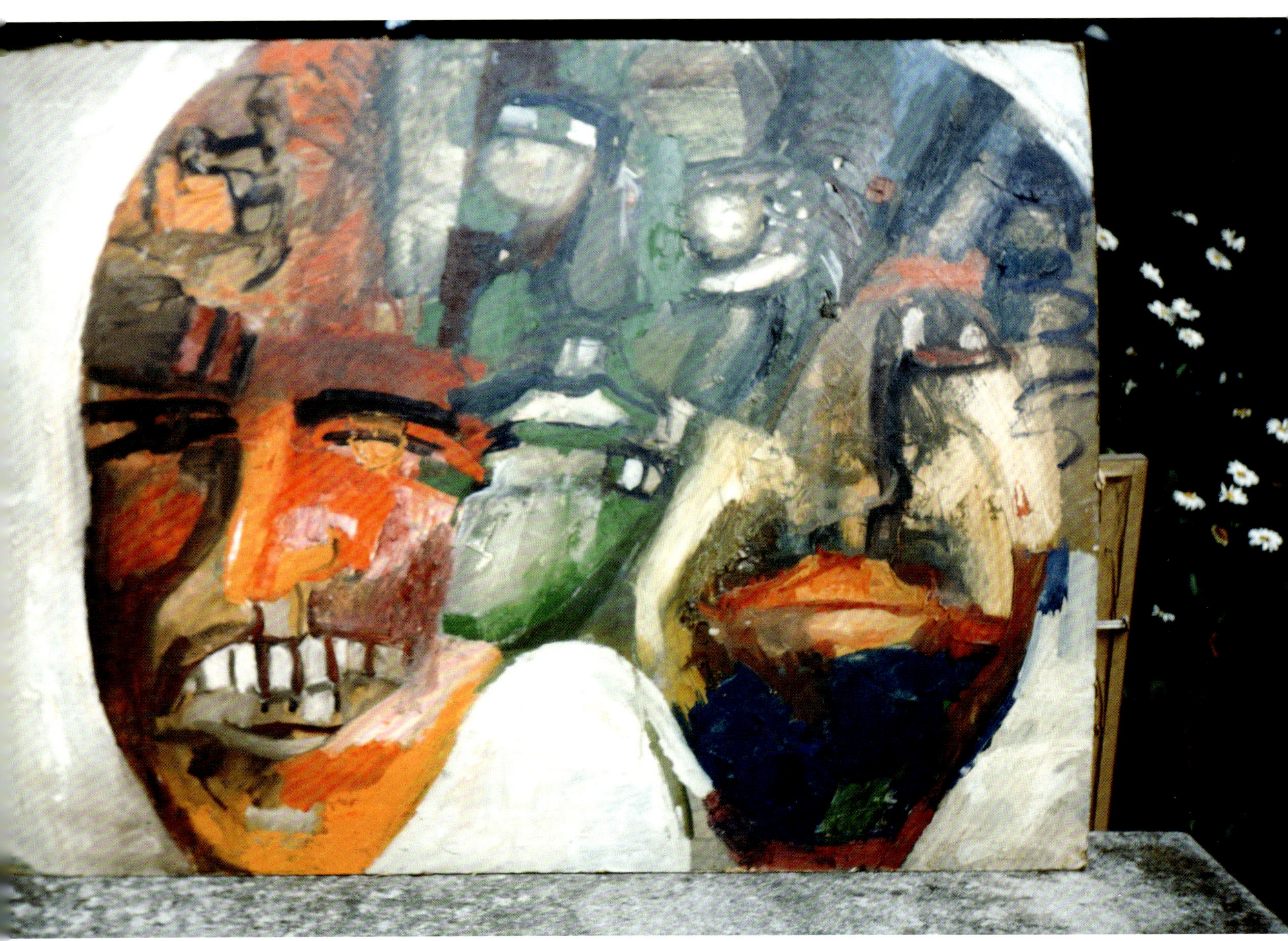

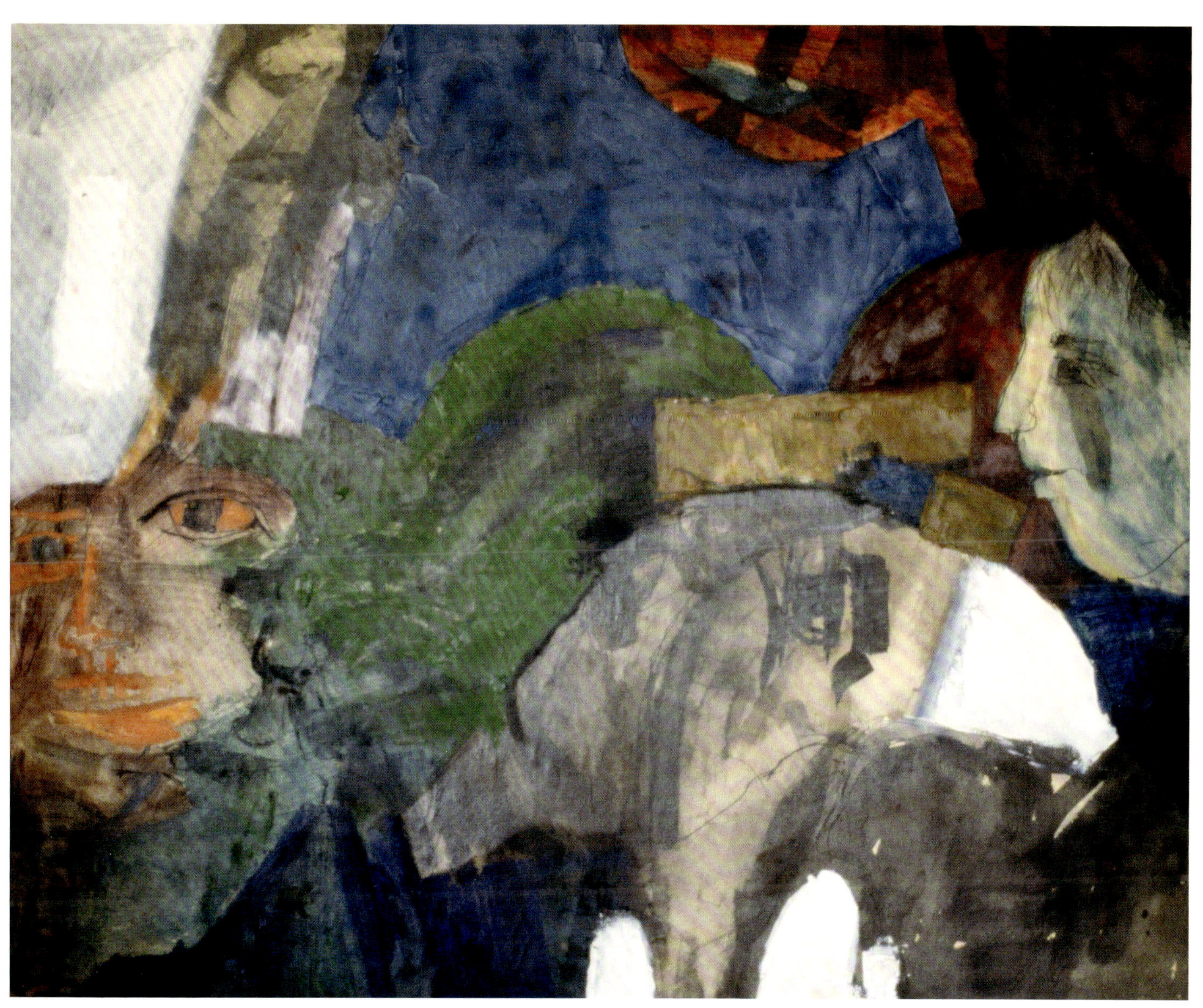

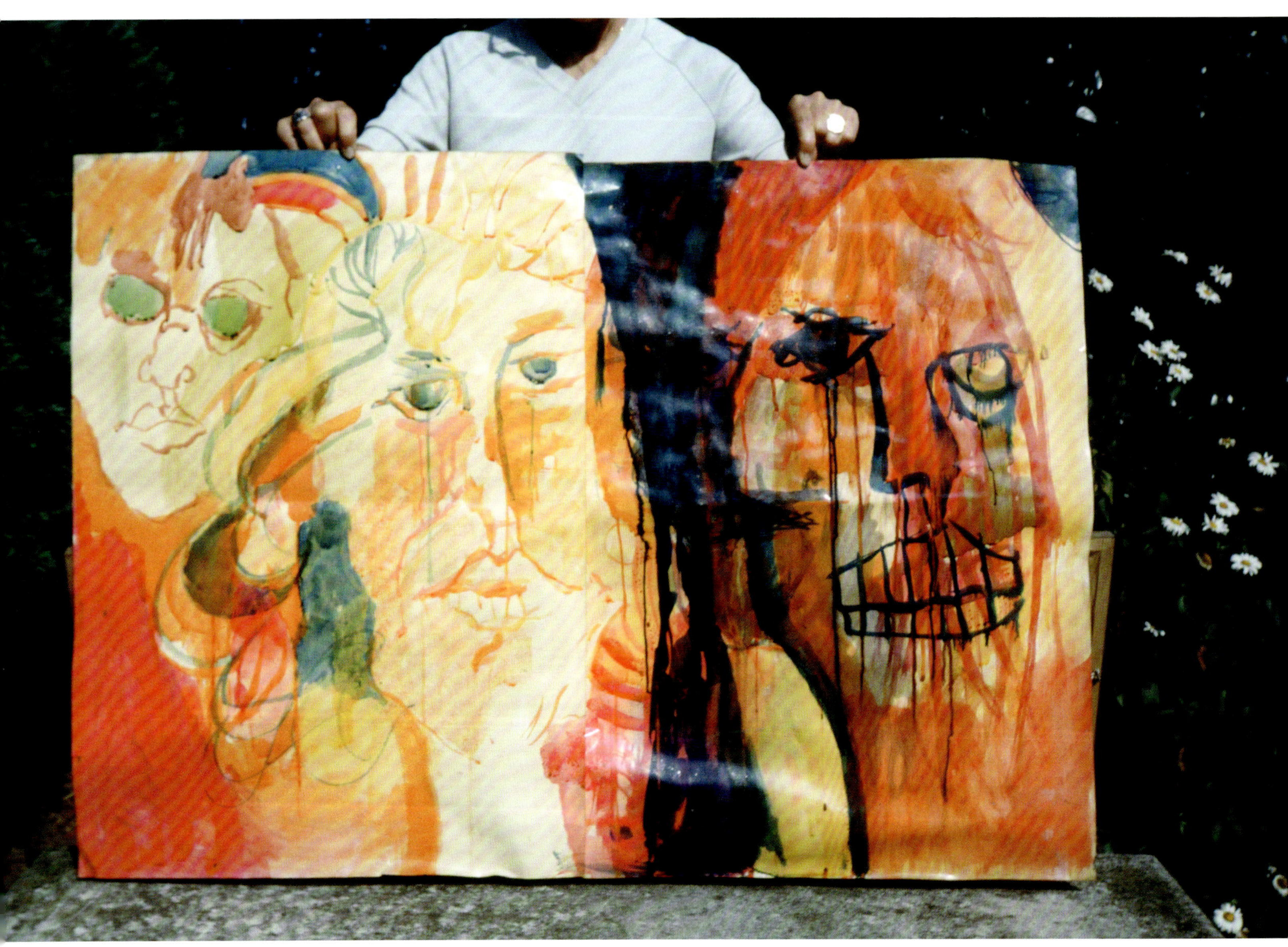

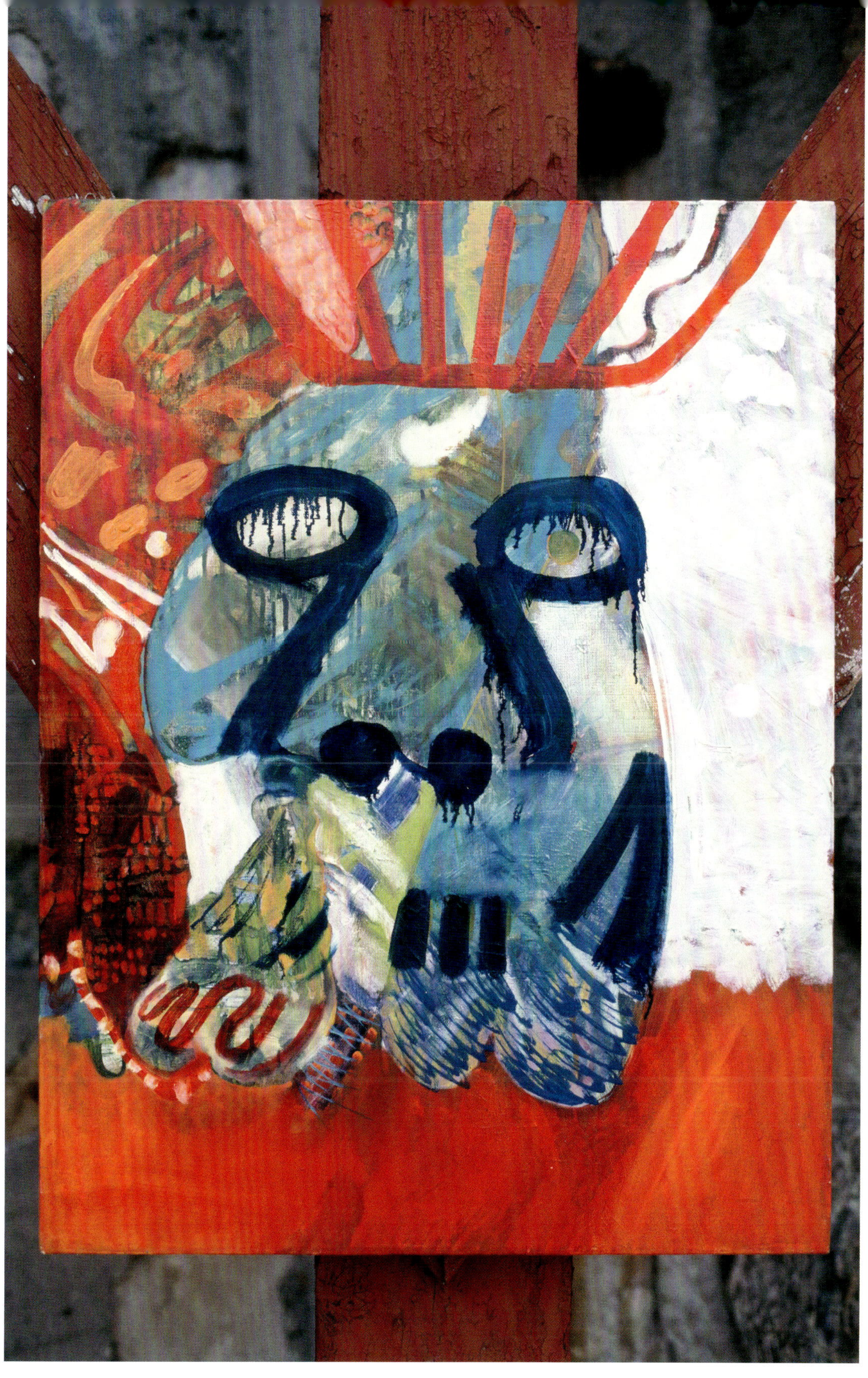

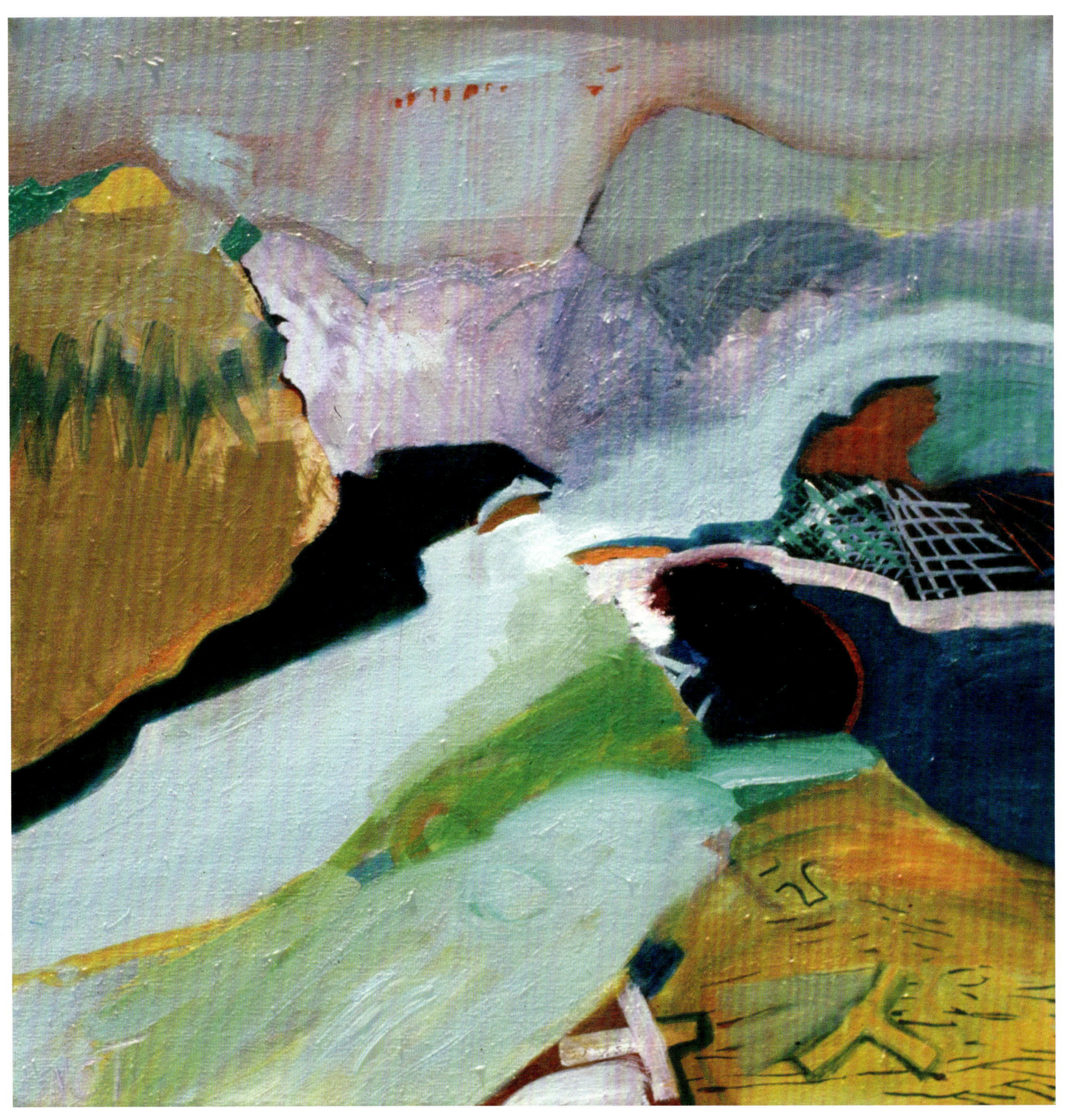

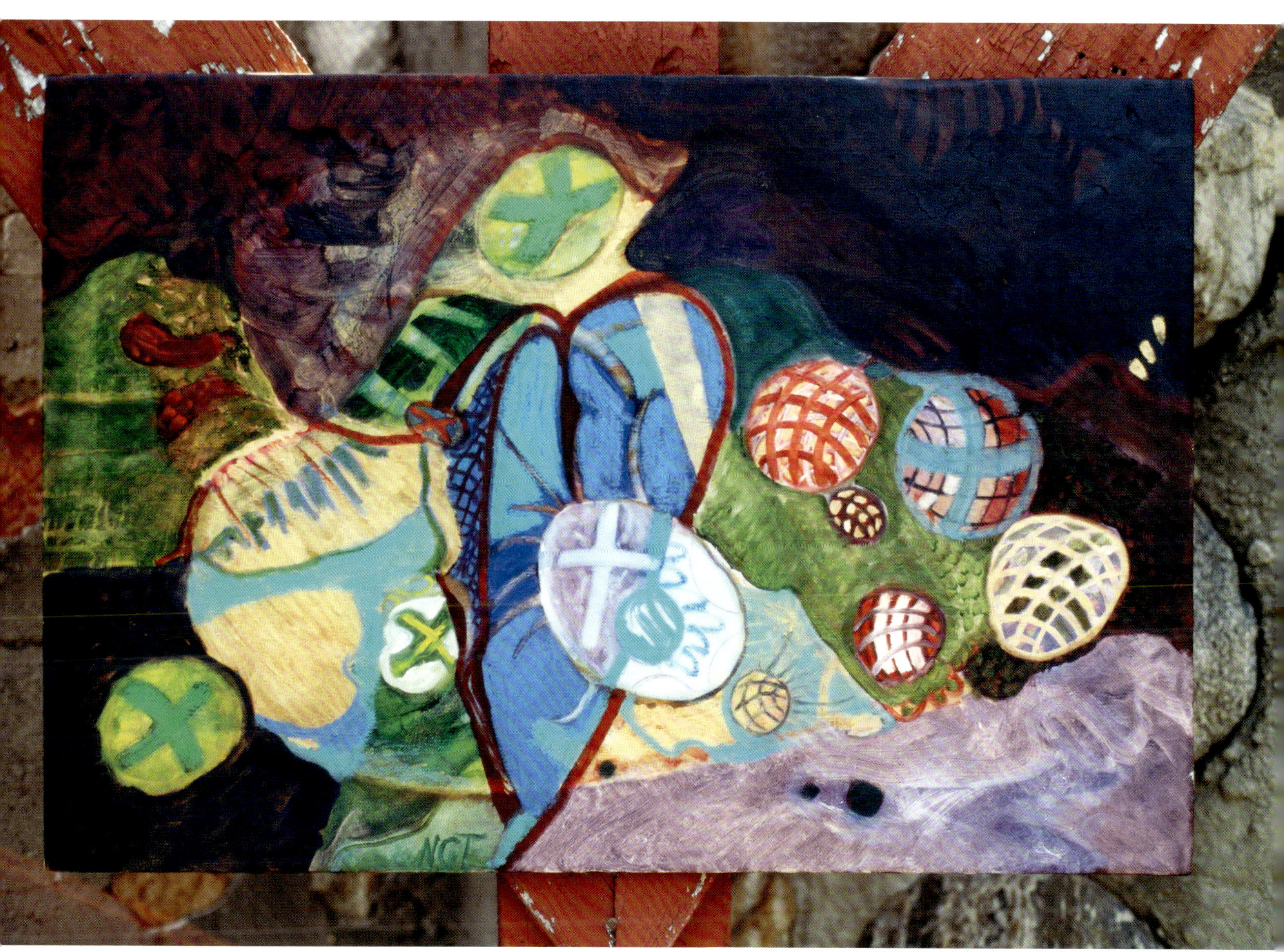

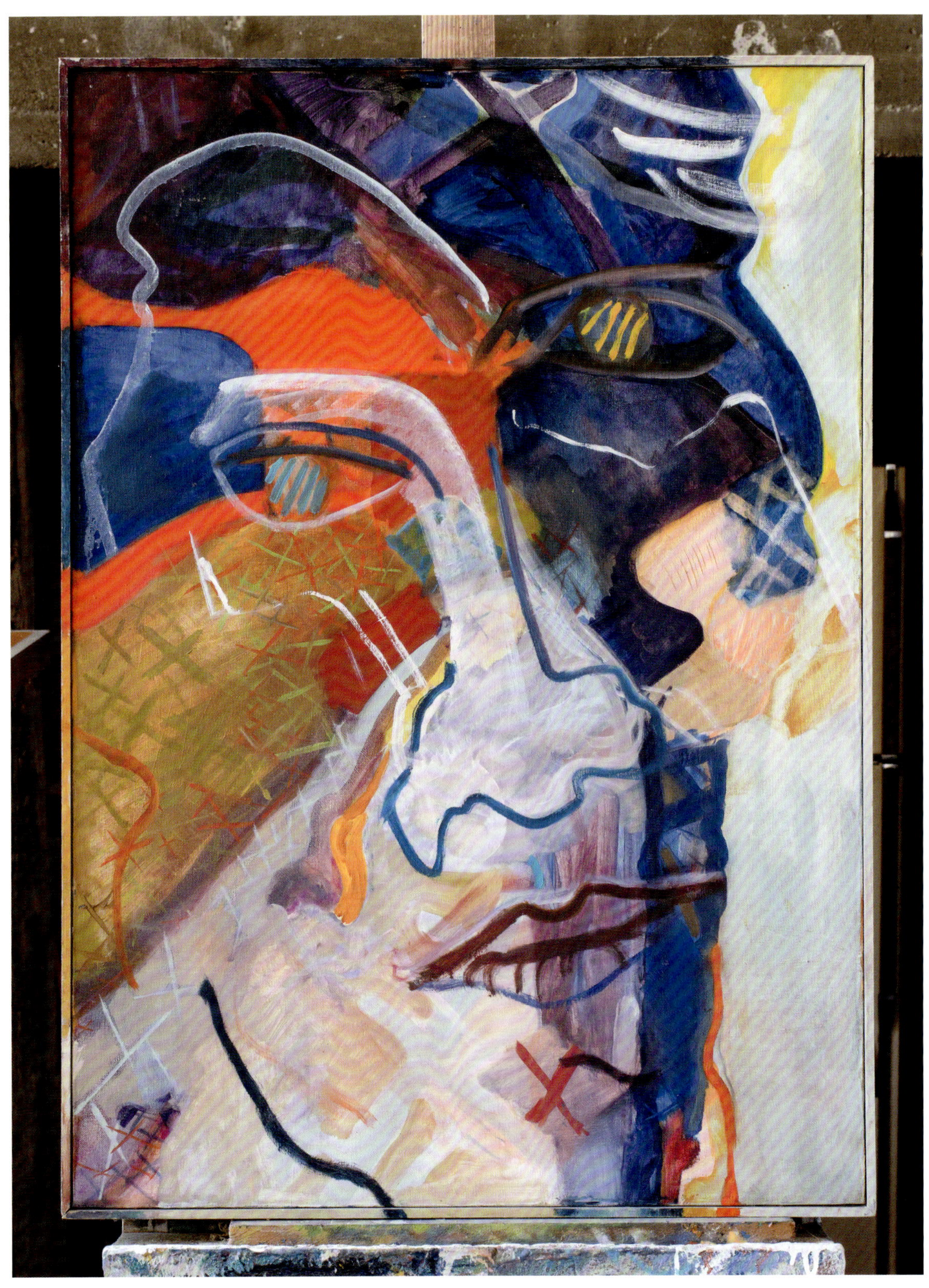

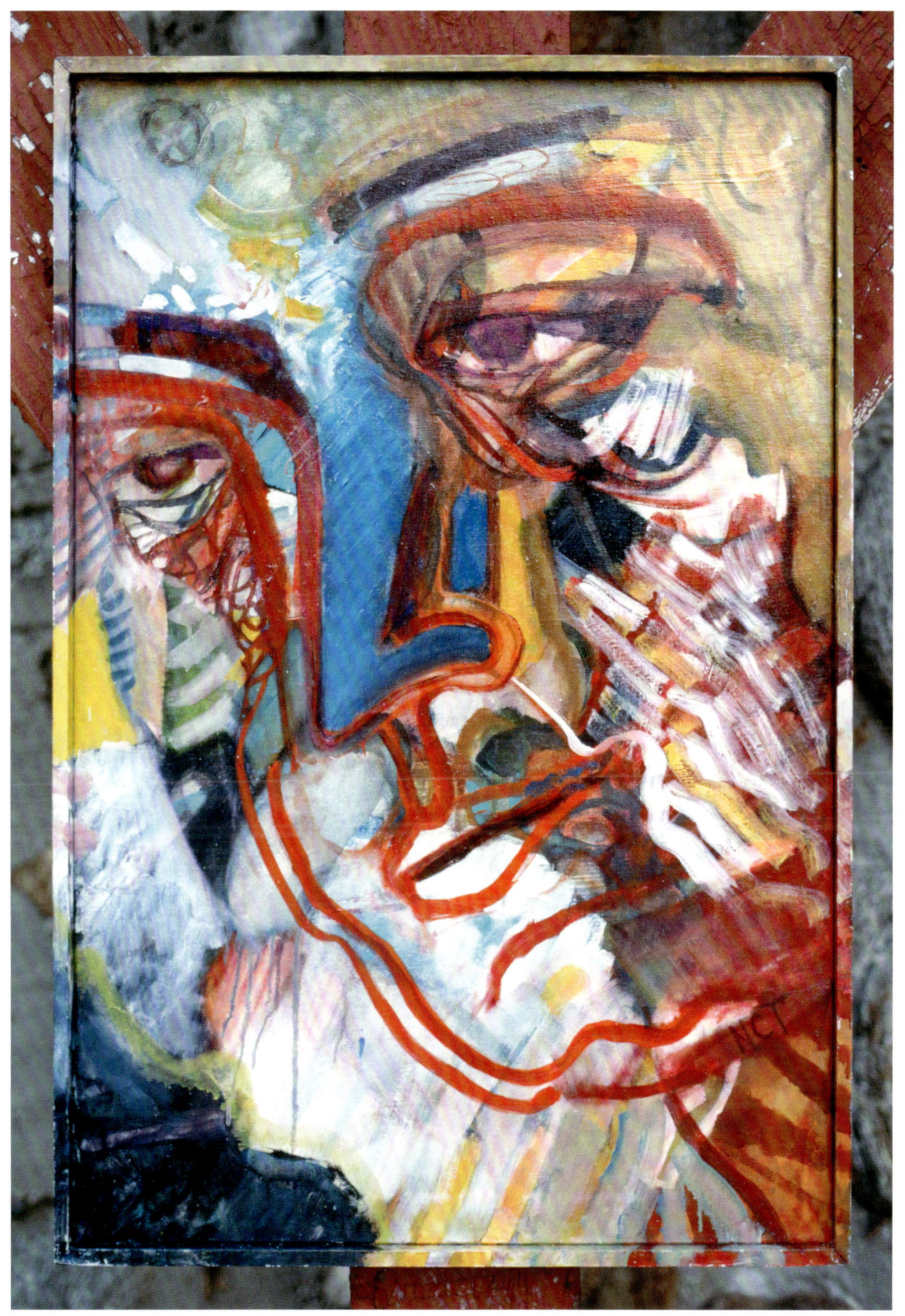

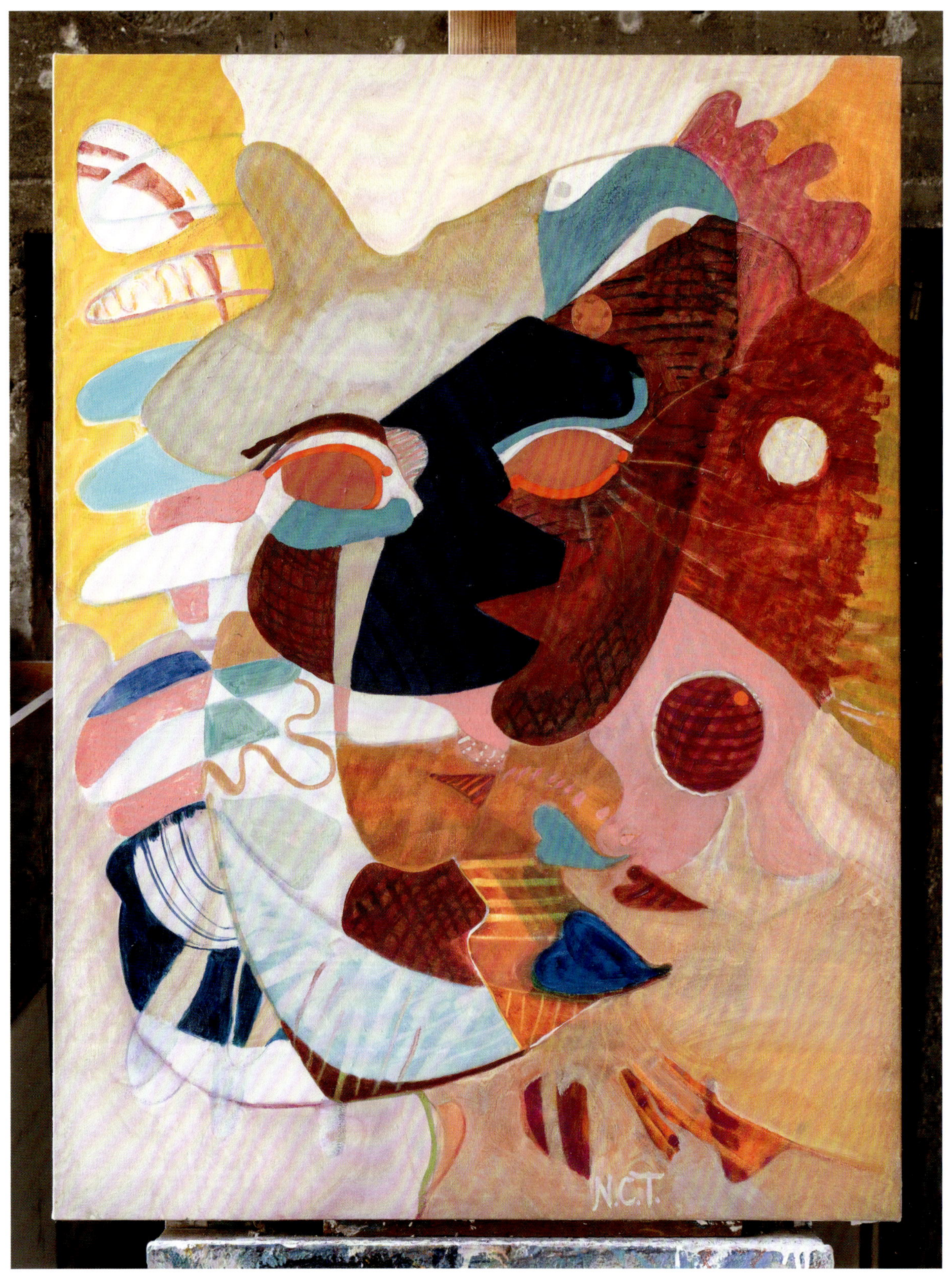

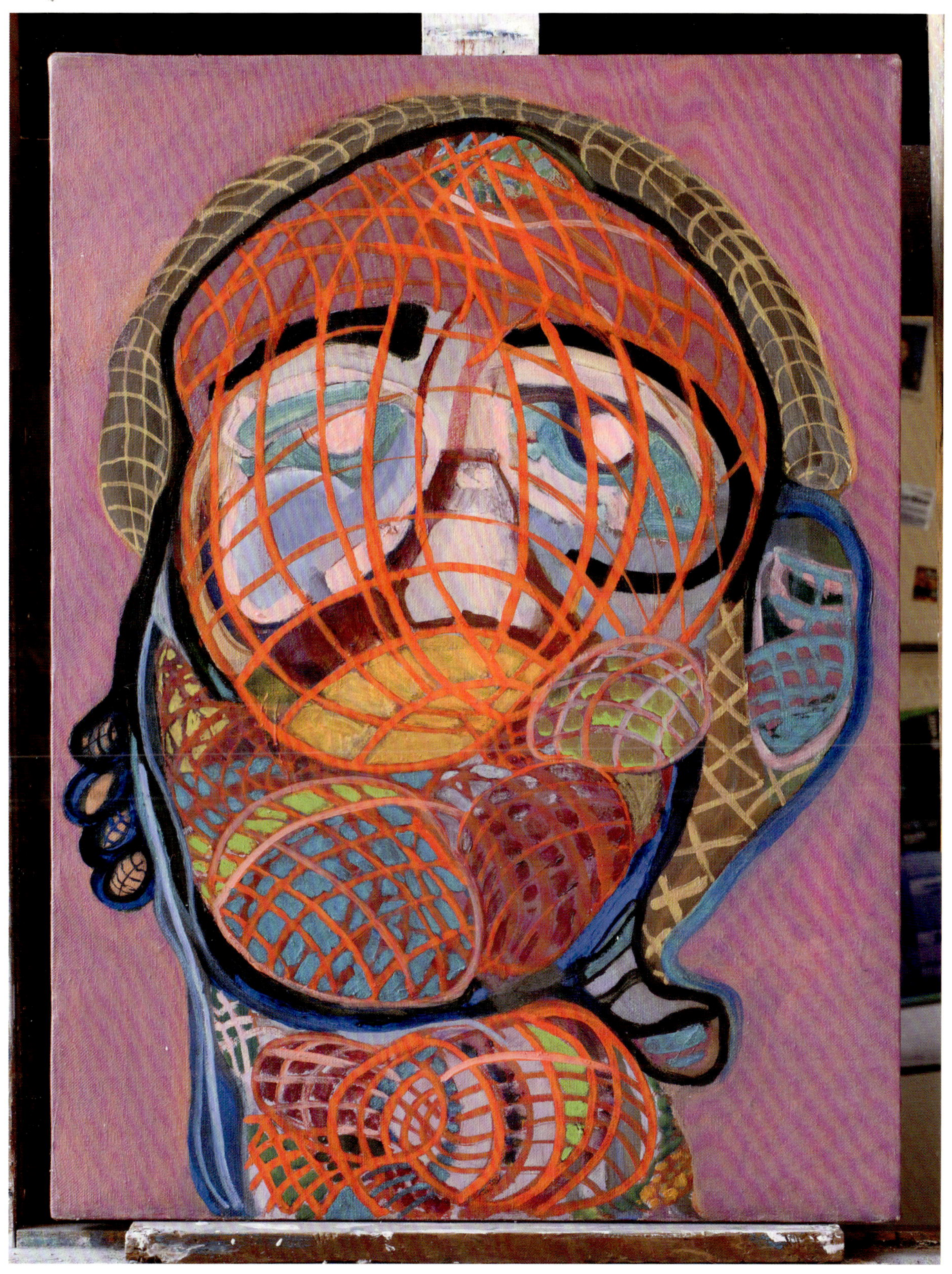

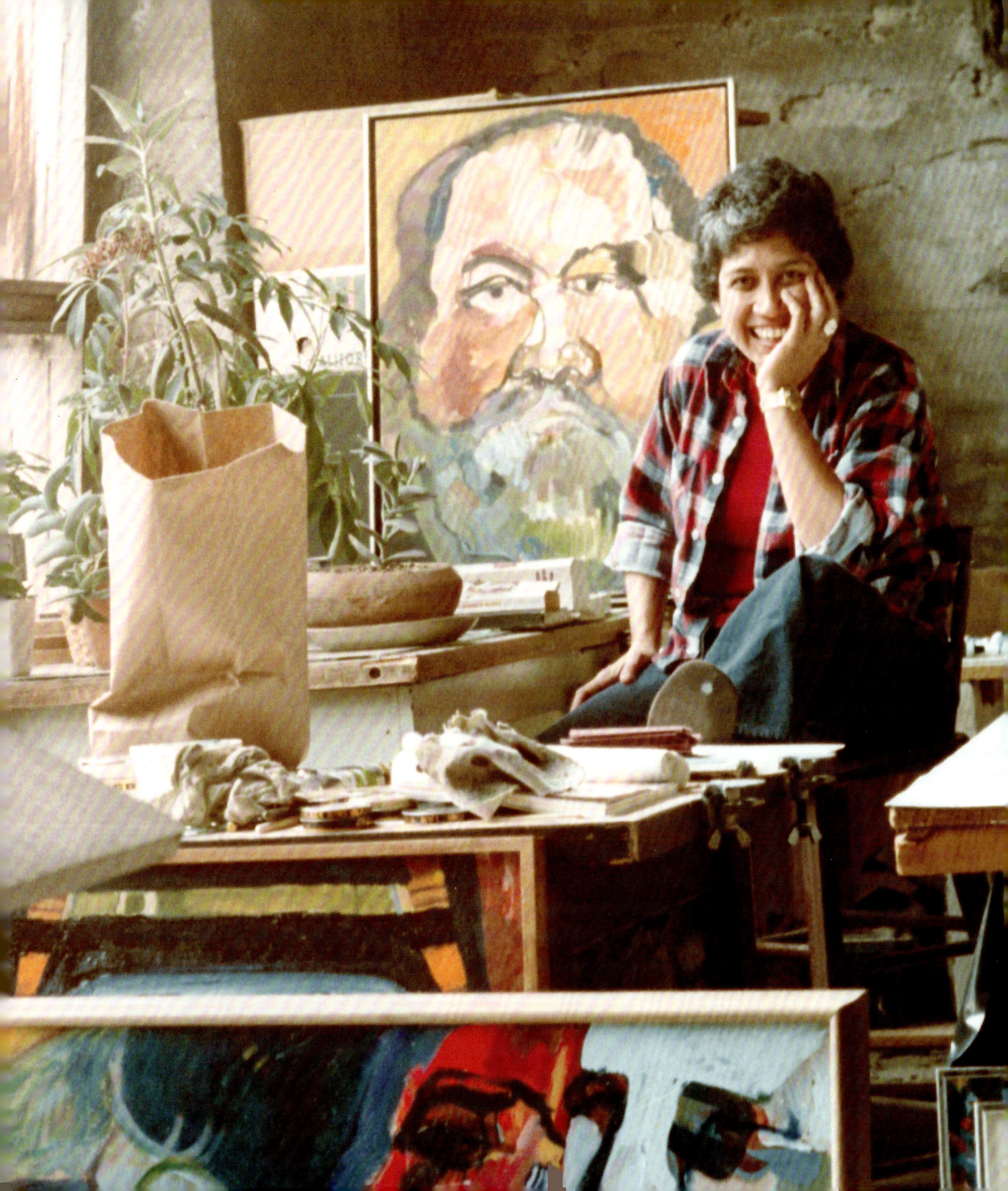

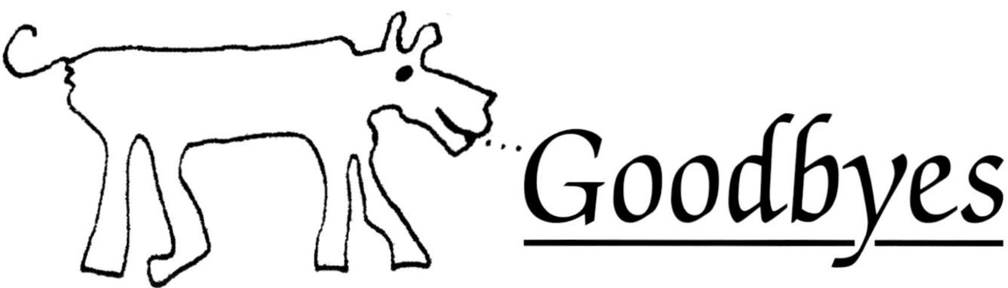

Goodbyes

VIRGINIA RIGNEY: Shortly after Norma's passing, I received a note from a high school friend enclosing Norma's obituary clipping from *The New York Times*. I have not talked with this friend for over ten years, and she has not seen Norma since their graduation in 1956. The note read, "Aren't we fortunate to have known her?"

CATHERINE McINTOSH: The thing that comes to mind the most when I think of Norma is her laugh and her smile. She would tend to be kind of grumpy looking, and then she would break out into a big smile and laugh if something had struck her.

BRIAN RANSOM: All of my kids independently said that the one thing they remembered most about Norma was how she would just light everything around her when she smiled. "She would just light up." And that's what all three of them said to me they remembered best about Norma, was just that explosion of laughter and brilliance coming out of her eyes and face. She was just a beacon of light, really truly.

KARIN SKIBA: Sometimes she could be abrasive, but I knew that was her way. Norma always seemed to welcome me, and I appreciated it.

BRIAN RANSOM: When Norma was dying, I was there until about a day and a half before she died, and then I had my ticket to go back. She was cogent enough that she recognized me and we were able to talk some, but she had decided that she was going to go with honor. So she had stopped eating. Although I snuck her a root beer float one night, because she asked for it. But then, the next day, my son Jacob was going to play a show in San Diego and he stopped by. My sons and Norma, there was an amazing bond there. They did a lot of duet stuff. Norma had just enough presence left that Jake said, "Would you like it if I played for you?" And so Jacob, the day before she died, I think, sat with her in the room and played a little drum they use in Brazil for the samba, a little timbau thing. And that was the last anyone saw her crack one of her big smiles.

AIDA PAVLETICH: Once, during rainy season, Norma called me to say that Chicken Creek behind her house, usually a slight depression in the earth, had become a river. For Norma, my ceremony brought an ocean rock to step across Chicken Creek when it was flowing, sand-washed pebbles to cairn her ashes in the field, a tub of ladybugs to carry off her dust on bright red wings up to Mount Baldy. I set their colors free into the sky to find her.

BRIAN RANSOM: With a lot of my art friends, there's a lot of sort of critical analysis. But Norma's stuff would just bubble up from way deep. It wasn't, like, up for discussion, as it were. It was just her meditations. I mean, you just look out her window and you can imagine seeing the view the way she saw it, but you never would—because you're seeing a normal mountain range, and she was seeing this sort of unbelievable explosion of lines, going across the sky.

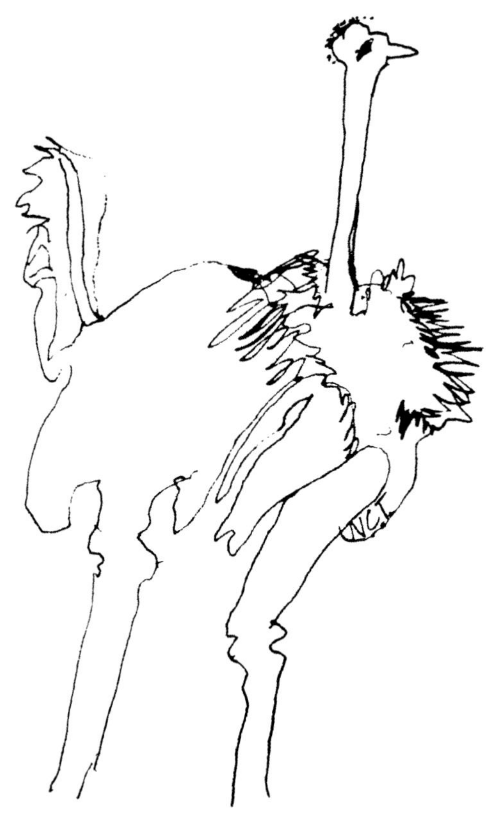

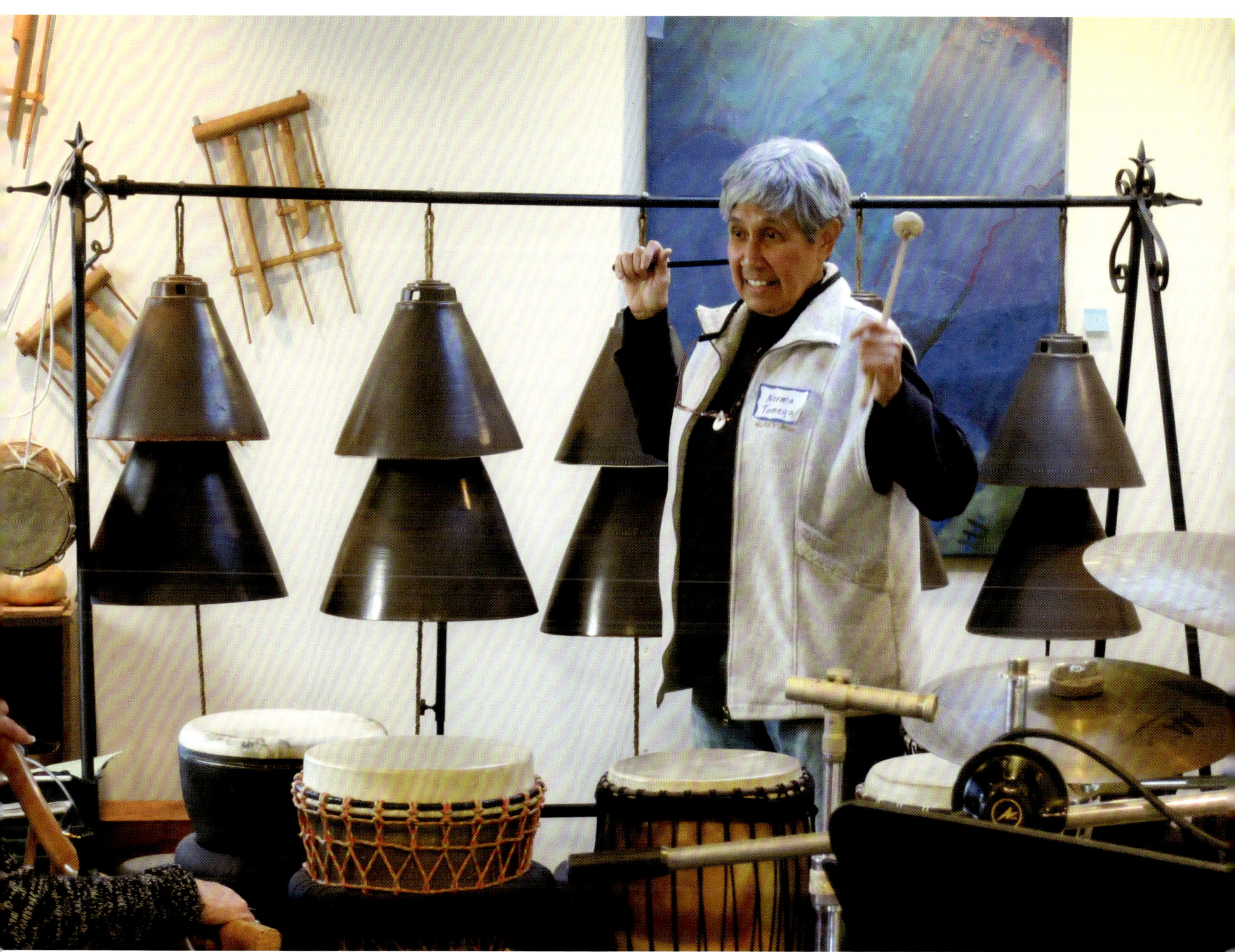

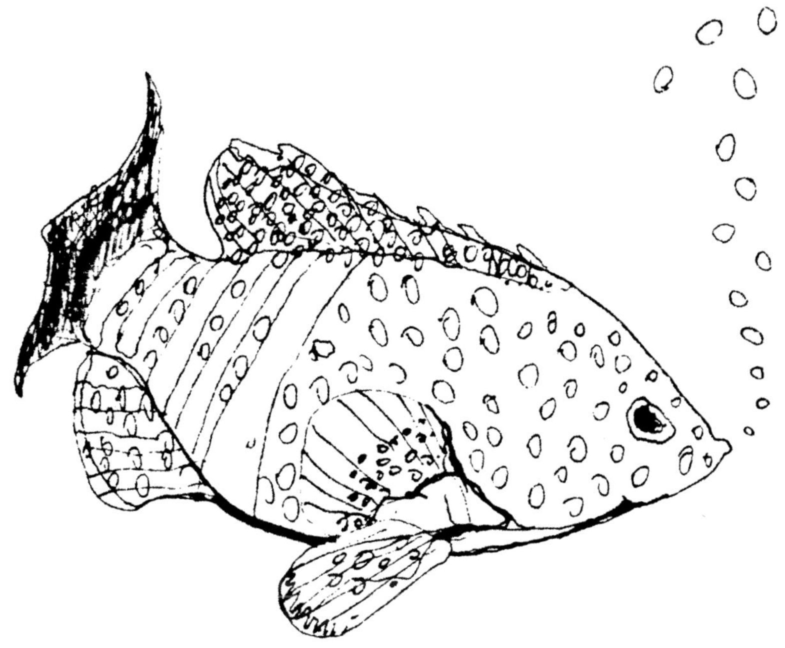

The reflections and documentation gathered for this collection represent an accurate but incomplete view of Norma Tanega's extraordinary life. Please use this as a guide to research parallel histories and share your discoveries. Future editions will benefit from your curiosity. We are grateful to you, the reader; to the contributors; and to Norma for her rich, complex legacy and the opportunity to explore the wonders she left behind.

First published in the United States of America in 2022
by Anthology Editions, LLC

87 Guernsey Street
Brooklyn, NY 11222

anthologyeditions.com

Introduction by Diane Divelbess

Editor: Mark Iosifescu
Design: Bryan Cipolla
Research, development, and dillydallying: Zonder Titel

Cover: *Self Portrait* by Norma Tanega, September 1984

Photography and artwork licensed courtesy of the
Norma Tanega Estate.

Additional images courtesy of Catherine McIntosh
(p. 143), Corinna Müller (pp. 2 left and center, 5),
Tom Skelly (pp. 96, 97), and Karin Skiba (p. 37).

The image on p. 31 appeared in *Melody Maker*,
July 9, 1966 © NME 2021; the images on pp. 32–33
appeared in the Ontario, California *Daily Report*,
March 19, 1981. Reprinted with permission.

First Edition
ARC 081

ISBN: 978-1-944860-35-6
Library of Congress Control Number: 2021949844